GEORGE WASHINGTON'S WORLD

by

GENEVIEVE FOSTER

with illustrations by the author

A quick glance through this book, stopping especially to look at the dramatic and arresting double-page illustrations before each section, will show what it does for the period during which the United States of America was born.

Through her two children of high-school age, Mrs. Foster discovered how difficult it is for young people to visualize the events of a period *in their relationship* to each other. With unbounded enthusiasm she set to work to give a picture of WORLD events during Washington's life. It was a long and strenuous piece of work, but her enthusiasm never flagged. One feels this as one reads the book, and the result is one of the most distinctive and unusual—we hope one of the most useful—books we have published.

An interesting feature is that the reader may follow the story of one character through the book; it is indexed to make this possible. Indeed, one can follow the characters through the pictures alone, seeing Napoleon grow from a tiny infant in the cradle to the would-be conqueror of Europe; seeing Benjamin Franklin grow old in the service of his country.

About the Author

Genevieve Foster is an artist who lives in Evanston, Illinois. She has illustrated many historical books for children, but this is the first one she has written. It is unusual for an artist to be able to do with words what she does with pen or brush—but Genevieve Foster's text has the same lively, vivid quality as her drawings.

Mrs. Foster is very serious about this book. She feels that present-day young people cannot understand events now going on, without a world view of the time when this country was first taking its place among the countries of the world. She writes not only of political events and personalities, but of the development of science, industry, literature, and art. The beginning of aviation, the discovery of oxygen, electricity, the invention of the cotton gin, the prevention of scurvy and smallpox, the reformation of the calendar, all take their place in her picture of world events.

GEORGE WASHINGTON'S WORLD

George Washington's WORLD

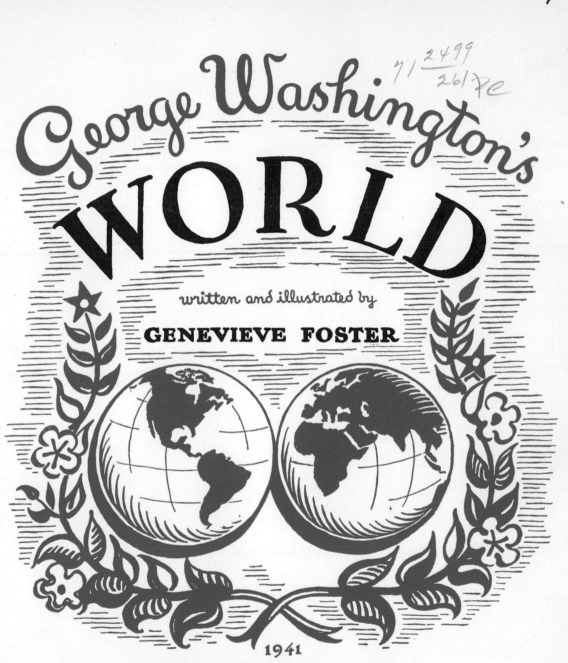

written and illustrated by

GENEVIEVE FOSTER

1941

CHARLES SCRIBNER'S SONS
New York

FOR JOANNE
AND
ORRINGTON, Jr.

CONTENTS

PART I

PART II

PART III

Fayette hunted his "were-wolf" · pirates sailed the Mediterranean · 500,000 Kalmucks went back to China · Japan was a feudal state closed to the world · California was settled · a hurricane brought Alexander Hamilton to America · Boston had a tea party · Paul Revere took his ride · the continental army was formed · etc.

I

WHEN GEORGE WASHINGTON WAS A Boy

People who were living when

JOHN HANCOCK
was practicing penmanship
in the Boston Latin School
(born 1737)

JOHN ADAMS
our second president was a
Massachusetts farmer boy
(born 1735)

DANIEL BOONE
was learning to hunt in
the backwoods (born 1735)

(1741)

VITUS BERING
exploring for Russia, crossed
the strait from Asia to America

BENJAMIN WEST
(born 1738) had his first paintings
admired by his Indian friends

He experimented
with Electricity

BENJAMIN FRANKLIN
a friendly printer (born 1706)
was the best known American

JUNIPERO SERRA
who was to help found California
arrived in Mexico from Spain.
(born 1709)

JAMES WATT
inventor of the Steam Engine,
was busy in his father's shop. (born 1736)

JAMES COOK
who was to discover Australia
for England, ran away to sea
(born 1727)

and Events that took place

George Washington was a Boy

CATHERINE "the Great"
then a German princess
went to Russia (born 1729)

BACH
the famous organist
born 1685, died in 1750

MARIA THERESA
became Queen of Austria
and mother of many children
(born 1717)

LOUIS XV
was King of France (born 1710)

VOLTAIRE (born 1694)
was writing against injustice

(born 1712)
FREDERICK "the Great"
became King of Prussia.

GEORGE II
though German born, was
King of England (born 1683)

GEORGE III
was being a good
boy (born 1738)

CH'IEN LUNG
had begun, in 1736, his sixty years
as Emperor of China (born 1710)

between the years 1740 and 1755

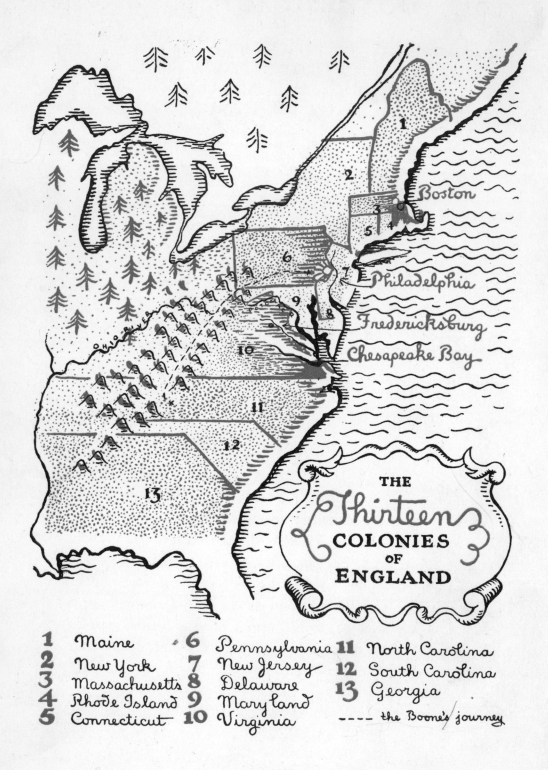

THE
Thirteen
COLONIES
OF
ENGLAND

Boston
Philadelphia
Fredericksburg
Chesapeake Bay

1 Maine   **6** Pennsylvania **11** North Carolina
2 New York **7** New Jersey   **12** South Carolina
3 Massachusetts **8** Delaware **13** Georgia
4 Rhode Island   **9** Maryland ---- the Boone's journey
5 Connecticut   **10** Virginia

A BOY OF VIRGINIA

ANOTHER YEAR had passed. It was April in Virginia. Warm spring sun shone down on the broad waters of Chesapeake Bay and on the Rappahannock River, one of those crooked blue fingers of the bay that point up into the green shores of Virginia, and along which the tide waters of the ocean ebb and flow.

The boy, George Washington, stood on the end of the plantation wharf watching a ship that was sailing away. Soon it would round a bend in the channel and before long be leaving the mouth of the river for the broader waters of the bay. Thence it would sail out onto the open ocean that stretched three thousand miles from there to England.

Now the ship was loaded with tobacco only, but a year from now,

5

on that exciting day when it returned, it would come sailing up the river like a treasure ship, loaded with fine things for all the family. There would be new furniture for George's mother, a mahogany bed, perhaps, with four tall posts, or a mahogany highboy, a fine suit for his father, plum colored or bottle green with cream-colored stockings, and, for him and his three small brothers, smaller suits made like their father's. There would be guns for hunting, polished and smooth with shining barrels, a doll with a china head for Betty, and best of all, thought George, a new bridle and saddle for his colt! But a whole year to wait seemed almost like a lifetime to a boy of ten.

To a Virginia planter like his father, a year was but the lifetime of a new tobacco crop, and his surprise each spring was not how many, but how few things the ship brought back, for unfortunately although tobacco was the planter's money, the buyers of London had the right to set its price. However, since it was against the law for people in the colonies to trade with any other country except England, the tobacco ship continued, year after year, to come and go.

"A year is a long time to wait," sighed George as the last white speck of topsail disappeared. "But some day I won't have to wait. I'll be on that ship myself."

George felt sure that when he was old enough his father would send him "home" to England to go to school and to learn the manners of a gentleman. His big half-brothers Augustine and Lawrence had both gone. Then Lawrence had come home and sailed away again with other soldiers to fight for King George against the Spaniards.

"I'll do that too," thought George, sticking his chest out and setting his feet down firmly like a soldier as he left the wharf. Then, seeing his small brother, he went bounding up the path and following the sweet spicy smell of hot gingerbread, disappeared around the corner of the house that stood among the pine trees on the hill.

Those pines about the house had given this the name of Pine Grove plantation, though most people, especially the colored folks, called it Ferry Farm. George had been born on the Potomac River plantation, but when he was just a few years old, the family had moved from there to Ferry Farm. At first he had just romped in the fields and woods, but when he was old enough to learn his numbers and his A B C's he had ridden down the road to Mr. Hobby's "old field school house." At first George had to sit in front of old black Peter on the horse, but a few years later there was hardly a horse on the plantation that he couldn't manage, and old Peter just stood by to chuckle.

"Look a' dat boy ride now! Tell you ain' no boy in all Vaginny kin ride a hoss like dat boy kin ride!"

One day in spring, when he was eleven, George Washington, although he was the son of a wealthy planter, suddenly found himself a poor boy, while his brother Lawrence on that same day became a wealthy man. That was because their father died, and it was the English law that a father must leave his property to his eldest son. So Lawrence had inherited the twenty-five hundred acres of plantation on the Potomac, and most of what his father owned, while there had been left to George and his mother and her four other children only the two hundred and fifty acres there at Ferry Farm.

"The Mercy only knows how we're going to get along," complained his mother, "but I suppose we'll manage. But from now on, my poor dear George, you will have to study out some way to make a living."

At first the family were not quite certain what to have George do. Some one, possibly Augustine, spoke of surveying. Lawrence favored having him go to sea, in the king's navy, if possible, or if not, on a tobacco ship. That sea idea sounded great to George. But his uncle

Joseph wrote from England that it would be a dog's life and his mother wept and begged him not to go, so, reluctantly, he unpacked his trunk that he had all strapped and ready, and stayed at home to go on with the surveying. He studied hard. When he was fifteen and had learned as much as his teacher knew about both mathematics and surveying, George left school and went to live with Lawrence at his plantation on the Potomac, which he now called Mount Vernon.

Besides his surveying instruments, George took with him a notebook in which he was copying one hundred and ten rules, such as these of "CIVILITY & DECENT BEHAVIOR IN COMPANY AND CONVERSATION."

Sleep not when others Speak, Sit not when others stand. If You Cough Sneeze, or Yawn, do it not Loud but Privately. Shew not Yourself glad at the Misfortune of another Keep Your Nails clean and Short, also Your Teeth clean

Even though he had not been able to go to England, George thought that with good rules like these to follow, he would get along so that Lawrence and Anne need not be ashamed of him. Anne was Lawrence's wife, the daughter of Sir William Fairfax, a cultured and wealthy gentleman, who lived on a neighboring plantation. In the Fairfax drawing-room, George tried especially hard to remember all his rules of good behavior, but since among the one hundred and ten there was not one to tell him how to be gay and witty with the ladies, he always felt shy and awkward, and his hands and feet kept getting in his way. "Such a well-conducted lad," the ladies said, "a pity he's so bashful."

With the men George was more at ease, and they all found him a good companion. Lord Thomas Fairfax, the oldest and wealthiest of the family and a cousin of Sir William, took a particular fancy to the lad. Many a morning the gaunt old Englishman would stand by while George practised his surveying. It gave him great satisfaction to see the boy taking as careful measurements of his brother's turnip patch as if he had been commissioned by the King to lay out a palace courtyard.

8

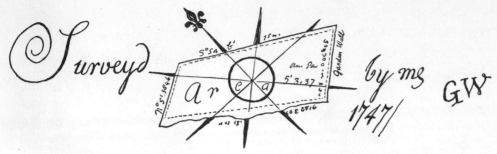

Surveyd by me 1747 GW

"That's a fine young brother you have, sir," he said to Lawrence. "One of these days we must give him a real chance at surveying."

Now Lord Thomas Fairfax was the owner of a tremendous plantation, thousands upon thousands of acres of land which lay in the valley between the Alleghany and the Blue Ridge mountains. Much to his annoyance, squatters from Pennsylvania were living on his land, but he could not collect rent from them nor drive them off, until boundaries were marked so that both he and the squatters knew which land was his.

So in March, 1748, he hired George Washington and young George Fairfax (William's son) to go with a guide and make the survey. It was George's first trip into the wilderness as well as his first job of surveying, and on that trip he saw and learned much that was later on to be of use to him. He learned about the country, and saw how the Indians and the traders and the people of the backwoods lived. Never before had he slept at night "in ye open air" in front of a fire, nor sat down to a meal of coarse food and had nothing to eat it with except the knife in his pocket. At the end of a month, in spite of rain, they brought back such careful measurements, that Lord Fairfax was enormously pleased and saw to it that George was made surveyor of Culpeper County.

With the first money that he earned and saved, the young surveyor bought five hundred acres of uncleared land and was the proud owner of his first plantation. Each year he bought more land, aiming in time to own a big plantation. The time came sooner than he thought. In 1752 his brother Lawrence died, and when the estate was settled, George Washington, then barely twenty-one years old, became the Master of Mount Vernon and an extremely well-established young Virginia gentleman.

DANIEL BOONE, A BOY OF THE BACKWOODS

WHEN GEORGE WASHINGTON was twelve years old, Daniel Boone was nine. Winters, the Boone family were all at home in one of the log cabins of a backwoods settlement about twelve miles from Philadelphia. But as soon as the grass was green in early spring, Daniel and his mother went to live still farther back into the wilderness, taking the cattle to pasture on some other half-cleared land. Through the long summer days it was Daniel's job to watch the herd and bring them back at sundown to be milked, but in the shadowy sweet-smelling woods the boy often quite forgot about the cows, he was so busy studying the tracks and trails of the wild animals and learning all the forest sounds. Small game he soon learned to bring down by throwing a gnarled root, and often came home after a day in the woods bringing a rabbit or a squirrel to stew for supper.

One early morning in autumn, Dan sat up suddenly in his bunk and listened. "Wild geese," he thought as he caught the faint weird honking sound again. Kicking back his buffalo robe, he slipped out onto the hard dirt floor of the cabin, ran to the door and looked out into the frosty morning. There, indeed, above the treetops was the dark flying arrow of the wild geese against the sky. That meant that the summer was over and any day now he and his mother would be driving the cattle home. Dan was anxious to go, for he was to be twelve that winter and his father had promised him a rifle of his own.

With the brand-new rifle on his shoulder and his dog beside him, Dan set out one winter morning, for the woods. For three days he did not come back. By that time not only his mother but his father and all the settlement were alarmed. "Indians," thought the older people grimly as they formed a party to search for him. Three miles back in woods they came upon an old deserted cabin. There inside sat Dan, calmly roasting meat before the fire, with the skins of animals that he had killed stretched out on the floor to dry. From then on Daniel spent weeks at a time alone in the woods hunting for meat and furs. When he had cured the skins, he would take them into Philadelphia and exchange them for whatever was needed. Like tobacco in Virginia, furs took the place of money on the frontier. So by his hunting, Daniel earned his living.

These are words he once carved on the trunk of an old beech tree:

CiLLED   D.Boon   ON
A.BAR
in ThE   TREE
Y EAR
1760

When Daniel Boone was eighteen years old, his family and their kinsfolk moved to North Carolina. They had heard tell how the land was fertile and game so plentiful that in a single day one man could kill five buffalo, or bears enough to make a ton of bacon. So they had packed their few belongings and started on their way. As they travelled south the sun rose over the Blue Ridge Mountains to their left and set behind the higher ridges of the Alleghanies. At night they camped in a circle around a blazing fire, on guard against a surprise attack from hostile Indians. Finally, on the western edge of North Carolina, they built their

11

cabins and laid out their new farm homes. Daniel Boone kept up his hunting for he was far more of a hunter than a farmer, and, judging from his spelling, he was certainly no scholar.

But he was a great backwoodsman. He may never have learned much out of books, but he knew all the mysterious signs of the forest, could reckon time and distance by the sun, and in the years to come was to mark out many a wilderness trail for others, less daring, to follow.

JOHN ADAMS, A FARMER BOY

JOHN ADAMS was also three years younger than George Washington. He was born up in Braintree, Massachusetts, a small village about ten miles from Boston. From the beginning his father, who was a farmer, had planned that his son John should become a minister, in Massachusetts villages a most important person.

One Saturday morning, John Adams, nine years old, short and fat and roly-poly, was up on the hill by the big rock hoeing in his father's garden. He suddenly bent down and tugged fiercely at a weed till his chubby round face was very red.

"Hard work" he puffed, taking a firmer hold on the obstinate weed. "Must be what the preacher means . . . he says it's hard to root out evil."

12

He tugged away till he got out every bit of the root down to the very point. Then he straightened up his back and turned to let the fresh east wind blow into his hot face. Coming in from the ocean it had a tingling salty smell. On a bright day like that, John could see the roofs of the houses in Boston Town, built on the ocean's edge ten miles away. Farther away, the deep blue ocean stretched up to the level of his eyes and met the bright blue sky. There wasn't the tiniest feather of a cloud in that clear sky. Nor was there any cloud in John's bright mind. Small John Adams could think very clearly. The things he liked stood out sharply from the things he disliked. One thing he did not like was to sit every Sabbath morning for three hours on a high hard pew and listen to a sermon. His feet went to sleep and prickled, and if he so much as nodded, he was bumped awake by a rap on the head from a pole kept by the sexton for that very purpose. Another thing John didn't like was to spend five more good days out of every week learning Latin grammar.

"Amo—amas—amat," he grumbled. "I love—you love—he loves. Love? Bah!" He hated Latin! At the very thought John hoed so hard that the hoe struck a spark of fire on a stone. So he whanged away again. Surprising how much fun John could get out of hating Latin! His father wanted him to study it, of course, so that he could go to college and become a preacher. About the preacher business he hadn't made up his mind, but he well knew that he hated Latin.

It was a long time before he screwed up enough courage to tell his father so. It was early one spring morning. Through the open door the smell of the lilacs by the well drifted into the low-beamed sitting-room.

John stood before his father. His short sturdy body rested squarely on both feet and he looked his parent straight in the eye.

"Father," he said, "I do not want to study Latin any longer."

"Well, John," his father answered, "if Latin grammar does not suit you, you may try ditching. Perhaps that will suit you better. My meadow yonder needs a ditch, and you may put by Latin and try that."

John was delighted. It had been easier than he had expected. With a shovel on his shoulder he trudged off to the meadow and began to dig. It was the longest forenoon that he ever spent. Digging ditches was hard work and by the time he went home for dinner he was so tired that he could hardly eat the good baked beans and steaming brown bread that his mother took from the fireplace oven. He was quite ready to return to Latin grammar, but he was too proud to say so. He dug stubbornly in the ditch all that afternoon and all the next day. That night he put his pride down deep in his pocket, and said to his father:

"If you choose, I will go back to Latin grammar."

With that he turned, clambered up the narrow stairs to his small room beneath the sloping roof and fell asleep at once.

The next day he went back to school and studied hard. When he was fifteen years old he was ready to go to Harvard College. His father was well pleased and looked forward to the time when his son John would be a preacher and the most important man in some Massachusetts village. John had mastered the Latin, but he still wasn't sure about becoming a preacher. He graduated from Harvard in the class of 1755 and gave his graduation speech in Latin so well that the minister of another village offered him his first job teaching the grammar school. That winter he did a great deal of reading and thinking, and definitely made up his mind that he was not fitted for the ministry. Uncertain what to do, for some time he said he felt bewildered, "like a boy in a strange country with half a dozen roads before him, groping in a dark night." But he added "My inclination was soon fixed upon the law." So for the next two years, while continuing to teach what he called his "troublesome little runtlings" to lisp their ABCs, John also studied law with a gentleman of the village.

His term over, he went home to Braintree, and there began to practise. Not much of a case, his first one: just an argument over an old broken-down horse, valued at two dollars, if it lived till April. But with that humble start, young John Adams became a lawyer.

From then on his knowledge of the law was always to be used by John Adams with honesty and courage, and was to enable him to give such service to his country that he would be made its second President.

14

JOHN HANCOCK, A BOY OF BOSTON

JOHN HANCOCK was a schoolmate of John Adams, and also lived in Braintree, Massachusetts, until he was seven. Then his father, who was the minister in the village, died. One day not long after that a fine coach had driven up in front of the Hancock house. John had kissed his mother and sister and baby brother, said good-bye to his friend John Adams and the other boys and gone away to live in Boston. All his friends in Braintree thought John was a lucky boy, because he was going to be adopted by his uncle Thomas, who, every one said, was the wealthiest man in Boston. John felt very proud sitting between his uncle Tom and his aunt Lydia on the seat of their fine coach and was glad that the boys could see him as it rolled through the main street of Braintree, and off down the road toward Boston Town, leaving a curl of yellow dust behind it.

The frogs were croaking in the marshes when they reached the edge of Boston, and pigs scampered out of the way of their horses as the coach rumbled through the narrow streets up to the top of Beacon Hill, and

15

stopped before the finest house of all. Candlelight shone through the fan-shaped window over the front door and when they stepped inside, it was into the finest room the little Braintree boy had ever seen. The floors were waxed and gleaming, the walls of panelled wood, and there was a broad beautiful staircase with a twisted handrail. A strange fire was also burning—not one of oak logs such as they used at home, but small black pieces of something John had never seen before.

"That is coal," said Uncle Thomas, "brought from England."

His uncle chuckled and his aunt smiled down at him and put her arm about his shoulders. They were both happy to have a small boy in the house and, after he had gone to bed, they said to each other that he should have the best of everything that money could buy.

Aunt Lydia was pleased to see how genteel the small fellow looked in his new clothes the first morning he started off to Latin school. School began at seven o'clock in the morning and lasted till late afternoon. The last hour was spent on penmanship. This meant not only learning to write but also how to cut and mend the goose-quill pens. John was quick to learn, and soon wrote so well that Uncle Thomas let him use his best quills and inkstand dish at home. He liked to practise writing his name. He would turn the end of the k around like this and run a long line back to the J in John:

John Hancock

Business took Uncle Thomas every day to the warehouse and the wharf. One morning he took his young nephew with him. Even before they reached the end of Fish Street or came in sight of the water, the air was full of strange exciting smells. Mingled with that of salt and fish, there was the piny smell of fresh-cut lumber, tingling spicy scent of cloves and cinnamon, and the sweet heavy odor of molasses. John followed his uncle through the office where clerks on high stools were adding up long columns of figures and out into the shadowy ware-

16

houses. From one end to the other it was piled high with bales and barrels and bundles and casks and boxes. Slabs of salt fish, bundles of furs, packs of boards and shingles ready to be shipped. And there were barrels upon barrels of molasses. John thought that there must have been a thousand barrels dripping with it. On the end of his finger it tasted even better than it smelled.

"Molasses comes from the West Indies," said Uncle Thomas.

The bright light was dazzling as they stepped from the shadowy warehouse out onto the wharf. On either side of the Hancock Wharf, other wharves jutted out into the water, and everywhere ships were being loaded and unloaded.

"Boston is the busiest seaport in the colonies." Uncle Thomas pointed to the far end of the wharf where two old weatherbeaten ships lay at anchor. "Those ships have been on many a voyage to India and China. They belong to the East India Trading Company. They bring us spices from India and tea from China. Ships bring goods from all over the world to these wharves in Boston Harbor."

Each year as John grew older he went more often with his uncle to the wharf. Sometimes they stopped at the Crown Coffee House on their way home, to hear the news. It was pleasant on cold winter days to gather round the thick oak tables in the cheerful candlelight and listen to the tales of the old sea captains and travelling merchants. The men of Boston also seemed to have important business to talk over. More than once John heard them grow excited talking about some laws they called the Acts of Navigation, which seemed to have a great deal to do with molasses. From what John heard, it seemed that if Thomas Hancock or any other merchant wanted to bring in molasses from the West Indies, he had to pay a big tax to the king on every barrel, because the West Indies belonged to Spain, and merchants in the colonies were not allowed to trade with any country except England. All the merchants seemed to agree that it was perfectly respectable to disobey such an unfair law and smuggle in the molasses in their own private boats.

When John was fourteen he went to Harvard College. There he was glad to see John Adams again, his good friend from Braintree. After graduation, beginning as a clerk in his uncle's shipping office, John Hancock soon became a successful merchant. Very courteous in his manner, very perfect in dress, his figuring was faultless, and his letters were always written in a very fine hand. His signature was particularly handsome. He now turned the end of the *k* in Hancock around in a sweeping curve and the long line back to the *J* in John was further embellished with a scroll.

That was to become America's most famous signature!

BENJAMIN WEST

BENJAMIN WEST was a Quaker boy. He was born in 1737 in a small Pennsylvania village not far from Philadelphia. His father was the innkeeper. As theirs was a well-travelled road leading to the west, the covered wagons of the German and Scotch-Irish immigrants were often to be seen drawn up in the courtyard of the inn, or rumbling by.

One noon Ben's father came in for his dinner with a worried frown on his usually calm face. His wife looked up with quick understanding.

"Have more of those poor people been through here going west?"

18

she asked as she poised her spoon above a steaming bowl of pepper pot.

"Aye. And well it is they did not stop for long. So little wish have they to pay a fair price for anything, 'tis no wonder they have trouble with the Indians." Her husband hung his broad-brimmed black hat on the customary peg and added, "If they would but buy the land and pay the Indians fairly for it as we Friends have always done, they, too, would find the red man friendly."

He walked over toward the fireplace and a gray cat which had been sleeping on the hearth rose and rubbed against his leg.

"Ah, Grimalchin, thee has no troubles, has thee?" he said as he leaned down to stroke the smooth arched back. "But what, indeed, has happened to thy tail?"

"That was Benny," explained the mother smiling. "That bit of fur he cut off this morning and fastened it into a goose quill to make a paint brush. I thought it did no harm."

At that moment a boy appeared in the open doorway, his small figure a slim silhouette against the yellow autumn leaves outside.

"See," he cried holding up both hands. "See what the Indians gave me!" In one hand he held a large lump of firm red clay, in the other a birch-bark cup filled with soft yellow clay. He had been, he said, to visit his special friends, the Indians. They had liked the drawings he had made of birds and flowers, so they had dug clay from the river bank and shown him how to make it into paint.

"Now with Mother's bluing I have three fine colors, yellow, red and blue. Now I shall paint really beautiful pictures."

One day a merchant from Philadelphia was visiting with Benjamin's father. The boy showed him a drawing he had made of baby Rose lying in her cradle, and the next time the man came he brought with him a beautiful box of paints with real brushes and three or four pieces of canvas. Ben was so excited he had to take the paint-box to bed with him that night, and the next morning early, instead of going to school, he slipped up to the attic and began to paint. When his mother found him, she was so pleased with the picture that she couldn't feel

19

it in her heart to scold him. Very strict Quakers in those days disapproved of painting pictures, but neither Ben's father nor his mother could see evil in it. Rather it seemed right that their boy should use the talent God had given him. So as he grew older, they did not interfere with his plans to be a portrait painter. At first Benjamin was happy to draw the faces of the village people for a few shillings apiece, but at eighteen, no longer satisfied, he set out for Philadelphia to improve his fortune.

Philadelphia was a Quaker city, often spoken of as the City of Friends; *Friends* being the name which the Quakers gave themselves. Young Benjamin West soon felt at home in Philadelphia. He liked the tidy red brick State House with its twinkling white-edged windowpanes, and the quiet shady streets, flecked with gold bits of sunlight which shone through the thick leaves of the elm and chestnut trees. He was interested in the long brown wooden shed made for visiting Indians, at one end of Chestnut Street, and in the busy Market Place that was to be found at the other end of the street along the Delaware River. The Market was such a busy place that it seemed as though every Quaker in Philadelphia must go there at least once a day to buy and sell. That was nearly true. The Quakers were such active merchants that they had made Philadelphia the largest and most prosperous city in the colonies. They had gold pieces aplenty in their pockets, and many soon hearing of the promising young painter, paid Benjamin West a guinea and a half to have their portraits painted.

Benjamin was pleased, but still he was not satisfied. He had the highest of ideals, the very loftiest ambition and he looked upon his profession as a noble calling.

"I am a painter," he once told an acquaintance. "A painter is a companion of kings and emperors."

"There are no kings and emperors in America," replied his friend.

"No, but elsewhere there are. That's where I intend to go."

And so he did and in England this young Quaker painter was destined to win fame and fortune, and to become the King's friend, as well as the only American ever to be made court painter to a king.

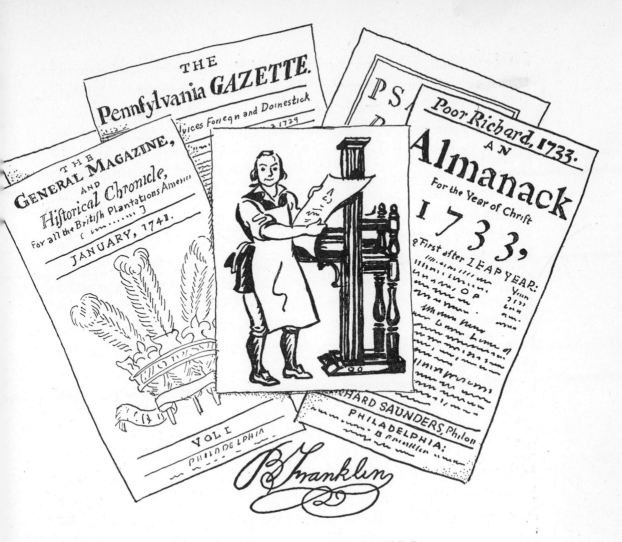

THE FRIENDLY PRINTER

PHILADELPHIA was called the City of Friends but the friendliest man in that City of Friends was not a Friend at all. That is to say, he was not a Quaker. He was the son of a candlemaker in Boston who had run away from home when he was seventeen and come to Philadelphia hoping to find a job in a printing office. Wet and windblown and dirty he had arrived one night—a hungry boy with just enough money in his pocket to buy two large buns to eat. He had slept that night in the Quaker meeting house, for he hadn't known a person in town. But he had a round ruddy face, a twinkle in his eye and such a quirk of a smile that before very long he had made friends with even the royal governor.

By 1732, Benjamin Franklin was a grown man and one of the busiest as well as the friendliest men in Philadelphia. He was then twenty-six and for two years had been the master of his own printing office down by the Market. He published a newspaper and that year, 1732, got out for the first time a surprising almanac, which not only foretold the weather, but was sprinkled full of wise and witty sayings supposed to have been written by a man called Poor Richard.

The next year he had spread out his business a bit, and opened a small shop next to his printing office, where everything was for sale from books and ink and goose-quill pens to codfish, soap, candles, cheese and "Senaka Rattlesnake Root." Deborah, his wife, tended shop and minded their two small boys.

Ben himself was usually to be found in the press room, dressed in a red flannel shirt, leather breeches and long leather apron. Moving in and out among the presses and cases of type, opening kegs of ink and poking in pots of glue, he was always busy at something. For Benjamin Franklin didn't know what it meant to be idle. If he were not writing a piece of news or one of Poor Richard's sayings, he might be carving a wood block, or showing an apprentice boy how to wash or sort or set up a stick of type. In the midst of things he might have to drop what he was doing and give advice to a neighbor on what to do for a rooster that crowed too loud or a smoking chimney. Though he already knew how to do more than enough to fill any man's day, he was always thinking up new things to do, and inventing new ways to do them.

Then, being as friendly as he was busy, as soon as he perfected a useful invention he told others about it so that they could make use of it too, and out of each grateful acquaintance he naturally made a new friend. So the busier he became the more friends he made, and the more friends he made the busier he became. So he grew busier and friendlier and friendlier and busier till he had made himself one of the most prosperous men in the town. Then, though he still edited his newspaper and his almanac, he no longer worked in the press room, but spent much of his time in the red brick State House on Chestnut Street, and busied himself with the affairs of the colony.

Even people in the other colonies who knew so little about each other had heard of Benjamin Franklin. All had read and reread his almanac year after year. It had become the fashion to quote Poor Richard's sayings and urge others to follow his good advice. So Benjamin Franklin was not only the friendliest and busiest man in the City of Friends, but he was also the best-known man in the American colonies.

After one of his visits to Boston, Benjamin Franklin returned to Philadelphia and at once began making experiments with the surprising new fluid or juice of which he had just heard, called Electricity. Night after night he worked away, producing weird blue sparks that lit up the dusty press room like miniature bolts of lightning.

"I verily believe," said he to himself, "that lightning *is* electricity."

So one day when the rain fell and the lightning flashed, he went out with a kite, a string and a key, and got what actually was electricity out of the storm clouds. Almost immediately came the idea, that an iron rod from the ground to the top of a steeple would attract and carry away the lightning that otherwise might strike and destroy the building. He tried out the idea, and then wrote an article in *Poor Richard's Almanac* telling how to make and use his new Lightning Rods, the first practical benefit to come out of the experiments with electricity.

News of the invention spread to Europe. Scientists discussed it. The King of France sent the inventor a letter of congratulation. The Royal Society of Scientists in London sent him a medal of honor, and not long after, from one of the universities in Scotland, he received a Doctor's diploma. From then on he was generally known as *Doctor* Franklin.

This is the first American cartoon. Benjamin Franklin drew it to show how important it was for the American colonies to form a union and how impossible it was for them to exist long, if they remained as they were then, thirteen little nations unfriendly to each other. Even though made up of people as different in their ways of living as Puritans, Quakers and Virginia Cavaliers, still the colonies had the same problems and difficulties due to life on a new continent, remote from Europe. They must join together if they wished to live.

He also wrote out a plan by which the colonies could form this union. For one thing, there was to be a council of representatives, which should have power to raise money to defend the colonies as a whole, from the Indians along the western border and from pirates or other enemies along the Atlantic seacoast. It seemed to him a good, sensible plan and, full of hope, Benjamin Franklin took it with him to an important meeting up in Albany, New York, at which delegates from the northern colonies were to meet and try to renew an old treaty with chiefs of the Iroquois Indian tribes. For many years these Iroquois Indians had been banded together into a union known as the Six Nations.

"Six nations of savages," thought Benjamin Franklin. "If they are capable of forming a union, it will be a strange thing if a union cannot be formed by ten or a dozen English colonies."

Other delegates were of the same mind, and all agreed to take his plan home with them to see how their own royal governor and assemblies felt about it. Not a single colony approved.

"Why should we pay good money to protect people on the frontier?" said those who lived on the seacoast. "Indians don't bother us."

"And why should we help to protect the seacoast?" replied the western settlers. "Haven't we troubles enough of our own?"

The colonies were as yet too jealous and self-centered to want any form of union. Benjamin Franklin was disappointed. Soon, however, the opportunity came for him to improve the roads, and that actually brought the colonies closer together than his plan of union could have done. For bad roads just as much as bad feeling kept the colonies apart.

This is how it came about: In the year 1753 the King appointed Benjamin Franklin the first Postmaster General of the American colonies. Hardly had he been appointed than he set out on what turned out to be a six-months' trip to inspect all the post offices from Massachusetts down to North Carolina. He returned brimming over with plans for improving the mail service, which he began at once. Before the first year was up, instead of taking six weeks to go one way, a letter could go from Philadelphia to Boston and bring back an answer in three weeks. In summer mail from New York came to Philadelphia three times a week instead of once, and once a week instead of once a month in winter.

Now a post rider who was to carry the mails with such speed could no longer be expected to get down from his horse to clear his path of a fallen tree, wade through the rivers or hack his way through the underbrush. And so the post roads were built. Those roads and that mail service were the first ties that drew the scattered colonies together, for when people could write to one another, could read newspapers from other parts of the country and even travel a bit themselves, gradually as the years went by they came to understand one another.

Then when the necessity arose to defend themselves from a danger shared in common, they were able to forget their differences and unite.

ENGLAND VS. SPAIN IN THE NEW WORLD

PHILADELPHIA was the largest city in the English colonies, but compared to Mexico City, the rich and splendid capital of New Spain, it was but a village. The colonies of Spain in America were also far larger and richer than the colonies of England. Just the thirteen colonies, the island of Jamaica, and a few other of the smaller West Indies belonged to England. But Spain's colonies extended from Texas and Florida, through Mexico, Central America, down the west coast of South America to the southern end of Chile. England eyed those vast possessions of Spain and her strong forts with envy. Spain watched England's growing power with distrust and hate, and since envy and hate breed war, war had broken out!

English soldiers had been sent to the Caribbean Sea, to Central and South America to fight the Spaniards. In 1740, England captured the Spanish fort of Porto Bello on the isthmus connecting North and South America. To celebrate the joyful victory a dinner was given in London, and that night, this song, now England's national anthem, was sung for the first time:

God save our Lord the King Long live our noble King God save the King Send him victorious happy and glorious Long to reign over us... God save the King!

Admiral Vernon was the English officer who had captured the fort. He was also the commander under whom Lawrence Washington, George's older brother, had gone to fight the following year, and for whom, when he returned, he had named his plantation Mount Vernon.

Now at the same time that England had sent Admiral Vernon to attack Porto Bello, Admiral George Anson had been sent out with orders to sail down around the end of South America and harass the Spanish settlements along the Pacific, and also to attack the Spanish trading ships. For Spain also owned the Philippine Islands, directly across the South Pacific from Mexico or "New Spain," and between those two colonies a Spanish trading ship went back and forth, known as the *Manilla Galleon.*

Admiral Anson had been obliged to set out with vessels that he insisted were too heavily loaded and unseaworthy, and so in the windy straits off Cape Horn many of them, as he had feared, were shipwrecked. More than two thirds of the crew also were lost on that voyage over, those who weren't drowned having rotted away with smallpox or scurvy. He was thus too crippled to attempt any attack on the settlements in Chile, so he cruised instead on up the coast, investigating the shore line and making maps. Charts of that region were much needed by England, for that was still unknown territory to the

English, and the Pacific Ocean was still to them a Sea of Darkness.

So Captain Anson proceeded, and halfway up the coast, as luck would have it, just off the colony of Peru, the *Manilla Galleon* hove in sight. Being almost alone upon the Pacific, the Spanish ships carried few guns for their protection, and so with his one remaining ship, Captain Anson was able to capture the *Manilla Galleon* and gain possession of the treasure in her hold.

Not in the hold, however, but in the captain's quarters, was found the greatest treasure, the prize of most immeasurable value. A packet of papers, but what a packet! In it were maps of all landmarks, harbors and islands in South America and the Philippines, and complete sailing directions for the trans-Pacific route! With the capture of that packet, all Spain's secrets of the Pacific lay revealed to England!

The War God

FRAY JUNIPERO SERRA

THE AZTEC INDIANS, a fairly civilized and very religious people, had ruled Mexico before the Spaniards came. Those early Aztecs had first welcomed their Spanish conqueror, in the belief that he was the "Fair God" whose return to earth they had long been expecting. But they had soon found to their sorrow, that while the gentle kindly men in the long brown robes had come to teach them new prayers and a new religion, the hard-eyed men in shining helmets had come to search for gold and conquer with the sword.

So the land of the Aztecs had become New Spain. Now in 1750, the Spanish conquerors lived there in elegance and luxury with descendants of the Aztec Indians for servants. And on the site of the old Aztec temple to the god of war, Mexitli, there had long been standing a great Spanish cathedral, with its cross of shining gold.

On New Year's Day of 1750, with their eyes fixed on that shining cross, two brown-robed Spanish monks of the Order of St. Francis came limping into the streets of Mexico City. Filled with the selfsame desire to bring religion to the Indians that the early fathers had had, they had left their home on the Mediterranean to come out to the New World. That they should be there, at last, he and his companion, caused at least one of them no feeling of surprise, for if ever there was a man with that unwavering faith that makes people able to accomplish what they set out to do, it was this man, Fray Junipero Serra.

Thin and pale he was from fatigue and hunger, for after a long sea voyage he and his companion had come two hundred miles from the harbor of Vera Cruz on foot. Beneath his dusty robe his legs were badly swollen, and an ugly festering sore had eaten deep into one foot and ankle, but his calm face fringed with the halo of dark hair showed no sign of physical suffering. His eyes were like those of a child as he looked up at the golden cross of the cathedral, which marked the goal of his long and tedious journey.

"To become one of these is worth all the pain and fatigue that we have suffered," said Fray Junipero to his companion a few hours later as they rose from their knees in the monastery chapel.

The Father Guardian and the monks also in turn expressed their delight at having among them Fray Junipero, whose reputation for piety and eloquence was not unknown to them, nor his eagerness to spread the religion of the cross among the Indians.

"Oh, for a forest of Juniperos!" exclaimed the Father Guardian. "Then would our work indeed go forward!"

When they asked him of his journey, Fray Junipero made light of the hardships, though the ocean voyage had been a bad one and uncommonly long. After but a few days' rest, he was eager to begin the work for which he had made the long journey to New Spain, but it was five months before the opportunity was given him. One holiday evening the monks were strolling among the peach and orange trees in the monastery orchard. "There is need," said the Father Guardian, "for more brothers to go among the Pames Indians in the Sierra Gordes. As we all know, they are a wild tribe, difficult to conquer. The field is one of the most trying, but the need is great."

"Send me, Father," cried Fray Junipero eagerly.

Accordingly it was arranged, and accompanied by his dear friend and devoted pupil, Palou, Fray Junipero set out again, and again on foot walked to the west coast of Mexico. There, in the mission at Santiago, he was to stay nine years. Not until after those nine years had been spent, and seven more of faithful service at another mission, was Fray Junipero to start on the great expedition with which his name will always be connected.

For it was Fray Junipero Serra, who was to carry the cross while others carried the sword, up into Alta California, to establish there a Spanish colony on the far opposite side of the great continent from that similar strip of land occupied by the thirteen colonies of England.

The Empire
Prussia
Silesia

FREDERICK, SOLDIER KING OF PRUSSIA

IN THE YEAR 1740, when George Washington was eight years old, a keen young prince by the name of Frederick became King of Prussia and sprang his first surprise on an unsuspecting world. Prussia was a very small nation and a comparatively new one. In 1700, Frederick's grandfather had been its first independent king. Frederick's father, the second king, very ambitious to make his small kingdom great, had built up for Prussia a large and powerful army, made up of rank upon rank of big burly broad-chested soldiers in high pointed hats and thousands of magnificent officers gleaming with gold braid and buttons. His scouts had scoured the world to hire and bring back the tallest men they could possibly find to form a corps of giants.

The Prussians were proud of that army. Every Prussian father had the ambition to raise a large family of sons to be part of it and every Prussian son was eager to learn the goose step and become a soldier. Every one, that is except Frederick.

Frederick, who now had become King himself and head of the army, never as a boy had had the slightest desire to be a soldier. And he certainly didn't resemble one. He was narrow chested and slim, with enormous blue eyes, a delicate mouth, and hair which he wore curled in the latest French fashion.

"He is a weakling, that Frederick," sneered the proud fathers of soldiers. "What does he all day, but read French books and tootle the flute? Never does he buckle on the sword and behave like a man."

"It's a disgrace to have such a son," stormed his father the King.

Stomping into Frederick's room one day he broke the detestable flute into splinters and threw the French books in the fire. So determined was he to make a soldier out of his obstinate son that time and again he beat Frederick severely and punished him cruelly.

At last, obedient, but with a heart turned to steel, a mind as sharp as a trap, and a distrustful glint in his strange blue eyes, Frederick had settled down to learn the grim business of war.

"Mein sohn . . . mein sohn . . . now he will make Prussia great," sighed the old King. "Now I die content!"

With the old King dead, every one wondered what Frederick the new King would do. All kinds of opinions were afloat, even a rumor of war, which the young King neither denied nor admitted. Finally curiosity got the better of one old general and he approached the King.

"Your Majesty," he began, clearing his throat with a series of small explosions. "May I ask what plans your Majesty makes for the future?"

32

Frederick looked up from what he was writing.

"Can you keep a secret?" he asked.

"Most surely, Majesty," answered the expectant general.

"So can I," said Frederick and turned back to his work.

When the door closed, he pulled out a map and ran his eyes thoughtfully over a section lettered, SILESIA. Silesia was part of Austria. Austria was the heart of the Holy Roman Empire. To its Emperor all the rulers, kings or princes of the little German states and free cities were supposed to owe their allegiance.

Frederick, however, merely looked with envious eyes upon the Emperor of Austria, and was pondering when and how he should take Silesia away from him, when news came that the Emperor of Austria was dead, and had left his throne to his young daughter Maria Theresa.

Frederick saw that his time had come. He made up some fine high-sounding story as to why Maria Theresa had no right to Silesia, and then simply marched in with his army of soldiers, flourished his sword in the air and announced that the land was his.

Maria Theresa, however, came from a long line of absolute monarchs and she had too much of the spirit of her ancestor kings to submit without struggle to being robbed of any part of her kingdom. She called on her soldiers and fighting began but though they fought for two years she was not able to recover the land she had lost. Her cheeks burning with anger, the young Queen was obliged to see Frederick keep Silesia and add it to Prussia.

At the outcome of the new King's ruthless adventure, Prussian generals were surprised and "hochmutig." Neighboring kings were dumbfounded and nervous, and the eyes of the world were on Frederick of Prussia. From then on whatever he did for the rest of his life was news!

 HEN THE WAR WAS OVER, Frederick had more time again to spend on his music and his books. Every day a concert preceded the King's evening meal in the palace at Potsdam. One evening in 1747, the guests were assembled, and seated, the orchestra in its place, the concert about to begin, when young Carl Bach, who was the King's accompanist, approached, bent and whispered a few words in his Majesty's ear.

Frederick rose at once. "Gentlemen," said he, "old Bach has come!"

Without being given time to change his travelling clothes the famous old organist was brought at once to the concert hall.

There the King gave him a theme for a fugue, which Bach worked out to his Majesty's great delight and to the amazement of all the distinguished musicians who were present.

After he left, Bach wrote out and developed the theme, adding a sonata that the King might play upon his flute, and sent him the manuscript, published later under the title "Musicalishes Opfer."

This is the way Frederick played it on the clavier:

and this is the way Bach simplified it:

РОССИА! _Russia_

CATHERINE: HER JOURNEY TO RUSSIA

WHEN FREDERICK II became King of Prussia, the little German girl who most of her life was to be known as Catherine the Great of Russia was eleven years old. Her name was Sophia Augusta Frederica, and she was a princess of Anhalt-Zerbst, a small state, bordering Prussia.

Sophia Augusta Frederica was a most unhappy child because she had not been born a prince instead of a princess. Ever since she could remember she had wanted to be a boy and learn to do the fine exciting things that boys were taught. Also she thought that if she had been a boy, her parents perhaps might have loved her as they did her brother.

Now as she was nearing fourteen there began to be talk of arranging a suitable marriage for Sophia with one of the neighboring princelings. It looked to her like a very drab and uninteresting future.

But with New Year's Day, 1744, her whole world changed. The family were seated at dinner, when a messenger arrived with a letter

35

addressed to her mother, who with fingers aflutter broke open the seal and read the following words:

"At the explicit command of Her Imperial Majesty, I have to inform you, Madame, that the Empress desires your Highness, accompanied by the Princess your eldest daughter, to come to Russia as soon as possible and repair without loss of time to whatever place the Imperial Court may then be found. . . ."

"The Empress of Russia . . . accompanied by your eldest daughter. . . ." Those were magical words! To Sophia, the very thought of Russia alone was exciting. It was such a strange and tremendous land, and now to think that she, Sophia, was invited to visit the Empress!

That same afternoon two hours later another letter arrived, this one from Frederick, the King of Prussia. He wished them to know that he was the one who had thought of arranging the match for Sophia "with her third cousin the Grand Duke Peter of Russia."

Such a journey, and such a marriage for a daughter of his did not meet with the approval of good Christian August.

But his wife, the Princess Johanna, was triumphantly happy. As soon as her own dresses were all in order, she was ready to start. Without having provided Sophia with a single dress fit to appear in at court, she hurried her daughter away.

It was a terrible journey to make at this time of year. Day after day they sat bundled up in the coach, with mufflers up to their eyes and their feet nearly frozen, jolting and lurching over the hard ruts and stony ditches. Their nights they spent in small filthy inns among dirty peasants, who sat drying their stiff socks against the only stove.

But Sophia scarcely heeded any discomfort, her heart beat so fast with excitement. All seemed hardly more than a dream, however, until they had crossed the Polish border and slipped over the frozen river into Russia. There bells rang, cannons saluted them, people cheered and generals kissed their hands. At St. Petersburg a thousand courtiers had remained behind to greet them. From there on, sunk deep in furs and satin cushions, they rode in the royal sledge of the Empress. Behind ten

36

swift horses they sped like the wind over the sparkling snow from St. Petersburg to Moscow. All four hundred miles between the two capitals the road was broad and smooth, for over that road 100,000 people who made up the court and its followers travelled twice a year.

It was the night of the Grand Duke Peter's sixteenth birthday when Sophia arrived in Moscow and, against the dusky winter sky, caught her first glimpse of the white walls, the colored spires and round onion-shaped turrets of that ancient oriental city.

Inside the battlemented palace of the Kremlin one splendid hall opened into another, a bewildering maze of red-and-gold enamel and purple hangings, arched and painted ceilings, and pointed doorways.

The Grand Duke Peter was first to meet them, but Sophia, the excited girl, took almost no notice of her future bridegroom, so eager was she to follow the messenger and meet the Empress.

No fairy godmother could have greeted her more warmly. For the first time in her life the Cinderella princess felt that she was wanted. "I love it here," she thought. "I love it. I belong to Russia!"

Then as she looked at the Empress Elizabeth, who stood for everything that she wanted to be herself, her mind grew firm, "The day will come when I too shall be as great as if I were a man!"

Immediately the ambitious girl set herself to the task of learning the language of her new country. June came and the day when she was to be baptized into the state religion of Russia and receive her new Russian name. As she appeared wearing a gown as red as her lips, embroidered in shining silver, people were startled by her beauty, and when she recited all her responses perfectly in their own Russian tongue she won for herself a firm place in their hearts.

So with that ceremony and that day, the German princess slipped out of her old name and left her old life behind as completely as a gorgeous butterfly slips from an old gray cocoon. As she left the church amid the cheers of the people it actually seemed to her that Sophia Augusta had never been real, and that she had always been as she was now, her Imperial Highness, the Grand Duchess, Catherine Alexievna!

Noble
Bourgeois
Peasant

THE KING OF FRANCE AND HIS SUBJECTS

THE NAME OF the King of France at this time was Louis, as it had been fourteen times before. This, the fifteenth Louis, was the most gorgeous, the most fashionable, the most bejewelled and lace-trimmed king in Europe—and the most utterly useless. He did nothing. He thought of nothing, he cared for nothing but his own pleasure, and he had whatever he fancied no matter how great the cost.

Louis XV lived at Versailles, about twelve miles from the city of Paris, in the most beautiful palaces in Europe built by his very famous great-grandfather, Louis XIV.

Before these palaces had been built at Versailles the King lived as the kings of France before him had, in the old palace of the Tuileries in the city of Paris. Then the nobles of France had lived on their country estates, in old castles, many of which had been built by their ancestors in the Middle Ages. There the peasants worked and tilled the fields as peasants always had, and paid the same dues and taxes and rents to their noble overlord as their ancestors had paid in ancient times when they needed his protection.

Louis XIV was an absolute ruler, but with the noblemen scattered all over the country it was difficult to keep absolute power over them. So when he had moved to Versailles he made the nobles leave their estates and also come to live at Versailles, where he could have his eye on them. To keep them happy he established for them many more honorary offices at court such as those of Lord High Chamberlain, Grand Master of the Royal Hunt, Lord High Steward of the Kitchen, to which large salaries and no work were attached.

By the time Louis XV became King, it was the well-established custom for all important noblemen to live at Versailles as near to the King as possible, and every waking moment to follow him about. There were two hundred attendants stumbling over each other in the King's bedchamber alone. From the time he awoke and held out his white hands to be perfumed and jewelled to the time when the Lord High Keeper of it put the nightcap on his head, the King was never alone. The courtiers were always there, to watch his every move and imitate it.

What the King did and had one day, *they* did and had the next. What he was, they became: the most fashionable, bejewelled and lace-trimmed noblemen in Europe, and the most useless. They danced, played games, chatted with each other and made love to the ladies. Every year their manners became more exact and fanciful, their clothes more delicate in color and more hung with lace, their wigs more finely powdered

39

and their furniture more full of curves and scrolls and more richly gilded. And all they did was play. But as too much play becomes monotonous, all their amusements grew tiresome in time.

"Life is boring," sighed the King. "Life is boring," sighed the noblemen, and yawned behind their white, jewelled hands.

Meanwhile, back on the estates, the peasants still worked and tilled the fields as they had always done. Only now each year they had to work even harder, for each year their lord at Versailles needed more money for his pleasures, to say nothing of the huge amounts needed by the King. So while the noblemen played, their overseers squeezed larger rents for the small fields, larger feudal dues and more enormous taxes from the peasants. When they had turned in their crops in payment, many peasants had barely enough left to keep from starving.

"Life is hard," they said as they scuffed off their wooden clogs each sundown and wiped the sweat and dust off with their rough brown hands. "Life is hard."

Between the peasants whose life was all work and the noblemen whose life was all play there was of course a very large middle class of people who worked for a living, but also had some time to play. The French name for them was *bourgeois*. They were the bankers, lawyers, printers, doctors, jewellers, watchmakers, tailors, shopkeepers, bakers, writers, musicians, . . . all the kinds of people who make up a town. A townsman is what the word bourgeois means. Some of them were wealthy, most of them were just hardworking and thrifty, but all of them hated to see such a large part of their hard-earned money go for taxes.

"Life is unfair," they were beginning to say. Why should thousands of people work hard for their money, in order that one king and a few extravagant noblemen should have it to squander?

It was plain to see that such an unfair condition of things could not last forever. That, however, did not trouble the King.

"It will last as long as I live," Louis XV would say. "After that," with a shrug of his shoulders, "what do I care what happens in France?"

40

PIERRE CARON, BORN A BOURGEOIS!

N O NO NO!" screamed Pierre. The small handsome French
boy clenched his fists and stamped his small feet violently.
"No, I will *not* become an old watchmaker. And I *will*
wear red heels and a sword at my side and be a nobleman."

"But my son," repeated his father Caron the watchmaker patiently,
"as I tell you, one may not wear the red heels and the sword, unless he is
born a nobleman. You are born a bourgeois."

So that was it! He had been born wrong! At last the boy understood,
but it made him wild with rage. He stamped out vowing that he would
never come into the old shop again!

It was a fascinating place, however, with its rows of ticking clocks

41

and watches and in a few days the boy was back again sitting as usual in the great window to watch the people pass. Sometimes a nobleman would drive by. Often a lackey in gold-braided livery would turn in at the shop door, come to bring or call for the watch of his noble master.

In the evening Pierre would give imitations of their haughty manners while his mother and five sisters laughed until they cried. For the boy was a natural actor, as clever as he was handsome.

Of all the family his father was the only one who was not entirely pleased with him. Honest Caron père would have been happier with a son less handsome and clever but more steady and reliable. At times he even feared that the boy was not quite honest.

When Pierre Augustin was fourteen years of age, his father said to him one day, "Now it is time that you should learn our trade."

"But I don't mean to be a watchmaker," replied Pierre.

"No? What would you then? What trade, tell me, is better than that of your father and your father's father?"

Since Pierre could tell him of no trade he wished to learn, and dared not confide to him the wild ambitions that stirred his blood, he sat down to the watchmaker's bench to work by day at the tiny springs and wheels that go to make up watches.

But evenings, when the lights flared on the corners of Paris, Pierre roamed about the city in search of excitement. One night he followed a party of young noblemen into a café and made himself so entertaining with his songs and verses, that they invited him, gay and witty fellow that he was, to join them at their table. Similar evenings followed, and the more Pierre saw of the carefree nobility, the more positive became his ambition to be one of them.

It would be difficult. But it was not impossible as his father believed. That he had learned from the gossip of the market women. Who, they asked, was Louis XV's favorite, the most important woman at court, but Madame de Pompadour? And who had she been born, but plain Jean Poisson (Fish), daughter of a bourgeois—a fish you might say, out of their own pool. And who, indeed, was now Master of the Royal Hunt but the son of a wealthy wool-comber who had bought his title?

Pierre thought over his own possibilities. He had no fortune to buy his title, but scientific men had also gained distinction at court. . . . Possibly he might invent something to attract attention!

In the coming days, Father Caron was amazed to see his son who had worked but half-heartedly suddenly apply himself in earnest. Pierre had set his mind on discovering some way of making watches keep more accurate time. Finally he succeeded. And the play began, the play of:

"HOW PIERRE THE BOURGEOIS BECAME A NOBLEMAN"

Act I took place on the morning when he set out for Versailles, taking the small watch which he had made showing the new invention, to present it to the King!

The anteroom to the King's bedchamber was filled with noblemen when he arrived. Though the elegant gentlemen ignored him haughtily, he was not embarrassed. His belief that he was cleverer than they were gave him assurance. Even the quiver of uncertainty that came when his name was finally called to enter the King's presence left him almost instantly. After the King had inspected with great interest the wonderful little watch he had heard about, Pierre was given an order to make another one for Madame de Pompadour. Back in the anteroom again the nobles crowded around him, each clamoring for the first watch to be made exactly like the King's.

Father Caron was more than pleased when his son returned with a hundred orders and when the words *Watchmaker to the King* hung outside his shop, the old man said an honest watchmaker could not wish for more. His son Pierre, however, had very different ideas. So the play went on.

Act II took place when he was able to buy the position of Secretary of the Royal Kitchens. Then when the King dined, it was Pierre's duty to be on hand. He followed in from the kitchens sixth in line, immediately behind the Lord High Steward and the Kitchen Chef, and followed by the meat bearers. With just the proper flourish, he lifted the silver covers and placed the serving of meat on the plate before the King. Then he was free to wander about until the next meal, to gossip, play the flute, and plan how to better his position, which he soon accomplished.

Act III took place when, after the man who had sold him his position at court had been most mysteriously murdered, Pierre Caron married the wealthy widow and took for his name that part of her country estate de Beaumarchais. Pierre Caron de Beaumarchais was his name from then on, and one which he was later to make famous as a dramatist.

Old Caron père was grieved. It was disgrace enough to have a son give up an honest business for an idle life at court. But worse it was to discard an honest name for a high-sounding one such as a nobleman might have, but to which a bourgeois had no right. But needless to say, even after his wife died, Pierre Caron went on as de Beaumarchais. Act IV then took place. Looking about for the next persons who might be of use to him at court, Pierre's shrewd eyes chanced to light upon the four daughters of the King. Dour, ill-tempered, unattractive girls they were, of whom Louis XV, their father, thought so little that he called two of them by the charming nicknames of "Rag" and "Sow." Having the idea that if he could brighten up their dull days he might benefit from it, Pierre arranged to give them music lessons. It worked like a charm. The poor neglected spinsters were so thrilled by his attention, that they helped him obtain the high title of Lieutenant General of the Royal Hunt, one at last which carried with it the coveted title of nobility!

Then at last, the French boy who had so rebelled at having been born a bourgeois, could wear his red heels and carry a dress sword at his side!

The fact that he had been able to do this is important not because it happened to *him,* but because it shows how the old order of things was changing and how the middle class was growing strong. In the days of the King's great-grandfather, Louis XIV, it would have been impossible in the way he did it, for Pierre Caron the watchmaker's son to have become Pierre-Augustin Caron de Beaumarchais the nobleman.

THE GREAT VOLTAIRE

ONE HOT JULY in 1753 a huge coach went bumping along the dusty road leading away from the ancient German city of Frankfort. On the seat inside, a wisp of an old Frenchman with pipestem legs and a great curled wig bounded about like an eggshell. At each bump he sniffed with increased annoyance, as the huge wig slid farther forward, and threatened to cover his eyes entirely. Those eyes that sparkled like bits of cut steel in the thin pointed face were most remarkable. So too was the smile, scornful but not unkind, into which his thin lips fitted together, and they belonged, those

45

eyes and that smile, to the most remarkable man in the world; for this eggshell of a man bounding along the dusty road in a huge coach headed for nowhere was Voltaire.

And it was because he was Voltaire, and the most remarkable man in the world, that he was headed for nowhere. He had no place to go. He had been born a Frenchman, but now the French King had decreed that he should never set foot on the soil of France again.

That was because Voltaire had said once more, as he had so many times in his long life, what he believed to be the matter with France. The first time back in 1717, when he was twenty-three and still known as François Arouet, he had been sent to the Bastille for doing so. The Bastille was an ancient gray stone fortress built in the Middle Ages in Paris and long since used as a prison. There in that grim dungeon young François Arouet had spent eleven months. There he had assumed the pen name Voltaire, and there he began to write at the fast and furious pace that he had kept up all his life.

Such a gift he had for stringing sparkling words into brilliant sentences and verse, that by the time he was thirty he had become the first poet of the age, had had his plays produced at court and was high in favor with the King. But then, for having displeased a nobleman, he found himself put back in prison, for after all, brilliant and celebrated though he was, Voltaire was but a bourgeois!

That time, released from the Bastille after fifteen days, Voltaire, obliged to leave France, had gone to England for three years. He had found much there that he approved. "In England," said he, "you do not hear of one kind of justice for the higher class of people and another for the lower. An Englishman is not exempt from paying certain taxes just because he is a nobleman. A government like that of ours in France, which permits a certain class of men to say, 'Let those who work pay taxes; we should not pay taxes because we do not work,' is no better than a government of Hottentots."

Voltaire had known better than to make public the *Letters* in which he wrote these words, but a printer, foolhardy or daring, had them

46

published. Immediately the royal censor ordered the book seized, and burned by the executioner, and Voltaire had to leave Paris again.

"That Voltaire," said some one who recognized the power of his words, "ought to be locked up where he could have neither pen, ink nor paper. A man of his humor is capable of destroying a kingdom."

Although Voltaire wished only to reform, not to destroy the kingdom, nevertheless, by teaching the people of France to think of securing justice, he planted the seed of the French Revolution.

So then, in 1750, Voltaire, banished from France, had accepted the oft-repeated invitation of Frederick of Prussia.

"My dear Voltaire," Frederick had written, "you are a philosopher. I am the same; what is more natural than that philosophers made to live together should enjoy this satisfaction?"

Upon his arrival, Frederick had made Voltaire his Chamberlain, and given him a gold key to wear around his neck and a handsome pension. In return Voltaire had to correct Frederick's verses every morning, and at night enliven the royal supper parties with his wit. At first all was peace and happiness. But soon sparks began to fly. Voltaire grew bored, Frederick resentful, and instead of two philosophers made to live together each regarded the other as the most irritable man on earth.

So Voltaire departed gladly. When he finally reached the old free city of Frankfort, and lay down to rest in the Inn of the Golden Lion, he heaved a deep sigh of relief. But he sighed too soon. Early next morning four doughty Prussians marched solemnly into his room, clicked their heels together, and demanded in the name of their "gracious master," Frederick of Prussia, that certain book of his Majesty's verses and that certain golden key which Voltaire had failed to return. Learning that both were in trunks which were to follow, the officers put the distinguished Frenchman under arrest until the treasures should arrive.

Weeks passed and so it was July before Voltaire, almost speechless with rage and exasperation, was finally free to leave old Frankfort and go bumping along the road to nowhere, wondering at what spot on earth he should next set up his writing desk and make his future home.

JAMES COOK, A BOY WHO WENT TO SEA

ONE SUMMER MORNING in England, the year George Washington was ten, thirteen-year-old James Cook, who was to discover a new land for his country, ran away to sea. Monday morning it was and very early, just past the dawn. The little fishing village of Staithes, at the foot of a high cliff, still lay in shadow. Clammy night mist hung about the tavern of the Cod and Lobster and the smell of fish lay heavy in the slimy narrow street.

Next door to the tavern stood a combination shop, half grocery and half dry-goods store. Nothing stirred, oustide the shop or in, except a few ants and cockroaches, which in the half light might have been seen crawling about over some stray crumbs of sugar near the scales. Under the counter lay a pile of rumpled sacks, and near by on the unswept floor a small neat bundle tied in a faded handkerchief. There was still no sound when the rumpled sacks began to move a bit; a hand came out, followed by a knee, a bare foot and then the tousled brown hair of a boy. The boy stood upright and stretched himself, picked up the small bundle from the floor, listened a moment, and then tiptoed to the door, lifted the latch without a sound, and stepped into the street outside. He turned and closed the door behind him quietly but very firmly, and without hesitating, he started up the steep zigzag flight of narrow wooden steps that led from the village up to the top of the cliff.

"No more," said James, "will I be weighin' out sugar or measurin' flannel. Now will I 'ave a sight of the sailor's fine wide world m'self."

When he reached the last steps at the top of the cliff, a bit of fresh breeze blew back the hair from his broad forehead, and the sun shone in his fresh eager face, as he turned toward the sea and went swinging along the high narrow path that led to Whitby.

In the distance James could see a ship slowly beating its way in, the very ship, perhaps, on which he would sail away for the Arctic Sea, for the West Indies, or some unknown land in the Sea of Darkness!

The sun was high; the town was wide-awake when James swung into Whitby. Back in Staithes, Mr. Sanderson, the grocer, was also awake. As he clattered down the narrow stairs into the shop he found to his surprise the floor was still unswept and the shutters closed. With a stick in his fist, he poked under the counter, prepared to give the lazy boy a sound thrashing. But the boy was gone!

"Men, ha' ye seen James Cook?" he called to a couple of sailors leaning against a post outside. "M' apprentice James Cook?"

But no one in the village had seen the boy that morning. Nor ever did again, for James Cook never came back to Staithes.

Life on shipboard was so hard in those days that in order to get enough sailors for the Royal Navy, what was known as the "press gang" went abroad along the docks, into grog shops and up and down the streets of London hunting for men to force into the service. Their common method was to grab a victim, drag him away, and if he resisted, clout him over the head. When he came to he would find himself on shipboard. This dreadful practice was so common that London children had for their favorite game "Impressing Seamen."

One spring night in the year 1755, a coal ship lay rocking at anchor in the river Thames. The mate, having heard that the press gang was abroad, lay low and did not go ashore. The next day, however, he took his belongings, left the ship, and of his own free will added his name, James Cook, to the list of able seamen in his sovereign's Royal Navy.

JAMES WATT, A CLEVER LAD OF SCOTLAND

ON ONE SIDE of the ocean the boy George Washington saw the tobacco ships as they were being loaded in Virginia. On the other side a Scottish boy, James Watt, saw them unloaded at the port of Glasgow. Next to London, Glasgow, Scotland, was the largest market for tobacco. James Watt lived in a small village near the port where the Virginia ships stopped to anchor and unload. His father made the first crane used to lift off their cargo of tobacco barrels, and one day James made a miniature model of the crane. Years later when he had become famous as the inventor of the steam engine, the relatives dusted off that little old model and displayed it proudly. In those later years it also delighted a cousin of his to tell her favorite story of how Jamie watched the teakettle.

According to her tale, the little boy often went to the city of Glasgow, to visit his Aunt and Uncle Muirhead. One day when they were all enjoying a dish of tea Jamie put down his cup and kept gazing at the steam that was coming from the spout of the small brass kettle, under which an oil flame kept the water at the boiling point.

"James Watt," exclaimed Mrs. Muirhead, "I never saw such an idle lad. If you have finished, take a book and employ yourself usefully."

James did not answer. He merely picked up his silver teaspoon, and held it close to the spout and watched the steam gather on it and form into drops of water. Finally he looked up and smiled shyly as he saw the others watching him. They all laughed. It was impossible ever to be cross at James, he had such a wistful way about him.

He never made them any trouble, they said, and often they took him with them in the summer to Loch Lomond. James liked it there. The nights were very clear and he could watch the stars. Out among the hills there were new rocks to be found for his collection, and on the windy heaths strange varieties of thistles, mosses, white and purple heather.

At home again after the summer was over, there was his father's fascinating shop to work in, where all sorts of intriguing tools and pumps and fittings for ships were always being made or mended. Though there were often as many as fourteen men at work, there was always room for James, and he was the pride of the whole shop.

"Look-a-that, noo!" the men would exclaim, pointing at what the boy had made. "Wee Jamie ha' a fortune at his finger tips."

Now in the city of Glasgow there was a university, which was both very old and very modern. The somber buildings, whose turrets had high pointed roofs that looked like candle snuffers, were four hundred years of age. But the teaching was very modern, because it included the study of sciences. It would have been the perfect school for James.

But in the year 1753, his father's business was so bad that James, who was then seventeen, felt that he should start out on his own to learn a trade and earn his living. He wanted to learn to make mechanical instruments, such as scales, compasses, surveying tools and telescopes.

So he packed his leather apron with some models he had made and went to Glasgow, only to discover that there was no one there to teach him.

"London is the place for you to go," a professor of science at the university advised him.

The radical idea of making that dangerous twelve-day journey on horseback down to London cost James a good bit of thinking.

"But I'll go," said he at length. "I'll work hard and learn it a' in one year's time and then return to Glasgow and set up m' shop."

James didn't know a soul in London when he set out to find a job in some shop where he might learn his trade, and he soon found that no one wanted to take him on.

"One year is too short a time," they all said. "We mechanical instrument makers belong to the Guild of Hammermen. Guild rules say that Hammermen apprentices have to serve seven years, not one!"

James kept on hunting. Finally on Finch Lane, near the river, he found a place where the master agreed to instruct him in return for twenty pounds and his work, of course. He had to take the worst bench near the door. In winter it was cold, and many days thick fog rolled in, which, mingled with the smoke from many chimneys, gave him a racking cough. A day in the shop began at seven o'clock in the morning and lasted till nine every evening except Saturday. After closing time, in spite of the gnawing pain in his back, James did outside work to earn pay for his board and lodging.

At the end of the year he was worn-out and half ill, but he had accomplished what he had set out to do. He left no better instrument maker in London, when he went home to Glasgow.

He arrived there full of hope, only to find that he could not open a shop or even rent a room. The Guild of Hammermen said that it was against the union rules; he hadn't served his seven years!

"Let me see what I can do," said his friend the professor.

At his suggestion, the university provided James with a room in one of their buildings, where he might sell his instruments and also work on his experiments, which he usually spoke of half apologetically as his "gimcracks." There the professors soon began dropping in to chat with him, and were constantly amazed at the skill and knowledge he had gained without a university education.

"I'll tell you there's not much that that young man James Watt does not know," they were soon saying to one another, "and certainly there's nothing you can think of that James Watt cannot make."

A KING BUT NOT A RULER

ENGLAND, SCOTLAND, IRELAND and the American colonies across the ocean all belonged to the little island kingdom of England. They were ruled over by Parliament and the King or by the King and Parliament, depending upon who had control. The struggle between the two had been going on for the five hundred years since Parliament had been created. And long before they had a Parliament to represent them, the English people had begun to struggle for the right to rule themselves. Their first victory had come in 1215, when King John signed the Magna Carta, and agreed that knights of the shires should be called together yearly to help him make the tax laws.

In the year 1740, Parliament had the upper hand. George II, who was then the King, was just as well pleased to have it so, since he was not much interested in what went on in England. In fact, he could hardly speak the English language, for he had been born a German, not an Englishman. His homeland was Hanover, a small state touching the North Sea and edging the west border of Prussia, the kingdom where his nephew Frederick II had just become the ruler. What that nephew Frederick was going to do in Prussia, how Maria Theresa would make out as Queen of Austria seemed more important to George II than what was happening in England. Once that little blustering pop-eyed King went home to Hanover on a visit and stayed away five years—quite regardless of his duties.

With such an indifferent King, Parliament naturally had grown stronger with each year of his reign.

Parliament was divided into the House of Lords, which was the older section, and the House of Commons, which was the more powerful one. Members of the House of Lords were noblemen, who inherited their membership along with their titles and castles, jewelry, silver soup tureens, coats of arms and whatnot, all of which were theirs for life.

Members of the House of Commons were elected from the middle class, that is, all those who were substantially well-to-do, solid bankers, portly landowners, rich tradespeople, but no poor people. People too poor to own property had not yet even the right to vote.

Ministers to head the government with the Prime Minister at the top were appointed by the King, but they had to resign if they were not supported by the majority in the House of Commons.

So, as was perfectly natural, there was a continual struggle going on between the Prime Minister and his party who were running the government, and those of the opposing party who wanted to get control and put their own ideas into action. That meant that exciting debates and speeches were always to be heard in the House of Commons.

One of the best speakers at this time was a man (about the age of Benjamin Franklin) whose name was William Pitt. When that man

54

rose to his full height and began to speak, every one paid attention. No one who saw or heard him ever forgot his ringing voice, or his sharp piercing eyes, or the long hooked nose that overpowered his stern face like an eagle's beak. William Pitt saw much that was the matter in England and he made enemies of both the Prime Minister and the King, by denouncing what they did. He declared that what went on in Prussia or Austria was none of England's business, and that the English had far better reserve their money and attention for their own affairs. He pointed out that the Prime Minister kept himself in power by bribing the members to support him. Otherwise, said Pitt, they would never put up with his weak, shilly-shallying, pusillanimous methods of dealing with Spain in the West Indies and with France in India and America. William Pitt was scrupulously honest in everything he said and did, and wholeheartedly concerned with what was best for England. Though he fell out of favor with the King, every speech he made and office he held won for him the increased confidence of the people. Their name for him was the Great Commoner.

Now in 1740, when Frederick II became King of Prussia, and William Pitt, the Great Commoner, made his first exciting speech in the House of Commons, the King's grandson, who was to be George III and the next King of England, was just learning to walk. Ten years later he had grown into a dull, obstinate boy, but a good boy and proud of being the first of the Hanover Georges to be born in England. His mother, however, was a German princess, who believed that German ways were right and had no patience with the English idea that Parliament should run the government instead of the King.

"When you get to be King, George," she told her son continually, "BE KING!"

"That's right," echoed George. "When I get to be king I'll BE KING, and a good one, too."

But it was to be ten more years before George had a chance to try. In those years there was going to be time for a member of Parliament, the Great Commoner himself, to act as "King of England."

BENJAMIN FRANKLIN LOOKS AND LEARNS

THE SUMMER SUN stood high in the sky one fine July day when a calash which had been rolling along the green-bordered road in southern England came to a stop on Salisbury Field, near the ancient ruins known as Stonehenge. Two men stepped from under the shade of the carriage hood and walked among the ruins.

"Nobody knows how many thousand years these huge stones have been standing here," observed the older man. "They were here when Julius Cæsar and the Romans came to England, and no one knows how long they had been standing then." He looked up as he spoke and anyone from Philadelphia would have recognized his pleasant face. For it was that of Benjamin Franklin.

Benjamin Franklin, with his son William, had but just arrived in England and was bound for London on important business.

For some time past things had not been going well in Pennsylvania. Arguments over taxes had arisen between the Quakers, the royal governor and the Penns, who still owned the colony. Benjamin Franklin had been appointed to go to London where the Penn family

56

lived, to see what he could do towards smoothing out the difficulties.

The big, dark, smoky city looked much as he remembered it, as they arrived toward evening, and the friends whom he had made when he was there as a youth he remembered well, and was eager to see again. He was also looking forward to enjoying the theatres of Drury Lane and Covent Garden, to seeing the great actor, David Garrick, to making the acquaintance of the celebrated author Doctor Samuel Johnson, to visiting in the coffee houses and to all the attractions which the fascinating old city had to offer.

But business came first, so he went to see the Penns without delay, but came away from that first visit disappointed. He was also to be disappointed about another idea which he had in mind.

People of Pennsylvania were not the only ones who were discontented in America. Virginia planters complained about the low price of their tobacco. Massachusetts shippers complained of the high import tax on sugar and molasses. Both were caused by the Acts of Trade, which were laws passed by the English Parliament, in which (and here was the important point) the colonies were not represented.

"And why should they not be represented?" queried Benjamin Franklin. The right to have their tax laws made by their own representatives in Parliament had been granted to the English people almost a hundred years before in the Bill of Rights. Why should English people now be made to forfeit that right merely because they lived in New England instead of Old?

Because of the great distance it would be indeed impossible for the colonies to send delegates to Parliament. But why, thought Benjamin Franklin, could there not be a Congress or Parliament in America composed of delegates from the colonies who would cooperate with the English Parliament and the King?

As soon as he visited one of the King's ministers, however, it was plain to see how far apart were their ways of thinking.

"You Americans have the wrong ideas," said Lord Granville. "You contend that the King's instructions to his governors are not laws.

57

But those instructions, Mr. Franklin, are, as far as they relate to you, the *law of the land,* for the King is *legislator of the colonies."*

Lord Granville's ideas about the colonies were not unusual. All nations believed that their colonies existed for the good of the mother country, and most nations governed their colonies much more harshly than did England. Actually, except for those regarding trade, most of their laws were made by the colonists in their own assemblies.

In fact, Benjamin Franklin found that the people in America were far better off than most of the people in the British Isles.

"I have lately made a tour through Ireland and Scotland," he wrote home. "In those countries a small part of society are landlords, great noblemen, extremely wealthy, living in the highest magnificence. The bulk of the people are tenants, living in dirty hovels of mud and straw, clothed only in rags. Most of the people of Scotland go barefoot, but three fourths of the people of Ireland live the year round on potatoes and buttermilk, without shirts. In the comforts of life, compared to these people every American Indian lives like a gentleman."

Life of the poor people in England was little if any better. In the mine districts it was common practice for women and children to carry up the coal on their backs like animals. In the London slums they lived in squalor and in constant fear. If a workman failed to squeeze a living out of his small wages and found himself in debt, he was in danger of being thrown into prison, his family with him or else left at home to starve. It was not at all uncommon to see a man swinging from the gallows for having stolen a loaf of bread. These people did not set their wages nor have any voice in saying what the law should be.

"What a contrast," said Benjamin Franklin, "to the happiness at home in Massachusetts and all New England, where every man is a freeholder, has a vote in public affairs, lives in a tidy warm house, has plenty of good food and fuel, with whole clothes from head to foot. Compared to the poor people in the British Isles it can truly be said that there are no poor people in the American Colonies."

II

WHEN GEORGE WASHINGTON WAS A
Soldier

People who were living when

"EMPIRE BUILDER"

WILLIAM PITT
gained an Empire for England
by winning war against France

WOLFE
captured Quebec and
England gained Canada

CLIVE
by his victory won power
for England in India

The Spinning Jenny
a machine to replace this old hand wheel was
being thought out by Jas. Hargreaves in 1763

PONTIAC
fought in vain to save
their country for his people

POMPEII
had been discovered and
was being unearthed

THOMAS JEFFERSON
was sixteen, the year George
Washington was married.

Mrs. MARTHA CUSTIS
became Mrs G. Washington in 1759

ROBERT BURNS
Scotland's poet, was but
a wee lad (born 1759)

and Events that took place

Washington was a Soldier

The three most powerful women in Europe:

ELIZABETH of RUSSIA
MARIA THERESA
Mme de POMPADOUR

plotted revenge on FREDERICK

THE SEVEN YEARS WAR

FREDERICK II
discovered the plot and began the war,

VOLTAIRE
was writing against war and hatred

GOETHE
the great German poet, was a school boy (born 1749)

Canton

CATHERINE II
was crowned Empress of Russia in 1761

CH'IEN LUNG
forbade "barbarian" traders from Europe to enter China

GEORGE III
was crowned King of England - in 1760

between the Years 1756 and 1763

Ch'ien

Lung

CH'IEN LUNG AND THE "BARBARIANS"

HALF WAY AROUND the world from the American colonies where the young nation of the United States had not yet come into being, lay the oldest nation in the world, the great and ancient Empire of China. There when George Washington was four years old, Ch'ien Lung, a young Manchu prince, had ascended the red Dragon Throne in the Purple City of Peking, to become China's Emperor. On that coronation day, as he stood in his embroidered robes and the princes of the realm kowtowed before him, Ch'ien Lung made a wish that he be permitted to reign for sixty years. If so, he vowed, he would then abdicate in favor of a son. With his wish granted, Ch'ien Lung was to go down in history as the last great Emperor of China.

63

That China might prosper under his reign, Ch'ien Lung from the beginning tried to fulfill what the Chinese held to be a ruler's foremost duty, that of setting a good example to his people. Faithfully he observed the ancient customs. Each year at the time of Winter Solstice he went to the Temple of Heaven and gave thanks for the blessings of the year gone by, and prayed to rule so wisely in the year to come that he might truly deserve to be called the Father of his People. In the spring, on the Day of Pure Brightness, he took his offering to the tablet of Shen-nung, the "divine" Farmer King, the one who had first taught the people of China how to till their fields.

These and all other time-honored customs, Ch'ien Lung faithfully observed, for though a Manchu and a descendant of one of China's conquerors, he was as truly Chinese as those whose ancestors had always lived within the Great Wall, and tilled their fields along Huang-Ho, the Yellow River.

Ch'ien Lung was steeped in China's culture, and proud of her long continuous history, one beginning twenty-four hundred years before the birth of Christ. At the time that Julius Cæsar found only wild tribes in France and England, China had been for centuries the eastern center of the world's civilization. When Rome fell, and the Dark Ages blotted out Europe, China's culture continued to go steadily on. In 1755, more books had been written and printed in Chinese than in all other languages put together.

No Chinese book of history, however, told of what had happened outside of Asia. To the black-haired people, China was truly, as they called it, "All-That-Is-Under-Heaven." In Ch'ien Lung's thought, Europeans were merely "outside barbarians," not differing greatly from the wild tribes of Asia.

Too many Europeans, he thought, were coming to China in these later years, bringing things to trade that Chinese people had no use for. They were becoming a nuisance, those red-faced people with their beaklike noses and their pale bulging eyes. Every year more of the "Holan devils," as the people called them, and more of the "red-haired devils," who called their country England, came pushing into China's harbors, sailing up her rivers, and clamoring in their loud voices for silk, for porcelains, and especially for tea.

In ancient days when travellers from Europe had come only overland, China had been well protected from them, as well as from the wild tribes on the western border, by the mountains, the desert and the Great Wall. But now that they were coming by water, a new means had to be found to protect the peace of China from these disturbing "devils." So in 1757, the Hongs of Canton were created.

"From now on," said Ch'ien Lung, "Canton shall be the only place in our empire where Europeans shall be allowed to trade."

Europeans, however, were not to be allowed to enter the city of Canton itself. Outside the walls, along the river, buildings called Hongs were built, where the Europeans might have their living quarters, their storehouses and their offices. A special group of Chinese Mandarins, the Hong Merchants, was appointed to carry on all the dealings with the foreigners. Since the Europeans were not allowed to learn Chinese, and since the Chinese cared to learn no more than necessary of that barbaric language which had so many difficult tongue-twisting sounds, business between the English and the Chinese was carried on in a ridiculous jargon which came to be known as pidgin English.

"No likee silk?" they would say, or "Me sellee number one tea."

The English were most annoyed by the whole arrangement. They protested but it did no good. Ch'ien Lung remained firm. It was best so. Foreigners had no understanding of China's laws and customs, nor did they follow the wisdom of her great teachers. Besides that, having nothing at first to offer that his people wanted, English traders had hit upon a dreadful drug that Chinese people could be made to buy. It was opium made from poppies grown in India. Therefore it seemed best to Ch'ien Lung to restrict the trade. What could "outside barbarians" from the Western Ocean bring to China but discord and evil?

So while the Hong Merchants dealt with the barbarians, the people of China were undisturbed by them. Life went on as it had for centuries. Chinese farmers tilled their neat fields and governed themselves in their small villages, as independently as people in Massachusetts, Pennsylvania, or Virginia. China was an empire, but it was at heart, as it had always been, a democratic country.

The farmers of China were still singing in the year 1755 the same old song good King Yao had heard his people singing 2000 years B.C.:

> "We rise at dawn
> And rest at sunset,
> We dig wells and drink,
> We till our fields and eat:
> What is the power of the Emperor to us?"

Back in England, wares brought from China were so popular that English manufacturers began to copy them. Dishes decorated with the well-known bright blue "willow" pattern were made by Mr. Spode and Mr. Wedgwood, while chairs, cabinets and lacquer screens were designed in Chinese fashion by the furniture maker, Thomas Chippendale.

सैन्धवदेश *Land of the Indus*

INDIA AND THE EUROPEAN TRADERS

INDIA, ALTHOUGH NEVER a united nation like China, was an equally ancient land whose beginnings are lost in obscurity. But as far back as records go, travellers and traders had been going to India.

When the European traders first went overland to China for tea and silk they also went to India for spices, and those travellers to India had brought back in their caravans not only ginger, cinnamon and cloves, but cottons spun as fine as cobwebs and the most dazzling and precious jewels. With those jewels, they also brought back almost incredible stories of the far more brilliant diamonds, the more beautiful

67

rubies and more perfect emeralds to be seen in the land from which they came. Palaces made of jasper and alabaster, idols of solid gold with eyes of emeralds, elephants with jewel-bespangled trappings on which the native princes rode and the still more fabulous riches of the Grand Mogul made India seem to those who listened like a land of magic, an enchanted land—and certainly a treasure house for traders.

The first traders from France and England had gone to India about the same time that their explorers had first reached America. Nineteen days after the Pilgrims landed on Plymouth Rock, an English trader had bought a site on the east coast of India and founded the first English trading post at Madras. A hundred miles to the south of Madras the first French trading post was founded at a place called Pondicherri.

From the first, greed for trade caused rivalry between the French and English traders, so they both had stationed soldiers at their posts, and both bribed or hired the native Indian rulers with their troops of "sepoys" to help them fight against each other.

About the time that George Washington had gone on his first surveying trip over the mountains in Virginia, a spirited young daredevil by the name of Clive had been made commander of the English trading post in India. Down at the French post there was an older governor, a very clever man, and very wise in the ways of India, but not such a ready fighter as young Clive. So in 1751, Clive attacked the French governor and defeated him and his Indian ally at Arcot, and then put another native rajah, one who was friendly to the English, on the throne.

Not long after that battle took place in India between the two nations, fighting also began in America between the French and English.

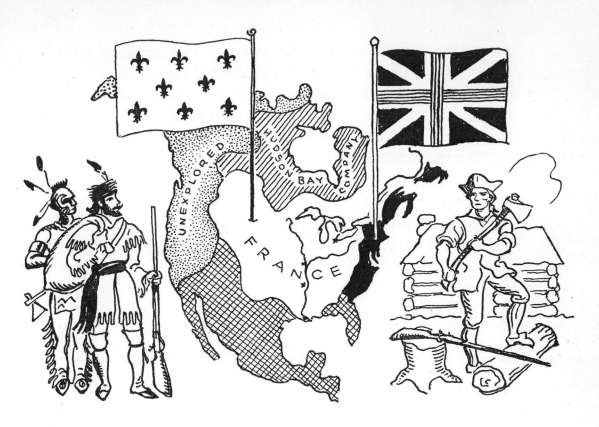

FRANCE AND ENGLAND IN AMERICA

RIVALRY FOR LAND caused the friction between France and England in America. The French, having first discovered the Mississippi, naturally laid claim to the great river valley. But that land was likewise claimed by the English, for when the King of England had granted charters to each one of his colonies, their land had been handsomely but vaguely described, as beginning at the Atlantic Ocean and extending from sea to sea. So disputes about the land constantly arose between the French and English and both bribed or hired the Indians to help them fight each other.

Now while the English had been establishing their thirteen colonies along the Atlantic seacoast, down through the center of the continent the French had built a string of forts, sixty of them in all, along the lakes and rivers from the mouth of the St. Lawrence to the Gulf of Mexico.

There the French voyageurs, explorers and traders paddled the rivers and roamed the woods, and lived among the Indians in easy friendly fashion. But the English settlers, in order to clear land for their fields, drove back the Indians, cut down the forests and destroyed the Indian hunting grounds. Consequently whenever war broke out between the two "paleface" nations the Indians were always more ready to help their friends the French.

About the year 1752, the French began building a fort near the Ohio River on land which the English said was theirs. A group of Virginia planters, who called themselves the Ohio Company, claimed that the land had been given to them by the King of England, and sent a messenger asking the French to leave.

Imagine the commotion then caused in France by the news that the English messenger who had been sent, a young man by the name of George Washington, had deliberately "murdered" thirty Frenchmen near their fort on the Ohio. And not only had the young Washington committed the assassination, said the French, but he had even signed a paper admitting that he had done the dastardly deed!

The French, stirred up to seek revenge for the so-called "murder" of their unfortunate comrades, summoned their Indian allies, and attacked the English. So it was that a war was started in America between France and England, later to be known as the French and Indian War.

from a portrait by Charles Wilson Peale

FRENCH AND INDIAN WAR BEGINS

GEORGE WASHINGTON had, of couse, not the remotest idea that what he was going to do would start a war, that crisp October morning (1753) when he stood in the office of Governor Dunwiddie in Williamsburg, Virginia. Nor could he have imagined in his wildest dreams that he would ever sign a document saying that he had committed murder.

All he knew was that he had instructions to carry a message to the French to abandon the fort which they were building on the land of the Ohio Company, of which land both the Governor and he himself owned many acres. He was also to locate a site where the Ohio Company themselves might build a fort, for according to their grant they were obliged to establish settlements on the land within ten years or lose their claim to it. Now, after four years, nothing had been done.

"How soon can you start?" the Governor asked that morning.

"Today, sir," answered George, and taking the Governor's letter, placed it carefully in his pocket, mounted his horse and within the hour was far down the road toward Fredericksburg.

A Dutchman of that village, by the name of Van Braam, who claimed to understand French, was engaged by Washington to go with

71

him as interpreter. A guide named Gist, two woodsmen, and two servants completed the party. Halfway there they were joined by an Indian chief called Half King, friendly to the English.

It was a difficult journey into the wilderness; in places not even the trail of a bison broke the underbrush. However, they reached the fort. The French received them courteously, though they quite naturally refused to leave land which they said belonged to the King of France, and sent back a letter by Washington to that effect.

The journey back was worse than coming, for by that time winter had set in, and it was so difficult for the horses that most of the way the men had to go on foot. Although he was nearly drowned in a river full of ice cakes, and barely escaped death from the gun of a treacherous Indian, in January, Washington was back in the Governor's office in Williamsburg. His diagram of the French fort, and his detailed report concerning the surrounding country were so satisfactory to the Governor that as a reward, his rank was raised from major in the Virginia Regiment to lieutenant-colonel.

On the first of April, 1754, George Washington, now lieutenant-colonel, set out again for the French fort, but this time in command of one hundred fifty soldiers and with strict orders to drive out the French, by force. Van Braam, the interpreter, was again with him, and again they were joined by the Indian, Half King. Before attacking the French, Washington was supposed to be joined by reinforcements. So, in a pleasant open spot, which he called Great Meadows, he pitched camp to wait for them, and while waiting built a small log fort, later known as Fort Necessity.

One rainy night toward the end of May, Washington sat writing a letter, when a sudden gust of wind spluttered his candle, and looking up he saw in the fitful light the dark wet face of Half King.

"French men on the way to attack you. Come with me," the red man motioned. Washington rose at once. Detailing forty men to go with him, he followed the stealthy Indians through the rain-drenched woods, until Half King suddenly stopped and pointed. There indeed through the dripping trees dark figures of men could be seen grouped about a fire.

To attack an enemy unaware was the Indian way, and so also the way of the wilderness. A hasty order was given to fire. At the sound of the shots the Frenchmen sprang to their guns, as Jumonville, their leader, and ten of the men fell dead. Then the other twenty, realizing that they were lost, surrendered.

The third of July was another rainy day at Great Meadows. That day Washington and his small number of Virginians, still waiting for reinforcements, were attacked by five hundred French and their Indian allies. The small garrison in Fort Necessity managed to hold out all day but by night the young Colonel, distraught and crestfallen by the turn of events, was obliged to surrender.

The French were content. They had avenged the death of their comrades, who, they asserted, had been only carrying a return message to the English. Merely sign their paper, they said, agreeing not to return to French territory for at least another year, and the Virginians might march home with the honors of war. Now, either Van Braam didn't read it carefully, or else understood very little French, because he handed the paper to his Colonel to sign, and Washington, in all innocence, signed his name to a paper on which the French words plainly said that he had "murdered" Jumonville and his companions.

It was humiliating for the young Colonel to return to Williamsburg that summer with his first success dimmed by this defeat. All fall it hurt his pride to overhear or imagine uncomplimentary remarks being made of him, and just or unjust criticism. And that winter back at Mount Vernon, to add to his misery, George was ill. He was in bed for weeks.

During those long gray winter days the one bright spot in his life was Sally Fairfax, lovely Sally, with her soft dark hair and her piquant beauty. Each morning as he lay there against his pillows, George found comfort in the thought that Sally might drop in that day or the next to see how he was getting on, have a cup of green china tea with him or regale him with a gay bit of news from the neighboring plantation. But when she did come and was actually in the room with him, her presence was almost as much a torment to him as a joy! It was tantalizing to have her so near and friendly, yet so hopelessly removed from him, and to know that the feeling in his heart must never shape itself in words. They would be words that Sally herself would never care to hear, for Sally was the wife of George William Fairfax, his best friend and neighbor.

But, as all things come to an end at last, the winter finally passed.

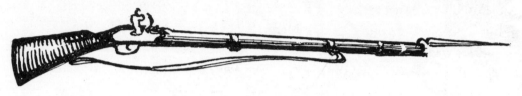

When spring came, George Washington, feeling somewhat better, started again for the fort on the Ohio. This time he went as adjutant on the staff of General Braddock, an English general who had arrived in America, bringing his fine English soldiers in their bright red coats.

General Braddock gave the Colonials to understand that he intended to make quick work of this little matter of the fort on the Ohio. Then he would go on to capture other French forts in a wholesale manner. Now General Braddock was experienced on battlefields in Europe, but unfortunately he knew nothing of fighting in the wilderness. Nor did the English soldiers. The Virginian soldiers under Washington knew what to expect, but the English soldiers had never been in the wilderness before. They had never seen American Indians, never heard their wild savage warwhoops nor seen their copper bodies smeared with war paint. English soldiers were trained to march in perfect formation, raise their guns waist high and fire without aiming when the command was given. That might be the correct way to conduct a battle in Europe, said the Colonial officers, but it was a poor way to use in fighting Indians. General Braddock, however, thought that a man of his experience needed no advice from "backwoodsmen." So they set out,

74

English and Colonials under his direction, on such an ill-planned expedition as could end only in disaster.

After creeping along for miles at the slow pace set by cumbersome baggage wagons (on one of which, by the way, Daniel Boone was teamster), Washington, seething with impatience, finally persuaded Braddock to send some of the troops on ahead. So, on the morning of July 4, twelve hundred English in their bright red coats, so conspicuous in the forest, and certain Virginia troops, were about ten miles from the fort, steadily advancing. Noon came, and they still went on, not knowing that, although not a leaf stirred on the bushes, all through the surrounding trees motionless figures crouched and from every angle black beady eyes were watching. Suddenly, a wild yell split the air, a yell such as the English general had never heard on any battlefield in his life before. Bullets whizzed from every direction as an enemy they couldn't see shot down the bewildered soldiers.

"Let them take refuge behind the trees!" cried George Washington as a bullet pierced his sleeve and his horse fell dead under him. But Braddock would not give the order for his men to break rank. So some

75

stood to be shot down like birds in a trap, while the rest stampeded in confusion and panic. Mounted on this third horse, Washington, heedless of danger, wheeled here and there, to rally his men. The Virginians did what they could in the losing fight, but soon the battle was over, and when it was, more than half the men lay wounded and dying, and their brave red coats, which a few moments before had formed such a brilliant target against the green wall of the forest, lay like a great pool of blood on the forest floor. General Braddock died of wounds a day or two later, and that his body might be safe from Indian scalp hunters, Washington saw that he was buried in the middle of the road where the wagon tracks would hide his grave.

Word of his heroism and bravery on that disastrous day made George Washington's return to Virginia that of a hero. But word of that bloody defeat went as bad news to England. And the next year there was more bad news to be received—that of a disaster in India.

At Calcutta, on a branch of the Ganges River, the English now had another trading post. There one hot day in July, 1756, a native prince, the Nawab of Bengal, who was friendly toward the French, attacked the English unexpectedly. Those who were fortunate made their escape down the river, but all the others were herded together for the night in one small room of the fort which had but two tiny windows high up in one wall.

The brassy sun had been burning hot all day, and that night the dead heat was so stifling that all but twenty-three out of one hundred forty-six English prisoners smothered to death in that small room, since called the "Black Hole of Calcutta."

"We are undone," wailed a member of the House of Commons, over the bad news. "What a prospect for England!" he moaned. "What a dreadful prospect!"

And soon the "dreadful" prospect grew even worse.

76

from a portrait..

SEVEN YEARS' WAR BEGINS

AUGUST, 1756, THERE WAS WAR in Europe! War that was to lay waste to Europe for the next Seven Years. Frederick of Prussia had started it again. This time having discovered a plot against himself he had taken the plotters by surprise. The plot he very scornfully dubbed the "Petticoat Plot" because it had been formed by the three most powerful women or petticoat wearers in Europe: Maria Theresa of Austria, Elizabeth Empress of Russia, and Madame de Pompadour, who since she did most of Louis XV's thinking for him, might almost as well have been the ruler of France.

Frederick had been King of Prussia for fifteen years, and in those years of tending strictly to business he had become the most powerful ruler in Europe: the most feared and the most hated. Maria Theresa, especially, enraged at having to watch him grow strong and Prussia grow rich, had finally suggested the plot to crush him and put his upstart nation back in the second-rate place where it had hitherto belonged.

"That monster must be punished for his deeds," said Maria Theresa, once more hoping against hope to recover her stolen Silesia.

"I will put eighty thousand men in the field and I will not make peace until he is defeated," declared the Empress Elizabeth of Russia, for who had better reason? Had not Frederick insulted her—thought his sister too fine to marry her nephew? Dah! Let him regret that now. Madame de Pompadour was also inclined to help Maria Theresa, so, though the idea bored him, Louis XV humored his lady in her whim and signed the pact which would send to battle thousands of men.

The plot had not proceeded even that far before wily Frederick, through his system of spies, got wind of it and sprang the trap before his opponents were ready. He called out his army and marched into foreign territory again, just as he had done fifteen years before in Silesia. Only this time the land he invaded was Saxony.

Saxony invaded, all the nations of Europe took arms against the invader: France, Russia, Austria, Sweden—all of them.

Except England. England supported Frederick, merely in order that little Hanover, the King's German homeland, might be safe. In too great danger of being captured by the French, George II had wanted England to help Prussia protect it.

And for once, to his surprise, the King found that William Pitt agreed with him, which was fortunate for George II, for Hanover, and for Frederick; because the Great Commoner, William Pitt, was now the power in England.

THE EMPIRE BUILDER

To HAVE WILLIAM PITT in power was likewise extremely fortunate for England. When she was at war with France in three parts of the world at once, when she was stung by defeat both in India and America, when the future looked black indeed for that budding Empire, it was her great good fortune to have at the head of her affairs such a completely patriotic man as William Pitt. William Pitt was brilliant, capable, forceful, energetic, and had the kind of confidence in his own ability that inspired others.

"I believe that I and no one else can save this country from disaster" he declared, speaking to a member of Parliament. Though he spoke more humbly, he was no less sure when he knelt for the first time after his appointment in the presence of the King.

"Give me your confidence, Sire, and I will deserve it," he begged.

"Deserve my confidence and you shall haf it," snapped our little German George in his best English.

William Pitt did all of that and more, for it was his energetic work that made secure the roots of the great British Empire. The very year he came into power, the fortunes of war took an upward turn for England. Good news came first of all from India, then soon after from America.

In India, Clive, that "heaven born general," as Pitt called him, inflicted a bad defeat on the native ally of the French, the Nawab who had smothered the English the summer before in the Black Hole of Calcutta. Clive's successful battle occurred in the grove of Plassey, about seventy miles from there. On a breathless July morning, the Nawab and his "sepoys" had attacked at dawn, but in the noon heat, resting in their tents, they were surprised by Clive and captured. This defeat at Plassey crippled the French, and with it the rule of England over India actually began.

Meanwhile Frederick II, with the help of money and supplies sent to him by England, was so far successfully fighting France and all of Europe in a useless war that was to last for Seven Years.

As for the French and Indian War: More soldiers had been sent to America from England, and new generals selected by Pitt to take charge.

Those generals also were successful. Joined by Colonials under the command of young Colonel Washington, they succeeded in 1758 in driving the French from their fort on the Ohio River, and so settling, once and for all, the fight over that small log fort that had caused so much trouble. It went up at last in crackling flames, set on fire by the French as they were leaving. In its place, the English built Fort Pitt, named in honor, of course, of the Great Commoner, and the settlement which later grew up around the fort became the city of Pittsburg.

The next year the English attacked Quebec. Quebec was the strongest French fort in America, believed to be almost invincible. It was no little log fort in the wilderness, but a strong stone fortress high on a steep wall of rock that rose two hundred feet straight up from the bank of the St. Lawrence River. Its commander was also one of the ablest and most courageous soldiers in America, the French general, Montcalm.

James Wolfe, a young man, but one of rare courage, was the general selected by William Pitt to sail to America and attack Quebec. So in June, 1759, English soldiers found themselves, under the command of young Wolfe, encamped on the St. Lawrence, not far from the fort.

Though their ships had managed to make the hazardous entrance, the river was rocky and treacherous, and first of all soundings had to be taken and a chart made of the river bed. That difficult and dangerous task was assigned to James Cook. He was discovered by Indians employed by the French, and just escaped by a leap to land as the canoes of the redskins reached his barge, but he had the records complete, charts so perfect that to this day there has never been need to make any others.

In the meantime, Wolfe had been pondering the best way to attack the fort. From the island across the river it was plain to see that although their guns might destroy the small village at the foot of the cliff, they could do no slightest damage to the fortress itself high on that steep wall of rock. The only chance for success was to attempt to go up the river past the fort, then find some way to reach the top of the cliff and attack the stronghold from behind. In spite of the great danger of trying to pass below the fort, where the French could easily fire down upon the boats and destroy them, General Wolfe decided that they must take the risk. He waited for a night when the sky was black and there was no moon. Then quietly, with the oars of their boats muffled so as to make no sound, the English soldiers poled their silent way up the dark river past the fort. Tomorrow, they thought, either they would be up in that grim fortress where the French now were, or they would all be dead. Then for a few moments, as their oars dipped the dark water, those in the general's boat heard James Wolfe repeat in his calm low voice the words of a poem which begins:

> "The curfew tolls the knell of parting day,
> The lowing herd winds slowly o'er the lea,
> The ploughman homeward wends his weary way
> And leaves the world to darkness and to me."

"Gentlemen," said Wolfe very simply when he had finished, "I would rather have written that poem than take Quebec tomorrow."

At last their boats reached the shore beyond the fort. They landed, and clambering along the dry bed of a narrow stream, they scaled the steep wall in single file to the top of the cliff. Before daybreak forty-five hundred men were drawn up behind the fort on a level stretch of ground, known as the Plains of Abraham. Completely surprised, at the first sight of those troops, the French knew that their cause was lost. The battle was short but so fierce that the Plains of Abraham were soaked with the blood of dying men. Twice wounded, the brave young Wolfe fought on until the fort was won.

"Now God be praised," he sighed as he fell, "I shall die in peace."

Montcalm, the courageous French general, also died and said as he was dying, "Thank God, I shall not live to see the surrender of Quebec!" Montcalm knew well that the capture of Quebec meant the end of the war and so the end of New France in America.

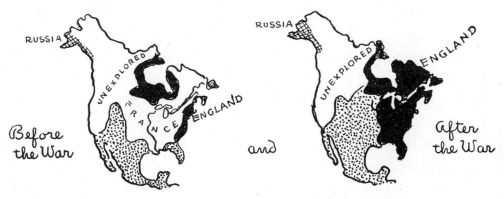

The victory brought joy to England, and more power and glory to William Pitt, the man who conceived the moves in this game of empire building, and to whom the credit, if credit it be, was due.

The King had long since given him his full trust and confidence, and fully recognized that William Pitt was the man in power, far more, indeed, than he who simply wore the crown.

"In dis country, Englant, de ministers are king," said little George. And truly, the people, *not* the King, held the sovereign power.

82

PONTIAC, THE PATRIOT

PONTIAC, TALL CHIEF of the Ottawas, stood in the doorway of his house of bark beside the river, deep in thought. War between the pale-face nations was over. Across the rushes and the water, above the log fort of Detroit, his eyes no longer saw the white flag with the lilies of France, but the red, white and blue flag of the English. And in that fort where his people had once sat beside the fire with their white brothers, there would be no longer any welcome for the red man. No place would be left for him beside the hearthstone.

Word had likewise come to the ear of Pontiac that the French had given away all the land in the great river valley to the English, land that was not theirs to give, but Indian hunting ground! Many times he and his braves had helped the French shoot down the red-coat dogs like pigeons, but now the French had gone. They had deserted the Indian, and given away his land!

But no, the French fur traders had said, all had happened while the

83

great French father slept. Some day the French would return in their war canoes, to drive the English back across the mountains.

And so as Pontiac stood there, and the wind swept over the rushes, a great plan occurred to him. The red man must be ready when the Frenchman came. All the Indians must join hands to help him. From the Hurons in the north to the Cherokees in the south, they must fight as one.

So Pontiac sent word of his plan to all the tribes. And the chiefs of every tribe listened when the swift runners came, carrying the wampum belt of red and black, and the tomahawk stained with war paint and, having heard, they promised to be ready at the appointed time.

Accordingly, when the sun had come back twice from winter sleep, and the moon was full for the fourth time, each chief called out his warriors. Then all the tribes at once, from one end of their land to the other, attacked the forts of their enemy and laid waste the settlements. But in the end the English proved too strong for them.

Fort Pitt was neither burned nor captured. At Detroit, their plan to enter the fort with sawed-off shotguns beneath their blankets was betrayed to the commander by an Ojibway girl. So the plot of Pontiac, the greatest conspiracy ever tried by savage people, came to failure.

Next spring, in the green corn moon, Pontiac and his braves paddled their canoes to a meeting-place on Lake Erie and there smoked the peace pipe with the English.

"Father, we have all smoked out of this pipe of peace," spoke Pontiac. "It is your children's pipe, and as the war is over and the Great Spirit and Giver of Life who made the earth and everything therein has brought us all together this day for our mutual good, I declare to all nations that I have settled my peace with you and taken the King of England for my father."

Another year found Pontiac far down the Mississippi at Fort St. Louis. Across from there, in the country of the Illinois, an Indian of the Kaskaskia tribe, bribed with white man's firewater, murdered Pontiac. So Pontiac died, one of the greatest Indians who ever lived in North America, a patriot who fought for his country in the only way he knew.

George R.

from a portrait by
Sir Joshua Reynolds

GEORGE III!

ENGLAND, ALREADY JUBILANT over her victories in America and India, found more cause for rejoicing in her new "patriot" King. For now, in 1760, came George III as King of England! John Hancock, Esq., of Boston, felt himself fortunate to be in London on the coronation day. A momentous day it was for him, for the young King, and for all the people who lined the streets in cheering crowds to see their young, new monarch pass.

Since early dawn, thousands of sightseers had been pouring into London; many of them had slept out all the night before to be sure to be on hand for the great procession. At last it came in sight. Guards on horseback lined the way; footmen in rich livery walked beside it, as the great coach, heavily carved and ornamented, rolled on in ponderous splendor to Westminster Abbey.

There in Westminster Abbey before the princes and nobles of the land, and according to an ancient custom, the actual crowning of the

85

King took place. It was a long and solemn ceremony lasting six hours and leading up to that most important moment when the King knelt and the Archbishop of Canterbury placed the crown upon his head. Then the trumpets sounded and the nobles cried: "God save the King!" Again trumpets sounded and the nobles cried: "God save the King!"

"God save the King!" they cried. "God save King George! Long live King George! May the King live forever!"

Only one thing was said to have gone amiss on that day of the coronation. Just as George III entered Westminster Abbey for the ceremony, the largest diamond in his crown fell out. Superstitious people shook their heads. "That is a most unlucky sign," they said; "'tis the sign of a great loss, just wait and see!"

John Hancock returned to Boston with glowing reports about the new King, and proudly displayed a gold snuff box which the King had given him—that King who, less than five years later, was to charge him with high treason and issue orders for his arrest!

The British Empire in 1763

and what it grew to be

GEORGE AND MARTHA WASHINGTON

THE NEXT WINTER in the little village of Williamsburg, Virginia, the Governor and the Virginia planters read in the *Gazette* a glowing and detailed account of the wedding of their new King, George III and his German bride, the princess Charlotte. Two years before that, on the sixth of January, 1759, another wedding of more personal interest to the Virginia planters had taken place—that of Colonel George Washington, the Virginia hero of the French and Indian War, and Martha Custis, the wealthiest young widow in the "Old Dominion."

From the moment that they had opened their eyes the morning of the wedding, that day had been one tingling with excitement for the widow's small daughter Patsy, who was six years old, and her brother Jacky, who was four.

"He's the bravest man in all Virginia," said Jack proudly, "and the biggest too, I reckon. He's two times as tall as Mama."

Martha Custis, who was to become Martha Washington, was a

round plump little body with bright brown eyes and round pink cheeks, a brisk and busy housekeeper. Although for days previous her house had been astir with preparations for the wedding, even on the very morning she found a few last-minute things to see to, before she was ready to be laced into her stays and have the quilted petticoat and the white silk wedding-dress slipped over her head.

It was a large and fashionable wedding. The Governor and members of the Assembly came up from Williamsburg, and most of the important planters and their families arrived in coaches or on horseback.

Patsy thought Colonel Washington looked handsome in his blue clothes and wearing his dress sword, as he stood beside her mother while the minister pronounced them man and wife.

After the wedding, George Washington took his little family to Mount Vernon, their new home on the Potomac. There almost at once Martha was busy every day with the many duties of her housekeeping. Besides the management of a house and servants she had to oversee the smoking and curing of meat, the spinning of wool, and the weaving of cloth, and the knitting of socks and making of clothes for the servants themselves. George also found plenty to do about the plantation. The fields and buildings neglected during the war had to be put in order. Of everything he kept careful account, and also a daily journal. These entries taken at random show how the busy days went by:

"Rid to Muddy Hole Doeg Run and Mill Plantations
"Began sowing wheat
"Tobacco ship'd on board *Deliverance*
"Try'd the new Plow
"Began stilling Cyder
"Surveying in Woods all day
"Went a Fox hunting. Catch'd two foxes
"Colo & Mrs. Fairfax din'd and lodg'd here
"Planted 20 young Pine Trees
"Went to Ball in Alexandria
"Fox hunting with Lord Fairfax"

Fox hunting was the favorite sport of Washington, as it was of most Virginia gentlemen. Hunting days would begin with an early breakfast by candlelight, and end with a fine dinner, and no doubt a toast to "His Royal Majesty, the King!"

In the spring of 1760 George Washington was elected to serve as a representative the following winter in the House of Burgesses, which met in Williamsburg. At his first appearance the speaker of the House turned to Washington and said he wished to compliment the Virginia hero on "his brave and steady behavior from the first encroachments and hostilities of the French and their Indians to his resignation after the happy reduction of their fort." Washington tried to reply, but could find no words, so the Speaker relieved his embarrassment.

"Sit down, Mr. Washington," he said. "Your modesty is equal to your valour and that surpasses the power of any language I possess."

THOMAS JEFFERSON AND HIS MOUNTAIN

THERE WAS A light fall of snow on Thomas Jefferson's mountaintop the day George Washington was married. George Washington was nearly twenty-seven years old that January. Thomas Jefferson was not quite sixteen. Young Tom's home was also on a plantation in Virginia, but one that was far inland from Chesapeake Bay and the Tidewater Country—back in the foothills of the Blue

Ridge Mountains. There in that new Up Country, his father, Peter Jefferson, had gone as a self-educated young surveyor to stake out his own plantation, and clear away the forests for his tobacco fields. There he had taken his gentle bride, Jane Randolph, from her father's home in the Tidewater Country, to live on what was then a frontier plantation. There, when his son Thomas had grown up into a tall sandy-haired freckle-faced boy of fourteen, Peter Jefferson had died, leaving the plantation to that boy of his.

That was how it happened that Thomas Jefferson came to own his mountain. A beautiful little mountain it was, round-topped and wooded, and to him the loveliest spot on the whole plantation.

Warm summer noons when he was sixteen, Tom and his friend Dabney Carr often cooked their dinner up there on top of the mountain —wild turkey or partridges roasted over the open fire, and cornmeal hoe cakes baked on a hot stone. When the fire was stamped out, they would either sit with their backs to the old oak tree, looking out over the valley, or one would lounge on his back in the grass while the other read aloud from some book of fine adventure. Captain Anson's *Voyage Around the World* was one of their favorites.

It always stirred in Tom a longing to see the far countries that the author pictured, but at the same time he believed that he would not find in all the world a lovelier spot than the top of his mountain.

"Some day I shall build a fine house up here," he would say to his friend, "and we can live in it always."

"And when we grow old and die," said the other boy, "let's both be buried here under this oak tree." So they solemnly promised that whoever died first would be buried there, by the other. There was no better place, those boys believed, to live or die than the top of their mountain. It was a narrow shut-in world down in the valley, but from the mountain the world stretched out to far horizons. Looking down from that height, the whole countryside was strangely beautiful. Rough rutty roads became brown ribbons, the muddy river was a silver thread lacing the trees and meadows. Even a farmer with an ugly face became but a tiny spot of blue or green crossing a red rust field. Everything found its place as part of one big beautiful pattern. That was why Thomas Jefferson loved the mountain so, and why he hated ever to leave it, even when the sun went down.

In the evenings he played his violin, with his sister at the harpsichord, or studied his books when the candles were lighted. Peter Jefferson would have been pleased to see how fond his son Tom had become of his studies and what a good student he was, for it had been the father's great wish and his last request that this boy of his, who loved the woods and outdoors as he did, should also be given what he himself had never had, a thorough classical education.

So, in the winter of 1760, the first winter that George Washington went to Williamsburg to serve in the House of Burgesses, young Tom Jefferson also went there to enter William and Mary College. Williamsburg was but a small town of about two hundred houses, but it looked very big to the boy from the Up Country as, with a pack of books strapped to his saddle and his fiddle under his arm, he came riding on his bay horse into the Duke of Gloucester Street. The Capitol building at one end of that wide and sandy street, the College buildings at the other, and the Governor's "Palace" facing the green, midway between, were the most splendid buildings Tom had ever seen.

The College of William and Mary had only two professors beside the president. One of them, a very kind, delightful Scotsman by the name of Doctor Small, soon singled out the new sandy-haired boy as an original thinker and one with a fine, keen mind.

He took Thomas one night after classes to meet Governor Fauquier, Royal Governor of Virginia. In that charming, courteous gentleman Tom saw at once an example of true culture to follow. The boy's fine mind must have made him interesting to the Governor as well as to Doctor Small, for the older men included him, together with George Wythe, a brilliant lawyer, in a club of four to meet once a week at the Governor's "Palace" for dinner and an evening's conversation.

As Thomas talked of science with Doctor Small, of literature and art with the Governor, of history and law with George Wythe, it was difficult for the boy to tell which study thrilled him most. All of them seemed to open to him such a wonderful new world, like climbing from a shut-in valley to a mountain-top.

Vacation times, on his way back and forth to Williamsburg, Thomas usually broke the fifty-mile ride on horseback by stopping the night at the house of a friend, a colonel in Hanover County. There at Christmas he chanced to meet one of the Colonel's back-country neighbors, a certain Patrick Henry, a gangling, good-natured fellow, flinging a merry jig on his fiddle. Henry told Tom that he too had a hankering after the law and reckoned he'd read up on it a bit himself and then come to Williamsburg and take examinations for the bar.

"I'll be looking you up when I get there," he drawled, as Tom rode off in the crisp winter morning.

And after a few months, true to his word, there in Williamsburg appeared the self-made lawyer. Primed with a smattering of facts, blessed with a persuasive tongue, Patrick Henry managed to pass the simple oral examinations, which gave him the right to practice.

Thomas might easily have done the same, but that was not Tom's ambition. What Thomas Jefferson wanted was a thorough knowledge of the law, which he decided, with so many other things to do and learn at the same time, would take him five more years of study. That he might waste no precious time, he made out a remarkable schedule for fifteen hours a day, and what was more remarkable, followed it.

The Governor's library was a treasure-house for Tom to explore. One portfolio filled with plans and drawings made by a famous Italian architect he pored over by the hour, tracing and making hundreds of sketches of the plain, simple columns and buildings in the old Roman style. There was the kind of house he knew he wanted to build some day on top of his mountain! Back on the mountain that summer he planned just where to place it. In time the house was built, and since it was the first one in America to be drawn on paper before being built, Thomas Jefferson is said to be America's first architect.

THE END OF THE SEVEN YEARS' WAR

IN EUROPE, the year 1762 marked the sixth year of the Seven Years' War, and a bloody war it had been. For Frederick, great defeats had alternated with astonishing victories against overwhelming odds, but now at last the King of Prussia knew that he was beaten. He stood absolutely alone, without even the help of England. For, after George II died and William Pitt went out of power, England had deserted Prussia. Outnumbered six to one, Frederick lost all hope. Berlin, his capital city, had been captured by the Russians, and hordes of Russian soldiers were clomping through its streets. The Austrians and French were steadily advancing. The ring of enemies was closing in around him, but like a trapped fox he fought on, savage with despair. Then just as he had lost all hope of winning, something happened, and at the last moment he was saved! It was simply this: the Empress of Russia died, and the new Emperor, unable to conceive of fighting Frederick, who was his beloved hero, called the Russian soldiers home.

At that, Louis XV, tired and bored with the whole business, also withdrew. The smaller states, one by one, dropped out, till there was no one left but Frederick and Maria Theresa, and, as she couldn't fight alone, that bloody war of greed dribbled away to nothing and was over!

The Treaty of Paris was signed in 1763. As far as Europe was concerned, nobody gained anything. Frederick did not keep Saxony, Maria Theresa did not regain Silesia. Things stood as they had before the war had started. That is, just as they were except that one hundred thousand men who had then been alive were now dead, and their widows and fatherless children were starving to pay for the war that had killed them.

But Frederick II was famous. From that useless and bloody war, that desperate struggle and those years of agony, he had gained the title of "Frederick the Great," and had come out of it more feared and hated by his enemies, more ardently admired by his followers. Those soldiers who lived to return never tired of telling stories of Frederick that have since been told and retold like legends.

A page boy told how they were once separated by a river from the Russians and he had been obliged to go with Frederick as far as that river to make some observations of the enemy lines.

"Stand here," the King had said, and laid his telescope on the page's shoulder while he took a squint. A Russian battery saw him and began sending a rain of bullets which whizzed about their ears and spattered the King's coat with mud. Frederick paid no heed but kept on looking until he had seen enough and then rode calmly back to camp.

Another story was told by one of two soldiers who had gone to get wood for the campfire which had burned down. It was the night after the battle of Leutchen, where Frederick had attacked the Austrians, and managed by quick manœuvres to come out victorious. It was a cold night in December. While the men were gone for the wood, the King stepped up to the fire to get warm.

"Get out of there," cried the man back with his wood, not recognizing the King in the shadows. "Every lazy bum wants to stand by the fire, but who gets the wood?"

"You're right, my son," laughed Frederick, "the place is yours."

Another cold night they were standing around the watchfire. It was after the battle of Torgau. Usually the King was out in front where all could see him, but in this battle the men had not caught sight of him. About dawn he came up, joined them at the fire and praised them for their bravery. One fellow bolder than the others asked the King where he had been himself while the battle was going on. On the left wing, said the King, and just then, having grown too warm, stepped back from the hot fire and unbuttoned his overcoat. As he did so a bullet fell from his uniform. Then they saw that his coat was full of holes and there was a slight wound on his chest.

"Good old Fritz," the soldiers shouted. "You're always with us! Long live King Frederick! Good old Fritz!"

GOETHE SEES BOTH SIDES

NOT ALL OF THE German people, however, were ready to cheer for Frederick "the Great." While some thought of him as a great king, others considered him an equally great scoundrel. This difference of opinion divided even members of the same family, as it did that of the poet Goethe.

Johann Wolfgang Goethe was just seven years old when Frederick of Prussia started the Seven Years' War, and each day he heard his father declare:

"King Frederick of Prussia is a wonderful man . . . a great general . . . a great hero!"

And as small Goethe listened so he also believed. For when Father Goethe spoke, his family harkened and when he set forth an opinion he gave them to understand that he spoke the one and absolute truth.

At their home in the old free city of Frankfort, the father's word was law, and there was no nonsense mixed with discipline.

Grandfather Textor, their mother's father, was a very different kind of man. He was genial and gentle, and small Goethe and his sister loved to go whenever they could to his old home on Freiburg Street to pay him a visit. He was an important person, too, the children knew, that grandfather of theirs, for he had a gold chain and a portrait of their Empress Maria Theresa which had been given him by the Empress herself, and at the ceremony when her husband had been crowned, Grandfather had been one of those honored to carry the coronation canopy.

Grandfather Textor was the Schöff or Imperial Magistrate of the old free city of Frankfort, that same city where to the good man's great disapproval Voltaire had been so disgracefully arrested by agents of Frederick of Prussia, at the Inn of the Golden Lion.

The old gentleman's mornings were always spent in the council house, but late afternoons he spent in his garden. There, in some sunny corner, he could nearly always be found tending his plants and flowers. He might be clipping the roses, sorting the tulip or hyacinth bulbs in a brown basket, or tying up a loose branch of one of the peach trees which he had trained in flat fan-shaped patterns against the warm south wall, so that, as he explained, each rosy piece of golden fruit might grow perfect in the sun. Grandfather Textor's voice was calm and deliberate and his ways were gentle. Never until the war started could small Goethe ever remember having seen him angry.

But the war changed everything. One dreadful Sunday when, according to custom, the whole family of uncles and aunts and cousins were at Grandfather Textor's for Sunday dinner, small Goethe heard arguments over Frederick of Prussia begin, and saw his hitherto loving family split up into two warring and unfriendly parts. To his dismay, he saw his grandfather angry! And worst of all, heard that gentle grandfather agree when an uncle denounced Frederick of Prussia as an unprincipled and untrustworthy tyrant—Frederick, that great King, whom he and his father knew to be a hero! It was unbelievable!

96

Never till that day had it occurred to the boy that grown people could possibly disagree about right and wrong. Right he had always supposed was right and wrong was wrong, and that all people, too, were either good or bad, and all other people agreed about them. The idea had never occurred to him that one man might have both a good and an evil side, and that it was often hard for those who judged him to see both sides at once. Good people, he believed, knew the right of everything. His father did. How could his grandfather be so mistaken?

Ever since he could remember, small Goethe had looked forward to Sunday dinner with his grandfather. Now there was such a lump in his throat when he even thought about him, that he no longer cared to go.

Not until the Seven Years' War had ended, was the boy able to listen to any criticism of his hero without becoming angry, or big enough to look at both sides of the question with an open mind.

Goethe was fourteen when the war was over, and that year, about Michaelmas, he left Frankfort and went to study at the University of Leipzig in Saxony. Saxony, being the battlefield, had had many of her towns reduced to ruins and her fields laid waste. So the Saxons to a man detested Frederick.

"I could praise him," Goethe tells us, "as little before the inhabitants of Leipzig as formerly in my grandfather's house. They were willing to let him pass as a distinguished man, but by no means a great one. 'There is no art,' they said, 'in performing something with great means, and if one spares neither money nor blood, one may well accomplish one's purpose at last. A truly great general would have got the better of his enemies much sooner.' They would cite infinite details that I did not know how to deny and I felt the unbounded reverence which I had devoted to this remarkable prince gradually cooling away."

And now came back to him the words of an inscription lettered on the wall above his grandfather's desk in the old Frankfort council chamber: "One man's word is no man's word:
       Justice needs that both be heard."

Goethe remembered reading only empty words. Now they held meaning.

97

CATHERINE: EMPRESS OF THE RUSSIANS

S O THE REASON that the Seven Years' War had come to such an
unexpected ending was that the Emperor of Russia called his
soldiers home. And that was because the new Emperor, a weakling and a coward, idolized the King of Prussia. Strange as it
may seem, although he was himself half Russian, Peter III hated Russia
as fiercely as his wife Catherine, born a German princess, loved the wild
exciting land that for eighteen years had been her home. Peter hated
Catherine also . . . he was jealous of her . . . and resentful. She was

98

beautiful and strong and intelligent; he was weak and sickly both in body and mind, and colorless to look upon, with pale stringy rat-tail hair that hung about a peaked face, pitted deep with marks of smallpox.

Like most cowards, Peter became overbearing as soon as he had the authority. The day he became Emperor, his first act was to swagger out dressed in a Prussian uniform and issue orders for the soldiers of what was now *his* army to leave Prussia and come home. When they returned, the Russian officers, already outraged at being called home after years of fighting just as they stood at the point of victory, were further infuriated by being ordered to lay aside their long green Russian coats, put on Prussian uniforms and ape the enemy they had been about to defeat. More than that, Peter III actually signed a treaty with Frederick the Great, to place certain of the Russian troops at the disposal of his hero.

Peter knew that Catherine sympathized with the soldiers and disapproved of what he did. But what cared he? A few drinks gave him courage to boast to his friends that some day he would lock her up or send her back where she came from.

One night at a banquet given to celebrate the new alliance of Russia and Prussia, more drunk than usual, Peter III made a display of himself by insulting his wife before all the five hundred guests who were assembled. Staggering to his feet, he pointed a wavering finger at Catherine and called her a

"Fool . . . Fool . . . three times a Fool."

Catherine's face turned white, but she kept perfectly silent.

The strength of the woman, to be able to take the insult and not reply, exasperated the weakling to fury. At another dinner Peter III insulted Catherine in public again, and when she again kept silent, he was beside himself with rage, and signalled one of the officers.

"Arrest the woman," he ordered, and only with the greatest difficulty was he persuaded by his uncle to recall the order.

Catherine rode unmolested to her apartments in another castle, the Peterhof, and retired for the night. That was the night of June 21, 1762.

Six nights later, a man was arrested—a conspirator, one of those hundreds of dissatisfied soldiers who were plotting to get rid of Peter III and put Catherine in his place. With that arrest the others feared that their plot was discovered. One conspirator arrested tonight meant more tomorrow. The time had come to act.

The Orlov brothers, Gregory and Alexis, bold savage fellows, fearless of danger, and devoted to Catherine, acted at once. Gregory dashed away to rouse his regiment of soldiers. Alexis rode to the Peterhof to notify Catherine. He reached her side at five o'clock the next morning. Catherine, roused from her sleep, looked up to see the scarred face and twisted lip of Alexis Orlov bending over her bed.

"Time has come," he said with his hand on her shoulder. "The carriage is waiting. All is prepared in the city."

Just a question or two, and Catherine slipped into a plain black gown, caught up her heavy dark hair with a comb, followed the man out into the dawn and rode away.

Halfway to St. Petersburg, they reached Gregory Orlov's regiment. Catherine stepped from the carriage and stood before the men.

"I have come to you for your protection," she said to them. "The Emperor has given orders for my arrest; he intends to kill me and my son." Her face was white as wax against the black of her hair and gown but her full lips were red as blood. It was the first time the excited men had seen her.

"Mother Catherine!" they cried. Passionately they threw themselves on the ground before her, kissing her hands, her feet, the hem of her dress. To a man they swore to protect her, and from their rough throats came the cheer:

"Hurrah! Long live our Little Mother Catherine!"

One regiment of soldiers after another joined them as they continued toward the gates of St. Petersburg. There bells rang. Thousands of people, puzzled and curious, poured into the streets. The procession reached the cathedral, the cross and the priest.

There, in the plain black gown, with her hair hanging loose, and holding by the hand her seven-year-old son, Paul Petrovich, who had been brought to her still wearing his nightcap, Catherine received the blessings of the priest and took the oath as Empress of the Russians. Just eighteen years it was since that June when she had stood in a red-and-silver gown to be christened Catherine Alexievna.

The people cheered, and the Palace doors were opened wide to receive her. That night, dressed in a uniform of the guards, and mounted astride a dappled horse, with oak leaves twisted round her soldier's cap, she rode at the head of fourteen thousand joyful soldiers to find Peter III and force him to abdicate.

The snivelling fellow tried to escape, but once caught, meekly signed the abdication, and let himself be shuffled away to prison.

Ten days later Catherine took from a breathless messenger two grimy sheets of paper. She unfolded them and read in the drunken, sprawling letters of Alexis Orlov that Peter III was dead. He had been murdered!

Murdered! Catherine thought quickly. The people must never know. They must be made to believe that their Emperor had died a natural death. The murderers could not be punished, for they were the men who had put her on the throne. A moment's hesitation only and Catherine refolded the grimy paper, placed it with its ugly secret in a hidden drawer of her desk and turned the key.

"Empress!" she said aloud. "Empress of Russia!" As powerful now as any *man* in Europe. But she would be more so. Russia was a vast empire, but she would make it more vast, more modern, more educated. She would better the condition of the poor, give the serfs more freedom. She would push Russia into a place in the affairs of Europe, and to a harbor on the Mediterranean. She put her ambition into words:

"If I could live to be one hundred, I should wish to unite the whole of Europe under the scepter of Russia. But I have no intention of dying before I have driven the Turks out of Constantinople, broken the pride of the Chinese, and established trade relations with India." Great as that was the ambition of Catherine II, now Empress of the Russians.

from a bust by Houdon

VOLTAIRE AND HIS PEN

As THE CLOCK STRUCK ten and the clear, clean sunlight of Switzerland in October swept every shadow from his very neat and orderly room, a wisp of a Frenchman in a gray dressing-gown and a cerise velvet nightcap sat propped against the blue damask pillows of a huge carved bed, writing furiously. Above him, to one side of the bed, hung the portrait of his old friend the King of Prussia, and on the opposite side one of the writer himself, painted the year he had come from his fatal visit to the unpredictable Frederick.

The face of the man himself had changed scarcely any from that of the portrait, though it was ten years since the likeness had been painted. The thin, scornful, kindly smile was just the same, the sparkle in his eyes appeared no less brilliant, as with a quirk of his head he looked up at his man who at that moment appeared in the door with a chunky bundle of letters. Placing his quill on the stand at the side of his bed he spread them fan-shaped on the counterpane before him, and speculated quizzically for a moment upon the various handwritings, in which was inscribed upon all of them his name *Voltaire*.

A round firm writing caught his eye, and breaking the imperial seal of Russia, he read his first letter from the Empress Catherine, dated October, 1763, in which she said:

". . . since 1746 when by chance your works fell into my hands I have never stopped reading them. Monsieur, one thing is certain that if I have any knowledge I owe it to you alone. Just now I am reading your essay on world history! I would like to learn every page of it by heart."

His history . . . well. "Remarkable woman that!" he thought.

Refolding and laying the letter neatly aside, he reached for another bearing the more familiar scrawl of Frederick of Prussia, for the "two philosophers" had again made peace through correspondence, since each agreed that the other was "good to read but bad to know." Voltaire looked at the letter a moment, and then laid it down unopened while with a frown he took up his pen:

"War is the greatest of all crimes," he wrote in his precise hand, "and yet there is no aggressor who does not cover his crime with the pretext of justice. It is forbidden to kill, therefore all murderers are punished unless they kill in large numbers and to the sound of trumpets. . . . Battles and revolutions are common to all history. . . . Take away the arts and the progress of the mind and you will find nothing in any age remarkable enough to attract the attention of posterity."

He tapped sharply on the floor with his cane, and when at the signal the man returned, Voltaire handed him the notes he had finished and indicated on which pile of manuscripts, on which of the five desks standing in the room he wished to have it placed.

"War is a crime, Wagniere," said he. "Take this past war fought on three continents at once, and over what? A simple dispute which two simple merchants would have settled in a couple of hours by arbitrators. But we Europeans, we squander men and money in the farthest corners of Asia and America. The natives of India compelled by force and cunning to receive our trading posts, and the Americans whose continent we have soaked in blood, regard us as the enemies of humanity who run from the ends of the earth to slaughter them and thereafter . . . to destroy ourselves!"

He stopped speaking, and looked to the window where outside two bronze leaves of a chestnut tree moved alternately against the blue square of sky and the white peak of a distant mountain. Ferney, this Swiss home of his, was a beautiful place, thought Voltaire. Here, though he had no crown, he lived like a king, a king whose pen took the place of a sword, and whose enemies were Ignorance, Injustice, and Superstition, not other human beings like himself.

"One should regard all human beings as one's brothers," he thought, and again he began to write:

"What! A Turk my brother? A Chinaman my brother? A Siamese? Yes, of course, for are we not all children of the same father and creatures of the same God? . . . O, God of all creatures, all worlds and all times. You did not give us hearts in order that we might hate one another, hands that we might slay one another. Do not let trifling differences in our poor languages, in our ridiculous customs, in our imperfect laws be signals for hatred and persecution among the puny atoms called mankind!"

He laid down his pen, and then hastened to read Frederick's letter before the clock struck the hour when he must dress, and meet some of the many guests who constantly came to pay him homage.

"Tell me," wrote Frederick in his letter, "what do you mean by writing a history of the wolves and bears of Siberia? I wish I could ignore their existence in our hemisphere!" And then at the end he added, "Good-bye, cultivate your garden, 'tis the wisest thing to do!"

"Yes," added Voltaire, "he who clears a field renders a better service to mankind than all the scribblers in Europe." And with a puzzling twist to his smile he glanced once more to where the leaves of the chestnut trees, that he himself had planted in his garden there at Ferney, moved against the sky. The clock struck eleven.

III

WHEN GEORGE WASHINGTON WAS A
Farmer

What other People were doing

JAMES COOK
landed in Australia in 1770, and claimed it for England

The STEAM ENGINE was invented in 1769 by JAMES WATT

JUNIPERO SERRA
established the first Spanish mission in California in 1769

DANIEL BOONE
led pioneers westward over the mountains into Kentucky

Oxygen was discovered by **PRIESTLEY** in 1774 and named by **LAVOISIER**

NAPOLEON BUONAPARTE
was born in 1769

LA FAYETTE
a French boy, born 1757, was hunting an imaginary wolf

ALEXANDER HAMILTON
as a boy in the West Indies, was already counting money (born 1757)

MOZART
"the wonder boy", born in 1756, was giving concerts in Europe

GOYA
a young Spaniard, born in 1746, was learning to paint

and Events which took place

while Washington was a Farmer

taken by Frederick "the Great" of Prussia

taken by Catherine II of Russia

POLAND was torn to pieces

taken by Maria Theresa of Austria

LOUIS XVI (born 1754) had to give up making locks, and become King of France in 1774

MARIE ANTOINETTE (born 1755) was sent by her mother, Maria Theresa, to marry Louis XVI

GEORGE III taxed his American Colonies into Rebellion.

SAMUEL ADAMS aroused Massachusetts

PATRICK HENRY was the orator of Virginia

PITT upheld the colonies

EDMUND BURKE plead in their behalf

BENJAMIN FRANKLIN was in England until 1775, representative for the colonies

APRIL 19, 1775 — at Lexington, the first shots were fired in the American Revolution

BENJAMIN WEST was court painter, and friend of George III

between the Years 1763 and 1776

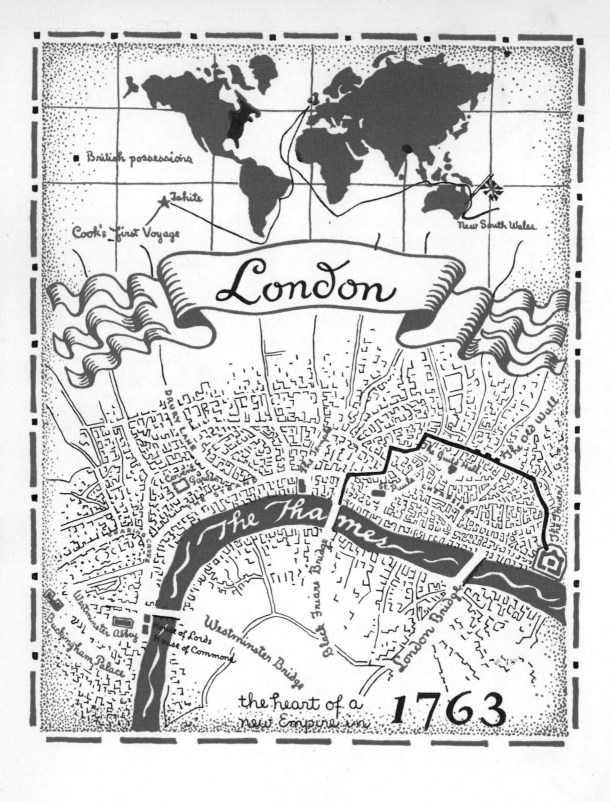

TO THE SOUTH SEAS WITH CAPTAIN COOK

FOR A SCORE of years after the Seven Years' War was over, George Washington continued to enjoy his life as a farmer at Mount Vernon. Meanwhile the world went on its way. The British Empire kept on expanding, rulers and statesmen kept on trying to adjust their difficulties, explorers looked for undiscovered countries, inventors worked out new devices, painters painted, writers wrote, and scientists and philosophers sought to advance man's knowledge of himself and the great world in which he lived. In 1768, this was the question puzzling the scientists of the Royal Society of London:

How far Distant is the Sun?

They knew that on June 31, 1769, the planet Venus was due to pass between the earth and the sun, and that if they could time that passage they could figure out how far away the sun was. The only difficulty lay in the fact that the one place where this phenomenon could be observed was on the distant island of Tahiti, in the South Pacific. Who was there both daring and skillful enough to undertake the expedition, they asked, and found that no one in the King's navy answered the requirements so well as a certain James Cook.

So in the summer of 1768, with ninety-five people on board, Lieutenant James Cook set sail for the South Pacific. His interesting journal tells of their experiences. At the Madeira Islands they were becalmed for days in scorching sun. At Rio de Janeiro, they were held under guard for a month because the Portuguese governor could not believe that people would be crazy enough to go so far just to look at a star.

As they rounded Cape Horn in an icy sea, some of the botanists who went ashore to look for new plants and animals lost their lives in a blinding snowstorm. Finally, however, after eight and one half months they landed on the warm, beautiful, palm-fringed island of Tahiti. They had no difficulty in setting up their small observatory, and then the night before the great day took ashore the astronomical quadrant. The next morning, it was nowhere to be seen! Without it their long journey had been made for nothing. A frantic search, however, prevented that catastrophe and brought to light the quadrant where some friendly but too-inquisitive natives had left it. So the crossing of Venus was timed successfully and recorded.

They then set out for home by way of the island of New Zealand, where James Cook gave to all the bays and capes the names which they still have today. At Queen Charlotte's Bay, they found remains of people who had been eaten by the natives, for the New Zealanders were cannibals: and human flesh "to them was a Dainty Bit."

On their next stop, Englishmen saw for the first time a strange leaping animal, which the natives called the "Kangooroo." They had reached the west coast of the island continent now called Australia. It was then August, 1770, and James Cook at once planted the British flag on that new land and claimed what he called New South Wales for England in the name of George III.

When James Cook reached home with not only his accurate report for the Royal Society, but also a new land to be added to the growing Empire, the journey was pronounced one of the most successful ever made. The King sent for him to congratulate him. His rank was raised to captain and everywhere he went he was now cheered and honored.

Is there an unknown Southern Continent?

This was another unsolved question. Some scientists still held the old theory that there must be one, to balance the land in the north.

"Otherwise," they argued, "the world would be topheavy."

To settle this question, James Cook made a voyage of twenty thousand miles, explored all the Antarctic and found not a southern continent, of course, but only what any experienced sea captain would expect, icy seas with mountainous waves, sleet, hail, and treacherous icebergs. But one danger which any other captain of those days would have expected, Captain Cook, hoped to avoid, and did. That was scurvy, the loathsome disease that up to this very voyage had always broken out on shipboard, and on a long trip usually caused the death of one half to three fourths of the crew. James Cook had come to believe that scurvy resulted from food the sailors had to eat, greasy salt meat boiled in dirty water, mouldy biscuits crawling with bugs, and no fruits and vegetables. So before starting on this trip he had planned very carefully what food to take. This time the men were given malt, sauerkraut and lemon juice, and as soon as they reached New Zealand were made to eat wild celery and all other green things that they could find.

On this voyage James Cook was gone three years and of a crew of one hundred eighteen men lost but four, and not one from scurvy. That was an astonishing record. A truly great discovery, for which he was made a member of the Royal Society and awarded a gold medal of honor; for, as the president said, "What inquiry can be so useful as that which hath for its object the saving lives of men?"

$$O_2 \qquad O \qquad H_2O$$

OXYGEN

O STANDS FOR OXYGEN, and is today probably the best-known symbol used in Chemistry. Before the year 1774, nobody had ever heard of the symbol, or of that most common gas, without which there would be no life on earth. Only a few scientists knew anything at all about the air they breathed or about the gases which composed it.

But about four years after James Cook discovered western Australia, Joseph Priestley, an English scientist and a good friend of Benjamin Franklin, discovered Oxygen. Though less exciting at the time, it was of more benefit to the world at large, because it opened up not merely another land, but a whole new field of knowledge. Almost simultaneously, as so often happens with discoveries, a Swedish scientist named Scheele announced that he had also found the gas.

The newly discovered gas started off with many peculiar names, according to different theories about the nature of it. Priestley called it "Dephlogisticated" air, Scheele named it empyreal air, still another called it vital air. The name Oxygen was given it by a young French scientist, the very brilliant Antoine Lavoisier.

Antoine Lavoisier also proved the Law that nothing is ever lost or created, but only changes form. Based on that law, he devised a new system of chemical terms and symbols, to replace the vague ones of Alchemy, and so is called the Father of Modern Chemistry.

Diagram of Engine
1769

THE STEAM ENGINE

THE YEAR 1769 was a most important one in the history of man, for that year James Watt took out his patent for the Steam Engine. That invention was to change a world of sails and homespun into one of steamboats, railroads and machines, and so make greater change in man's life, than any so far since the world began. Often after James Watt commenced to work on his invention, success seemed very far away. Completely discouraged, he untied his leather apron one Saturday afternoon in 1765. Daylight had dimmed and it was not worth while to waste a candle.

"Och, Robinson, I tell ye, mon," he said to the student professor of chemistry who had stopped in at the shop as he often did, "of all things in life, there's nought more foolish than inventing."

But the next day *the idea* came to him. Simple and natural, like all great ideas, it left no doubt or question in his mind.

Monday morning, bright and early, found him back in his shop again, and after classes Robinson came upon his friend bending earnestly over a "little tin cistern" which he was holding in his lap.

"Of course, if you can solve that condensing problem," Robinson began, and then stopped when James Watt looked up with a new expression on his face, and interrupted:

"Ye need not fash yersel' aboot that, mon, any longer. I can noo make an engine that shall not waste a particle of steam."

He knew that he had solved it—that problem which for two years he had been working to correct. Two years before, in 1763, he had repaired for the university a steam engine of a crude type, which some years before had been worked out by a blacksmith named Newcomen. A few of these Newcomen engines were being used for pumping water out of coal mines, but even repaired in their best working order the clumsy things were of little use. So much time and energy were lost in condensing the steam between the strokes of the piston, that actually the steam engine as a practical working machine did not exist. Since he had first seen the Newcomen model, James Watt had given the problem of condensing the steam a great deal of thought and had tried out many impossible solutions before finally the correct idea flashed upon him. The idea, of course, was the important thing, but without patience and perseverance given to its development, it would have come to nothing, as many great ideas have. James Watt, however, had the combination that it takes to make success, and, after four years of working on the model, he took out a patent for his Steam Engine in 1769. Then he worked five years longer on the models, perfecting the valves, boring more accurate cylinders, testing, rearranging, and minding an infinite number of details before they were ready to be put into manufacture.

Finally, in 1774, he became a partner of a prosperous man named Boulton, who had founded the Soho Iron Works, and then at last after nine years of previous work, Watt's steam engines were manufactured.

By 1776, the new Watt engine was acclaimed by everybody as a great success, but the inventor was just as modest as he had always been. He still did the work and let others do the boasting. When they asked him how and where the idea came to him, he would smile half shyly and reply, in his Scot's tongue:

"It was on the green of Glasgow. I had gone to take a walk on a fine Sabbath afternoon, early in 1765. I had entered the green by the gate and had passed the old washing house when the idea came into my mind that as steam was an elastic body it would rush into a vacuum and if a connection were made between the cylinder and an empty vessel that the steam would rush into, it might be condensed there without cooling the cylinder. . . . I had not walked farther than the golf house when the whole thing was arranged in my mind."

By 1776, his old friend Robinson had returned from Russia, and was working on the first set of *Encyclopedia Britannica,* which was then being compiled. The year after James Watt had taken out his patent, Robinson had gone to Russia as assistant to an English admiral who had been asked by the Empress Catherine to come and suggest reforms in the Russian navy. While Robinson was there, James Watt had also received an invitation from Empress Catherine to go to Russia as "Master of Iron Ordnance to her Imperial Majesty."

"Me gae tae Russia!" James Watt had exclaimed. Even the proposed salary of one thousand pounds yearly had not been enough to tempt him to undertake such a journey, or leave his well-established business. This was his reply to Robinson:

"I find myself obliged to decline acceptance of it, both from being sensible that I by no means merit your recommendation, and from my advancing somewhat in the estimation of mankind here as an Engineer."

HIS MAJESTY GEORGE III

"WHAT SORT OF PERSON is his Majesty?" asked Benjamin West as he rode to Windsor Castle beside the Archbishop Drummond on a day in 1763. Though the young American painter had but recently arrived in London after three years' study in Italy, he had already won the support of the Archbishop. That man of the church considered the young Mr. West's ambition to paint religious as well as historical pictures most commendable, and had offered to introduce him to the King.

"What sort of person is his Majesty?" repeated the Archbishop thoughtfully. "His Majesty, George III, is a young man of great simplicity and frankness, I should say. Cautious in forming private friendships, but when he has taken an attachment, not easily swayed from it."

116

Benjamin West

And so Benjamin West found George III, a man about his own age, simple and unaffected in his manner, who received him very graciously and then introduced him to Queen Charlotte. The Queen complimented him on the historical painting which he brought to show them.

"I've thought of another historical subject you might paint for me," spoke up the King. "I will read it to you from the Latin."

After Benjamin West had listened to the story of how the great Roman general Regulus had invaded Africa in the first war against Carthage, he agreed to paint the picture. When it was finished to the last eyelash it so exactly suited the King's taste that he ordered several others, commissioned Benjamin West later to paint religious pictures for the royal chapel at Windsor Castle, and made him court painter at a salary of a thousand pounds a year. He also offered him a title, but, as the distinction to be gained by signing himself Sir instead of Mr. Benjamin West seemed hollow to the simple Quaker, compared to that earned by his paint brush and pencil, he refused the honor.

He also refused to allow the King to make him the first president of the new Royal Academy of Painting, which in the year 1768 George III decided to establish and support. So the honor went, as Benjamin West felt it should, to Sir Joshua Reynolds, for whom he felt a sincere admiration and whose masterly portraits he recognized as work that he himself could never equal. Doctor Johnson, known all over London for his witty remarks, was appointed Professor of Literature in the new Academy, and Oliver Goldsmith was made Professor of History. This being a new position with no duties and so no salary, poor improvident Goldsmith, who never had a shilling in his pocket, said it was like a ruffle given to a man who needed a shirt.

Benjamin West's paintings look conventional enough today, but when the "Death of Wolfe" was first

Sir Joshua Reynolds

117

displayed, it caused a great to-do. It did not follow the ridiculous but well-established custom of that day that all historical characters should be painted in flowing Greek robes, no matter when or where they lived, which in this case would have included even the American Indian! The Archbishop was truly upset about it; so too at first glance was Sir Joshua Reynolds, and the King asked for an explanation.

Benjamin West replied that he considered it was the duty of the painter to be as truthful and accurate as the historian.

"I believe you're right, quite right," said the King, convinced, and having settled that matter to his satisfaction, he turned back to the more pressing question of how to raise money and what to do about the trouble that was starting in his American colonies.

George III had hardly removed the crown used in his coronation than he had begun to stir up trouble, both in England and America, by his firm determination to "be king"—to rule as well as reign.

George III was a young man of good intentions, but unfortunately, he was so sure that he knew the one and only right way to do everything, from boiling a piece of beef to ruling a kingdom, that he felt in need of no advice. First he dismissed William Pitt, and then appointed one Prime Minister after another till he found the perfect "yes man."

Parliament, also, he remade for his convenience. Whig and Tory were the two great political parties in England at that time. The Whigs stood for giving more power to the people, the Tories for more power to the King. George III, therefore, by using bribes at election time replaced many unfriendly Whigs with friendly Tories who would vote for the laws he wanted passed.

Laws for raising money came first, for the government still had to pay for the Seven Years' War. Since the colonies would benefit most from having the French driven out of America, it seemed reasonable to the King and his Parliament that from the colonies should come a large share of the cost.

"We can double our revenue from colonial trade," some one suggested, "if we enforce our old Acts of Navigation and put an end to smuggling. Every one knows that smuggling sugar and molasses and wine from the Spanish West Indies is common practice among colonial shipping merchants, especially in the port of Boston."

So to help catch these smugglers, customs officers who collected the duty in American ports were sent Writs of Assistance, which were papers giving them the right to "search any man's house or property for smuggled goods and also to arrest the owner."

That law, put in force, raised an uproar in Boston. James Otis, a lawyer, defended some of the merchants who had been accused, and John Adams said that "every man in that crowded audience went away as I did, ready to take up arms against Writs of Assistance." After that, warships were sent to catch the smugglers.

Control of the fur trade was also thought of as a way for raising money, and a law was passed forbidding any one in the colonies to carry on fur trading without a signed permit from the King.

"We must pass another law," added some one else, "to make the settlers stay east of the Alleghany Mountains. Settlers cut down the forests where the fur-bearing animals live and thus destroy them."

So in 1763 a proclamation was issued in the name of George III forbidding the colonists to make any settlements whatsoever west of the Alleghany Mountains, and as an excuse proclaiming it to be his royal will and pleasure to reserve that land for the Indians!

Still not content, two years later, in 1765, Parliament passed the Stamp Act, and then trouble really began!

Stamps about the size of postage stamps were sent to America with orders that the colonists buy and stick them on newspapers, almanacs, playing cards and so forth. Stamped paper was also sent to be used for all business papers such as bills, bonds, licenses, and deeds to property.

 Now Writs of Assistance to prevent smuggling didn't worry the western settlers, because they weren't engaged in shipping. Ship owners of Boston had no desire to settle west of the Alleghanies, so the act to preserve the fur trade was of no concern to them, but the Stamp Act was a different matter. The Stamp Act hit everybody's pocketbook and roused the wrath of the colonists from Maine to Georgia and from Kentucky to Cape Cod.

It was not the amount of the tax that made them angry, but the fact that here was a tax to which they had not given their consent, a tax which they had not voted upon in their own assemblies.

"No freeman, according to the laws of England, should be made to pay any tax to which he has not given his consent," said John Adams in an indignation meeting held in Faneuil Hall in Boston.

John Adams well knew the English law. He knew how the people's right to tax themselves had first been granted to them more than five hundred years before in the Magna Carta. How they had fought a revolution lasting fifty years to keep from losing that right, after which it was again guaranteed to them in 1688, in the great Bill of Rights. Those were the laws of England to which he now referred.

Down in Williamsburg, Virginia, there was great excitement in the House of Burgesses. It rose to a crisis one May morning when Patrick Henry, the back-country lawyer, shambled forward and began to speak. George Washington was there; young Thomas Jefferson, still a student with his law books under his arm, was standing in the doorway.

"According to the rights of Englishmen," began Patrick Henry, "the people of Virginia are not obliged to obey the Stamp Act." His voice grew tense with emotion as he neared the climax. His excited thoughts turned to other rulers who, like George III, had been too eager for power. "Cæsar," cried Patrick Henry, "had his Brutus, Charles I his Cromwell, George III——"

"Treason," shouted the chairman of the meeting, for as every one knew, Cæsar had been stabbed by Brutus, and Charles I beheaded.

"And George III, continued Patrick Henry, "may profit by their example. If that be treason, make the most of it."

In New York City that fall delegates from eight or nine of the colonies met in what they called a Stamp Act Congress. They discussed their grievances sensibly. Then they composed a letter to the King in which, as loyal subjects, they humbly petitioned his Majesty to grant them the rights and liberties of all Englishmen.

from an old caricature of George III looking at a picture of Oliver Cromwell

While these gentlemen discussed the Stamp Act calmly, citizens miscalling themselves "Sons of Liberty" seized and destroyed the stamps, insulted the distributors, plundered and wrecked their houses, until all of them were forced to resign, some even to leave the country.

George III was red in the face with rage over such rank insubordination of his subjects. The "King's friends" felt the same. Others in Parliament sympathized with the Americans. William Pitt declared that he was "glad that the Americans had resisted." Lord Grenville, on the contrary, said they had done wrong in resisting, that "the Parliament of England had full power to make laws to bind the colonies," tax laws included. William Pitt took a broader view. This is what he said:

"When two countries are connected like England and her colonies the greater must necessarily rule, but must so rule as not to contradict any rights that belong to both."

Had his words been heeded then, the United States might still be part of the British Empire, for William Pitt had stated the very principle to which the great British Empire now owes its unity.

Benjamin Franklin, who was still in England, was summoned one day to answer some questions before the House of Commons.

"If the Stamp Act is not repealed what do you think will be the consequences?" was one of the first questions as might be expected.

"A total loss of respect and affection the people of America bear to this country and all the commerce," was the ready answer.

As to the commerce that was true. The colonists refused to buy goods from England until the Stamp Act was repealed. In a short time English merchants felt the loss and complained to Parliament.

"Our trade is hurt . . . what . . . have you been doing? . . . our trade is hurt; pray remedy it, and a plague on you if you don't."

So the Stamp Act was repealed and there was much rejoicing in the colonies, but not for long. A new law was soon passed known as the Townsend Act, which stated that the colonists had to pay a tax on many of the articles which they had always hitherto imported free of duty, such as glass, lead, paper, paints, china, and tea.

The agents in London who handled Virginia tobacco soon received word not to send back in return any of the goods on which there was a tax. In no time the English business men spoke up again:

"Our trade is hurt," said those who sold glass and lead and paper and paints. "We have lost half a million pounds."

"What about our tea?" moaned the managers of the East India Trading Company. "It lies rotting in the warehouses, while Americans buy tea from Holland."

Finally even King George and his yes man, Prime Minister Lord North, admitted that these taxes also would have to be abolished.

"But there must be one tax left to keep up the right," they declared, still maintaining firmly their right to tax the colonies.

Then Lord North, proposed his *tea trick*. The idea was to repeal all other taxes except the tax on tea, but make the price so low that even with the tax it would be cheaper than the tea from Holland. Then if the Americans bought the cheap tea and paid the tax, it would be the same as admitting that Parliament had a right to tax them.

"It's a capital idea," chuckled the King, "a capital idea," and with Lord North, sat back most complacently to watch the happy outcome.

Benjamin Franklin distressed to see trouble increasing between the colonies and the Mother Country, drew this melancholy female, to show what a plight England would be in, should she lose her colonies.

One day unexpectedly he was honored by a request from William Pitt (now Lord Chatham) to call upon him.

"Does America want to be independent?" asked William Pitt, coming to the point at once.

"No," said Benjamin Franklin, which at this time was definitely the truth. "I have never heard in any conversation from any person drunk or sober the least expression of a wish for separation." It was the common rights of Englishmen, *not* independence that Americans wanted.

In further conversation, William Pitt said that he intended to bend every effort to bring about a repeal of the laws that were objectionable to the Americans.

Going home from that interview, hopeful for a peaceful settlement, Benjamin Franklin quite unwittingly wrote a letter, the outcome of which was to widen the breach between England and America. The letter seemed innocent enough. It was merely one of introduction for a penniless Englishman, a Quaker by name of Thomas Paine, to carry with him to Philadelphia where he hoped to find a job. Thomas Paine, it seemed, had tried his hand at being a corsetmaker, a teacher, a tax collector, a tobacco dealer, and what not, with equal lack of success. But he was a man of ideas, and his piercing eyes burned bright when he talked of astronomy, mathematics, philosophy and the great unchanging laws of the universe. He had no love for George III, and was to push ideas of "Independence" for what he chose to call the "United States."

123

FREDERICK THE MISER AND LOUIS THE WASTER

A S SOON AS the Seven Years' War was over, every nation was
faced with the damage it had done. Frederick "the Great,"
who was crafty and wise, set to work immediately to make
Prussia prosperous again.

When he laid down his sword, he opened his ledger and worked as
hard at peace as he had at war. He squeezed every cent of taxes from
those who could pay and spent the money to rebuild ruined villages,
make better roads and erect fine public buildings. From the farmers
whose fields had been trampled down by battles, he took no taxes for the
next six years. Corn no longer needed to feed the soldiers was distributed
among the poor, and for quick food he enforced the cultivation of the
then unfamiliar potato. Up and down the country he rode, peering into
every corner of the kingdom to see that his commands were being carried
out. Not one of his minor officials did he trust!

Each year he appeared wearing the same old blue uniform, and
each year it was dirtier, the red facings more streaked and faded and
the waistcoat more spotted and stained with snuff. But whose business
was that? He wore what he pleased.

He wore what he pleased, did what he pleased, ruled his country
the way he pleased and cared not a whit what the people were saying
about him.

One day in Berlin, he saw a crowd in the street. Riding up to see what held their attention, he found that it was a caricature of himself as a tax collector grinding away on a coffee mill, picking up every bean. He turned to his groom.

Hang that thing down lower on the wall where people can see it better," he said, and then jogged off with his wisp of a pointed pigtail sticking out behind over his narrow shoulders.

Frederick the Great was crafty, and after the war was over he cut down expenses by discharging many of his faithful officers regardless of the fact that they had no other means of livelihood. One of those discharged was an officer who had once been an aide-de-camp on Frederick's staff. He had also been chosen as one of a class of specially talented young officers to be given extra training in the higher tactics of war under the great general himself. Then he was suddenly dropped. His name was Baron Frederick William von Steuben.

He did not protest. It was no use for an officer to protest. Frederick had only one answer: "Kann sich zum Teufel scheeren." "He can go to the devil."

Baron von Steuben fortunately found his way to America instead.

The treasury of France had been empty enough before the war, but after that unfortunate struggle with England, France was bankrupt. But her King did not care, not so long as he had money enough to spend on himself and his beautiful women.

Madame de Pompadour, no longer young nor beautiful, died, and was buried one rainy day in 1764. Louis XV merely yawned and took another favorite, a woman both young and beautiful, but one of far worse character, known as Madame du Barry, whose whims and luxuries were to cost France many millions of francs before her time was up.

And France was bankrupt. It actually looked to the King and his friends for a time as though they had exhausted every possible means of raising money, until a shrewd somebody hit upon a brilliant idea. The scheme was that a company should be formed to buy up all the wheat and grain in the country, store it in their warehouses until there was a scarcity of food. Then, they could sell it at an enormous price and make an enormous profit! It worked perfectly.

Starving people went without bread, but Louis XV, their King, bought rare and beautiful jewels for his mistress, Madame du Barry.

No one dared say that the King did wrong. No one dared raise any objection to what he might choose to do, for no one who opposed the King in any way whatever was safe.

The Parliament of Paris, which was the court of justice, refused to submit to him entirely, so he did away with it, and sent hundreds of the members into exile. Individuals who spoke out of turn or appeared suspicious were hurried off to the Bastille and left there without trial, till they grew old and gray and their teeth fell out.

Almost any one, by the way, who wished to rid himself of an annoying relative or acquaintance might have him put into prison by simply buying a *Lettre de Cachet,* which was a warrant of arrest, in the form of a letter stamped with the King's royal seal.

Sending his subjects to prison was a convenient way for Louis XV to raise a little more spending money, but it was a dangerous way. The money of France was exhausted, indeed, but so too very nearly was the people's endurance. Royal edicts could not keep their mouths closed and their fists down much longer. And Louis XV knew it.

"*Après nous le deluge,* as the Pompadour used to say," he thought. "After us the deluge!"

"But so long as it comes *after* I myself am dead, what of it?"

MARIE ANTOINETTE, THE LITTLE AUSTRIAN PRINCESS

MARIA THERESA of Austria had gained nothing at all from the Seven Years' War. She was still left with the problem of how to protect Austria from her enemies. Particularly was she anxious to keep a friendly alliance with Louis XV, the King of France. To secure that, it appeared most desirable to her to promote a marriage between his grandson, the Dauphin (the French Crown Prince), and her own youngest daughter, the youngest but one of her sixteen children.

Marie Antoinette, the little Archduchess of Austria, was a lovable child, with golden hair and blue eyes, a gay smile and a warm heart, but she never would learn her lessons. She wanted only to laugh and play. She would slip away from her French teacher, hide from her reading master, and instead of practising on her harpsichord she would skip gaily off on her twinkling toes, to dance and play in the sunny courtyard.

One October day when she was seven, little "Toinette" was called in from her play to hear a small musician, just a few months younger than she was herself, play the violin and harpsichord. He was starting on a concert tour of Europe with his father and sister. People spoke of him as the "wonder child," but his name was Wolfgang Mozart.

Many days thereafter they spent playing together, the little Archduchess and the small musician. One day, crossing the polished floor, he slipped and fell, and Marie Antoinette quickly helped him up.

"You are good," said the small Mozart. "Some day I will marry you," he added with a smile.

Queen Maria Theresa smiled too, but as he climbed up into her lap she thought, "Ah no, if all goes well it will not be you, my little one, that my Toinette will marry, but the future King of France."

And, as she had so eagerly desired, in time all went well. The formal proposal from Louis XV for the hand of the Princess came when Marie Antoinette was eleven, and when all the wedding arrangements had been agreed upon to the most minute detail, the marriage day was set for the spring of 1770, and a special messenger from France, forty-eight carriages, each drawn by six horses, and one hundred seventy-seven bodyguards were sent to fetch the now precious princess.

As the magnificent coach, specially built for the occasion, covered with glass, painted with scrolls and crowns of gold, carried her little girl of fourteen out of sight, Maria Theresa, who had been so eager for that marriage, was sad with the vague premonition of evil.

"She is so young and heedless," she prayed. "God grant that no harm befall her."

It was a long journey of six hundred miles between the old home and the new. Marie Antoinette watched the hours go by on the small watch her mother had given her, smiling at the thought of all the joyful hours that would be hers at the gayest court in Europe, smiling at the thought of how gay and charming the French prince was sure to be, and smiling out at the dear good peasants of the villages who gathered in their festal dress to strew the path with flowers, as she passed.

When they had been travelling nearly a month, the horses came to a stop in a beautiful wood not far from Paris, where in the dappled sun and shade stood the coaches of the royal family who had come that far to meet her. In a twinkling, Marie Antoinette slipped from her seat and hastened over to the King. In a rustle of silk, she made a deep graceful curtsy, then looked up with expectant eyes . . . and there was her prince—a great awkward fellow, staring solemnly down at her with large pale blue near-sighted eyes. He kissed her dutifully on both cheeks, with no change of his expression, then, following her and his royal grandfather, clambered stolidly back to his seat in the coach and never ventured so much as a word till they reached their destination. On closer acquaintance Marie Antoinette discovered that there were only two things that Louis the Dauphin ever wanted to do—make locks and go hunting. Good days he went hunting, rainy days he hammered away in his smithy making locks, and his young bride soon found that she would have to make her own amusements.

That she found very difficult. Almost everything she wanted to do seemed to be contrary to some rule of etiquette, or was declared, by her lady-in-waiting, as unbecoming conduct. She couldn't run and play tag with her husband's young brothers, she mustn't have a dog, she mustn't ride horseback. She mustn't do this or that. What then could she do? This is the letter she wrote her mother:

"I get up at half past nine or ten o'clock, dress and say my morning prayers. Then I have breakfast and go to see my aunts. At eleven, I go to have my hair dressed. Next comes the levée. I rouge my cheeks and wash my hands before the assembled company; then the gentlemen withdraw, the ladies remain and I dress myself in their presences. Now it is time for church. If the King is at Versailles, I go with him, with my husband and my aunts to mass. After mass we have our dinner in public, but this is over by half past one, for we both eat very quickly. Then . . . I retire to my room, where I read, write, or work. Needlework, for I am embroidering the King a coat, which gets forward very slowly, though I hope that with God's grace it will be finished a few years from now.

At half past six my husband goes with me to my aunts. From seven to nine we play cards, at nine o'clock we have supper. We sit there for the King who usually comes at about quarter to eleven. While waiting, I lie down on a big sofa and go to sleep. That is how I spend my day."

It was a dull life instead of a gay one.

By May, 1773, Marie Antoinette had been in Versailles three years and had never seen Paris. The spiteful old aunts, Adelaide, Sophie, and Victoire (there were only three of them now, instead of four), had seen to it that she was deprived of that pleasure. So at last she plucked up courage to ask the King himself.

"And why not?" said the King, and told her to set the day.

So on the eighth of June, Marie Antoinette and the Dauphin made their first and joyous entry into the city of Paris. The procession of their coaches passed through flower-strewn streets, under flying banners and triumphal arches, among crowds of people who pressed close to the carriage to catch a glimpse of the golden-haired girl who would one day be their queen.

"How beautiful she is!" they exclamied, "and as kind-hearted too. Good times are sure to come again when they are king and queen."

Salutes of welcome were fired from the Bastille, as the procession wound slowly through the cheering throng to the Tuileries, the palace where the kings of France had lived in olden times. There the two young people stepped out on the balcony overlooking the garden.

"*Mon Dieu,* how many many people!" Marie Antoinette gave a little gasp of astonishment as she looked down on the upturned faces.

"Madame," said one of their attendants, "you see before you two hundred thousand persons who have fallen in love with you."

Marie Antoinette wrote Maria Theresa about the thrilling day:

"Last Tuesday," she said, "there was a festival which I shall never forget. We made our entry into Paris. Darling Mother, I do not know how to describe the transports of delight and affection shown us. How fortunate to be in a position where one can gain so much affection at so little cost. Such love is precious . . . I shall never forget it!

from a portrait

LA FAYETTE, A YOUNG FRENCH NOBLEMAN

STANDING AMONG those who cheered Marie Antoinette that day there must have been a young French nobleman, a boy of sixteen, who in a few years was himself to be as popular as she was then, and to become a hero both in France and in America. He had been born on September 6, 1757, in the ancient castle of his ancestors, deep in the woods of France. Late that afternoon, the mite of a nobleman with his fuzz of red hair and his wee clenched fists had been baptized with the very long name of Maria Joseph Paul Yves Gilbert du Motier, Marquis de La Fayette.

At the time of christening, the young father was at war, and two years later, when he was killed in battle, his baby Marquis became lord of the castle and head of the rather poor but very noble family of La Fayette. The young mother had gone back to her father's home in Paris, having left her small son to be brought up by his grandmother La Fayette, and as he grew older to be taught his prayers and lessons by the village priest. Fortunately these never lasted overly long, and the active red-haired boy had ample time to spend as he liked best,

131

wandering through the deep forest which surrounded the castle and in places came almost up to its old gray walls.

Not far from the castle, and skirting the village at the foot of the hill, spread the fields of the tenant farmers where the boy always saw the peasants at work. Whenever he passed by, those peasants pulled off their caps and bowed to him humbly, for he was their lord.

Their worn faces made the boy's heart ache.

"Poor ones," he thought, "their life is hard." He often wished that he could help them. Especially, tucked in his well-curtained bed on winter nights, when outside the wind whistled about the chimneys and he could hear the howling of wolves in the distant hills, he thought of the peasants. How the wind must be blowing whirls of snow through the cracks in their huts, and how close the wolves must be!

He always wanted to help the peasants, but there seemed to be nothing a boy could do until one day he heard of the werewolf and its horrible deeds. No common wolf, that one, said the peasants, but a man who turned himself into a wolf in order to feast at night on human beings. Any man or child who disappeared, they knew, had been seized and devoured by the terrible beast.

"Ah-ha!" thought the small La Fayette. Here at last was something for him to do. "I will kill that terrible wolf!" he vowed. "And how the poor folk will shout with joy when they see me come dragging the creature home!"

So already picturing himself a hero covered with glory, the small eager hunter went peering through the forest day after day.

But his search for the weird and impossible creature came to a sudden end, as he returned from the forest one evening to find a strange coach in the driveway and learned that the traveller who had arrived was his mother, Madame de La Fayette.

His mother! La Fayette rushed to greet her. Then he found that she had not come to stay for a month or two as she sometimes did, but to take him back with her to Paris. He was old enough now, she thought. "And quite tall, too, for eleven," she added with a smile.

La Fayette hated to say good-bye. He kissed his dear grandmother many many times on both cheeks, and his aunt and his cousin, before he rode away from the old gray castle of Auvergne to live in his grandfather's palace in Paris. There life was very different.

This grandfather, who was a wealthy man, saw to it at once that his young grandson was enrolled in a fine school for young noblemen, entered into the same class in horsemanship as the Dauphin's young brother, Count d'Artois, and sent to the dancing master. It was hard at first for the boy brought up in the country to feel at home in Paris.

The dancing school for one thing. The polished floor was very slippery and his new shoes with the red heels were very stiff. When he and his feet and his dress sword got all tangled up in the steps of the minuet, and the young ladies of nine or ten giggled behind their fans, he wished he were home in the forest.

And then the poor people in the streets, streets which were filthy with slops and slime. They were not like the peasants at home in the fresh open fields. They never bowed to him nor even doffed their caps when he rode by in his grandfather's coach. Instead some even muttered and shook their fists. And in bed at night it was not the distant howling of wolves that he heard but the howls of starving people hungry as wolves themselves whom the police were driving from the streets. They had no bread to eat. The King and his friends had bought up all the wheat. It made the boy miserable to think about it. But life moved so fast, he had little time to think.

When he was fourteen, his mother and grandfather died within one week, leaving him both an orphan and an heir to millions. Two years later, the same year that Marie Antoinette and the Dauphin made their "joyous entry" into Paris, La Fayette was married to Adrienne de Noailles. The marriage had been arranged by his grandfather with the Duc de Noailles, member of a most important family at court, whose palace in Paris stood opposite the Tuileries.

After the marriage of his fourteen-year-old daughter, the Duc arranged a place for his young son-in-law at court, in the suite of the Dauphin's brother, and was completely dumbfounded when shortly thereafter La Fayette was suddenly dismissed from the position. The Duc did not know of course that the boy had purposely brought about that dismissal because he had no taste for life at court.

Versailles was not where he belonged, he said to himself.

He didn't want to be a silly courtier. His father had been a cavalry officer. All the great La Fayette ancestors had served their king as soldiers, and not as idle fawning courtiers pouring perfume on his hands. He wanted to do as his ancestors had done. It was his dream to fight for some great noble cause, and like the knights of old, to conquer and return with flying colors.

So a command was arranged for him by his father-in-law, and when he was seventeen, La Fayette set out with a high heart to join a regiment of soldiers stationed at the town of Metz.

That was the spring of 1775, and that spring the Duke of Gloucester, brother of George III, was visiting in France, and also on his way to Metz. It was his story of the rebellion in his royal brother's American colonies that was to inspire La Fayette to fight for the cause of American liberty, and so bring true his dreams of glory.

134

ITALY: THE LAND OF BEAUTY

THE SPRING that Marie Antoinette went to France to marry the grandson of the King, her young friend Mozart was touring Italy with his father, who had taken him there to study, for Italy was a land of beauty, a land where people had always gone to study music and painting. Not only painters and musicians but people in general went there to enjoy the performances of the famous Italian operas at Naples or Milan, to marvel at the paintings and sculpture in the Vatican, to visit the ruins of ancient Rome, or just to enjoy the fruits and flowers, a warm sun and a blue sea.

When he was young, Sir Joshua Reynolds had travelled to Italy on a ship that was going to the Mediterranean to fight the pirates. Unfortunately, he had spent so much time studying Michelangelo's ceiling in the Sistine Chapel that he had caught a cold in his ears that left him deaf. That was why he always carried the black ear trumpet. Benjamin West had studied in Italy, before going to England. There the aged cardinal had been astonished to learn that any one so fair as the young painter could come from America, a land which he pictured as a barbarous one, inhabited only by red-skinned savages.

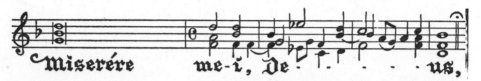

Mozart, who was fourteen, began by giving concerts in a northern part of Italy which belonged to Austria. From there he went to Rome to study the beautiful music of the church. It was a warm, flowery, lovely day when he and his father arrived. The dome of St. Peter's Cathedral had been freshly gilded. As it was the Wednesday before Easter, they went directly to the Sistine Chapel to hear the choir sing Allegri's "Miserere." That composition had never been written down and those who sang it were forbidden to do so on pain of excommunication. Mozart listened to it once and then was able to write it down almost note for note from memory.

After leaving Rome, Mozart went to Naples, the city most famous for the opera. From there he wrote his sister of seeing Mount Vesuvius, "smoking furiously."

Naples was always full of visitors, eager to see the old volcano and especially curious to visit the ruins of Pompeii. In 1748, the interest and curiosity of the whole world had been aroused by the accidental discovery of that old Roman summer resort, which had been buried by an eruption of Mount Vesuvius in the year 79.

While war was going on in Europe it was difficult to travel, but as soon as central Europe was no longer a battlefield, and there was no longer danger of being blown up at sea by enemy battleships, curious travellers came in great numbers like visitors to a world's fair, to see the ancient relics at Pompeii.

"The wonder is," related the travellers when they returned home again, "that you can see everything just as it was on the day the volcano erupted. Loaves of bread in the bakers' ovens, cakes, baskets of fish in the market place, all turned to stone."

They retold the story of how it had been discovered by an Italian peasant digging for a waterway there on the hill beside a vineyard, when his spade had hit upon a peculiar stone.

Not only sightseers, but artists and architects went to view the ruins, and furniture and house decorations like those found in Pompeii shortly became the fashion in Europe.

Robert Adam, the well-known English architect, visited Pompeii with an Italian friend, Piranesi, sometimes called the Rembrandt of Architecture because of his beautiful drawings. This is simplified from one he made of visitors viewing the ruined Temple of Isis in Pompeii.

Veduta del Tempio d'Iside quale oggi esiste fra gli avanzi dell'antica Città di Pompei

137

CARLOS III, King of Spain in 1770, had been ruler in Naples when Pompeii was discovered, for the southern part of Italy then belonged to Spain. This is Carlos III as he was painted by the great Spanish artist Francisco José Goya. In 1770, when Mozart went to Rome to study music, Goya, who was then twenty-three, also went to Rome to study painting. There, for fun, one moonlight night, as the tale is told, he climbed the dome of St. Peter's Cathedral just to scratch his name on the topmost stone.

Brimming over with high spirits was young Goya, and so full of life that wherever he went wild tales were told of his escapades. Like all Spaniards, Goya loved the bullfight and, going to Italy, is supposed to have worked his way to the seaport as one of a troupe of travelling bullfighters. In fact, from the time he was able to scramble up and down the narrow streets of his little native town in the foothills of the Pyrenees, or draw pigs with a charred stick on her sunny walls, up to the time he died at well over eighty, Goya was as full of life as any man could be. And so too were his paintings. In them you see almost brought to life again all the people who were living in his eighteenth-century Spain.

Spain, like Italy, was a land of color and beauty. Also like Italy, which once had held the center of a great empire, but was now a divided land, Spain, too, as a nation was living on glories that were past. Carlos III did much for his country, but he could not restore her power in the world. For many years, to his chagrin, even Spain's Fort Gibraltar guarding the Mediterranean had been held by England.

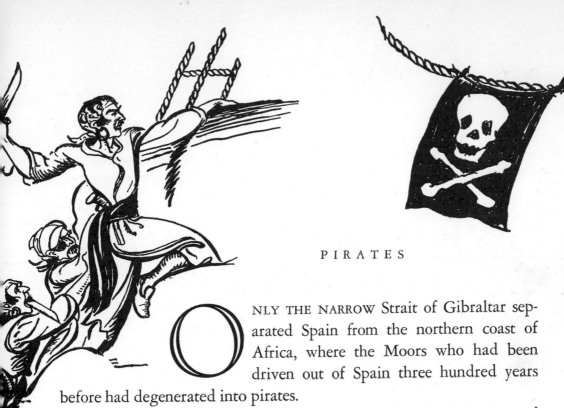

PIRATES

ONLY THE NARROW Strait of Gibraltar separated Spain from the northern coast of Africa, where the Moors who had been driven out of Spain three hundred years before had degenerated into pirates.

Their great chief was the Dey or ruler of Algiers. He supported himself in royal splendor by means of piracy, and his swarthy Algerians with daggers in their teeth were the terror of the Mediterranean. From their small swift vessels they would attack a European ship, rob the hold of its cargo, strip the passengers of their clothes and then take them back to labor in Algeria as slaves.

All the nations of Europe, supposedly so powerful, cringed before the pirate chief and allowed themselves to be blackmailed by him. Every one of them sent yearly tribute as a bribe to make him leave their ships alone. No change was to be made in the cowardly custom until after 1800. Then a small, weak nation, the United States of America, was to refuse to pay the shameful tribute.

The Dey of Algiers, the Pirate Chief, was a Turkish soldier, for Algiers belonged to Turkey. So too did the neighboring states of Tunis and Morocco, also pirate headquarters. In fact, except for Spain, France and Italy, every country bordering the Mediterranean Sea from Italy around to the Strait of Gibraltar belonged to the Empire of Turkey.

THE EMPIRE OF TURKEY

I N THE GREAT DAYS of Rome, when all the land around the Mediterranean Sea belonged to the Roman Empire, the Turks had been but wild tribes roaming the plains and mountains of western Asia.

But in 1763, three quarters of the land around the Mediterranean belonged to the Empire of Turkey, and the dark-skinned Turks, with their turbans, their prayer rugs and their crescent-shaped swords, were part of Europe. Their capital was Constantinople, that old illustrious city on the Black Sea, where Europe and the continent of Asia meet—a city of round-topped mosques and pointed minarets, where five times a day could be heard the voice of the muezzin calling the faithful Mohammedans to face the east in prayer. There in his seraglio, behind the Sublime Porte—the great gate closed to all intruders, surrounded by the veiled women of his harem, the eunuchs, officers and janissaries—lived the emperor, Sultan Mustapha III.

To him and all Turks, theirs was not the Turkish but the Ottman Empire, named for the great leader Osman, who had first gained a foothold for his people in Europe and united his warlike followers into an empire. Though each sultan was crowned with the wish that he might be as good as Osman, most of them, unfortunately, took their pattern instead from the cruel, merciless ways of Mohamed II who, peace-loving fellow that he was, had sliced off the head of his younger brother when he succeeded to the throne, so that he would have no disturbing rival, and then decreed that every following emperor should also murder his younger brothers in order to have a peaceful reign.

Mohamed II had captured Constantinople, then pillaged and sacked the city, and murdered the inhabitants, except the fairer women and the stronger men, whom he made into slaves.

That capture of Constantinople occurred in the days when Columbus was a boy, but ever since then the people of Europe had hated and feared the Turks, and there had been continual struggles to push them out of Europe and back into Asia where they came from. They had stood their ground, however, and in 1683 Turkey might well have conquered all of central Europe if it had not been for Poland. The Turks had attacked the state of Venice and had advanced to the very walls of Austria's capital, Vienna, when Polish soldiers, hastening to the rescue, drove them back. . . .

POLAND

I N THE YEAR 1772, Poland, which had once been one of the strong nations of Europe, had grown weak and so, an easy prey for her powerful neighbors, was ruthlessly torn to pieces by them and divided! There were three who took part in the dastardly deed: Catherine of Russia, Maria Theresa of Austria, and Frederick of Prussia.

141

For Catherine it was merely part of her plan to push Russia farther into Europe. "If you don't gain you lose," was her remark.

Maria Theresa, however, wept over having been persuaded to take part. "I feel shame to show my face," she sobbed. "I know that I am weak and friendless and so I let things take their course."

"Snivelling again," sneered Frederick. "Always in tears but always ready to take her share!" He admitted that it was the act of pirates. But what of it, if you could get away with it?

Those who took no part in it were not entirely without guilt, for they stood by and saw it done.

And the Poles themselves were also partly to blame—the noblemen, that is, for there was no other class of people in Poland except the rich noblemen who owned the land and the peasants who tilled it, except, of course, the merchant Jews who had no privileges.

The noblemen belonged to the Diet or Assembly and had the right to elect the king, but any one of them had the right to veto any law that was made, so there was practically no government at all. Also they were all so jealous of one another that they usually invited a foreigner to be king. Some of the nobles realized the weakness of their government and wanted to reform it.

Those patriot nobles, among whom there were a Count Pulaski and his sons, appealed to Catherine, as a good neighbor, to help them. Catherine agreed to do it. Instead, however, since it suited her purpose better to keep Poland weak, she saw to it that a man named Poniatowski, who was in love with her, was elected King of Poland, and then she helped not the patriots, but the other side. Seeing that they were betrayed, the patriots took up arms, but what chance had they against the Russians, and the Prussians and Austrians who by that time had also marched into Poland? Young Casimir Pulaski's father and brothers were killed. He was sentenced to death and had to flee the country. He made his way to Turkey and five years later reached America.

Thaddeus Kosciusko, another young Polish nobleman and soldier, also left for America about this time. And a merchant, too, Haym Salomon, a small, mild-mannered man whose genius lay in handling money.

All three, leaving a homeland where freedom had been crushed, were to give their whole-hearted service in the war for American Independence, a war fought in order that liberty and justice unknown to Poland might flourish on the soil of a new land.

ENTER NAPOLEON BUONAPARTE

AND NOW ON AN ISLAND in the Mediterranean, in the year 1769, a child was born who was to become a greater general than Frederick II, a greater statesman than William Pitt, a more autocratic ruler than Louis XV, more greedy for power than Catherine II, a more despotic emperor than the Sultan of Turkey, and more passionately idolized and bitterly hated than any one of them, and the worst pirate of them all.

Of the two large rocky islands that lie between Italy and the southern coast of France, the northern one is Corsica. It had been one of the Italian free states. But in 1769, Corsica's soldiers had been overpowered by the French, and the people, hot-blooded, fiery Italians, with ready daggers at their hips, had lost their independence.

One of those who had been forced to lead his countrymen in retreat was a proud young Corsican nobleman by the name of Buonaparte. To him and his beautiful dark-eyed wife there was born in August of that year 1769 a baby son. With his tiny tight-clenched fists and his hungry mouth he looked, to his beautiful young mother, much like her other babies—like any baby. Her pet name for him was Poli-one-e.

THE EMPRESS AND THE SULTAN

BEFORE I DIE, I shall have driven the Turks out of Constantinople!" declared Catherine, the Empress of Russia positively, and the Sultan of Turkey knew that it was no idle boast. Off and on for years Russia had been battling Turkey for a warm harbor on the Black Sea. Russia's only seaport lay in the Baltic and was ice-bound almost half the year. The Sultan also knew that Russia's Catherine coveted Constantinople, because that city controlled the entrance leading from the Black Sea to the Mediterranean. She was only waiting, he felt sure, for a convenient time to strike.

So all of a sudden, in a spurt of anger or bravado, the Sultan himself declared war on Russia (in 1768). He had been urged on by the French, who didn't like to see Russia edging into the affairs of Europe, and looked with concern on Catherine's growing power.

To rouse Russia was a reckless thing for the Sultan to do, for the Empire of Turkey was not strong and united as it had been in the days of Osman and Mohamed. It had long been showing those signs of decay that all old empires do before they go to pieces. Sloth, treachery, vice and ignorance were eating at its heart. Even the warlike spirit seemed to be disappearing. The Turkish soldiers were not much more than a rabble. Still using their old-fashioned weapons, they had fallen far below the standard of European soldiers.

The Russian soldiers were also a crude, half-civilized horde, it is true, but their officers were subtle and well trained. They pounced down on the Turks, completely routed them and drove them from the Crimea, (that ragged, square-shaped peninsula in the Black Sea).

At the same time more Russians sailed from the Baltic, down around to the Mediterranean, up into the Adriatic and there burned the Turkish fleet. The Sultan Mustapha had been warned that they were coming, but he pooh-poohed the idea, saying it was impossible.

"There is no way," said he, "to get from the Baltic Sea to the Mediterranean." His idea of the Atlantic Ocean was slightly hazy.

Turkish ignorance of geography didn't, however, much exceed that of the Russians about naval affairs. Most Russians had never seen an ocean-going ship—Alexis Orlov was made Grand Admiral of the Russian fleet before he had ever set foot on a battleship!

The victory over the Turks was due to experienced English naval officers, who had been engaged by Catherine. Alexis Orlov, however, took such pride in the victory and was so thrilled at the glorious sight of the Turks being roasted alive in their battleships that he wanted it perpetuated. So after the war was over he went to Italy and ordered a picture of it painted.

"But I have never seen a ship explode," objected the artist.

"No? I'll have one blown up for you to see," said Alexis, and he did. What was one ship more or less to him?

At the treaty of peace, the Russians got Azov and a few other fortresses, a toehold at last on the Black Sea. The Crimea was put under an independent ruler, whose rights Catherine agreed to respect, but did so with an eye to gobbling it up at some future date, as she had Poland.

But the city of Constantinople still belonged to Turkey. Russia however would be back again to try for it, for said Catherine, now that the "cat had been aroused, it would not rest until it had eaten up the mouse."

CATHERINE II had also expressed a desire to "break the pride of the Chinese." Instead, her own pride must have been hurt by a humiliating event that took place about this time in eastern Russia. There six hundred thousand people, oppressed by Russia's rule, left their unhappy home and went back to their forefathers' home in China. This was a strange event. No other such migration of a whole people has occurred in modern times, and no other migration has ever taken place from east to west, back to the ancestral home.

The people were the Kalmucks. A hundred years or so before, their ancestors, weary of war on the border of China, had come to find a new home in Russia. Russia had been glad to welcome the Kalmucks, only asking them, in return, to protect the border where they were against the wild Tartar tribes. For long years all went well. Then the Russian officials began to mistreat them. The Kalmucks dared not complain, for it was a state crime to protest.

"Our people no longer find peace here," said their leader Ugashi. "We will return to China."

In secret they made preparation for the journey, moving their herds, to pasture, gradually eastward until they were safely over the border. Then dividing themselves into two groups they started the long trek across Asia, one going north along the border of Siberia, the other far south to avoid the Gobi Desert.

Chief Ugashi sent word ahead to Emperor Ch'ien Lung that his people were coming. Thousands died on the way, but those who survived were received in China like long-lost children who, having suffered much in the land of the barbarians, had returned home, able at last to appreciate and value the blessings of a truly civilized country!

JAPAN — AND THE "PASSING WORLD"

OWARD THE RISING SUN from China lay the islands of Japan, and Chinese in their junks approaching the great harbor on the outer ocean could see for many miles the snow-white peak of Japan's sacred Fujiyama. This drawing from "The Wave" by the great Japanese artist Hokusai shows Mount Fuji in the background.

In the year 1776, the year of the monkey in Japan, where the years are named for animals, Hokusai was sixteen. Late winter days might have found him designing a "surimono" or greeting card for the new year. But with spring and the breath of wild cherry blossoms in the air, the restless boy was probably drifting along selling red peppers or calendars in the streets of Yedo.

Yedo is Tokio today, and today European visitors may climb to the shrines and temples of Mount Fuji, sixty miles away. But not when Hokusai walked the streets of Yedo. Then, Japan was closed to the world, and had been so for more than a hundred and fifty years.

In those years England, the small island kingdom off the coast of

147

Europe, had been putting down strong roots of what was to become a great world empire. But Japan, the similarly small island off the coast of Asia, had been wrapped up in itself as tight as a cocoon, and was to find, many years later when she wished to expand into a great empire, that the days of exploration were over and that there were no lands to conquer not already claimed by civilized nations.

At the time that China built the Great Wall, and Rome was the center of civilization in Europe, England and Japan had both been inhabited by tribes not far removed from barbarism. Later, about the same time in both countries, feudal lords had come into power who fought against each other and kept their countries in an almost constant state of war. Now in 1776, England was a constitutional monarchy still at war, but Japan was a feudal state, just as it had been, except that the country was at peace.

Powerful daimos, or feudal lords, still retained their armies of trained warriors or samurai, but they no longer made war on each other, for they had been subdued by the military overlord or Shogun. There was an emperor, the Mikado, but he was just a decoration, of no more use than a feather in a hat. The real head of the state was the Shogun. Under him everything in Japan ran as smoothly as a clock. Every act of life followed a perfected pattern, even to the small matter of lifting a teacup to the lips or placing an iris in a bowl.

That he might keep his power over them, the Shogun demanded that the daimos with their attending samurai leave their country estates, and spend at least six months of the year in Yedo.

To supply the wants of these gorgeous daimos and their trains of haughty samurai, there had grown up in Yedo a large middle class of people, bakers, wigmakers, weavers of silk, jewellers, tea-house keepers, puppet makers, fishmongers, all kinds of artisans, merchants and craftsmen. The splendid lords looked down upon these common people, but the common people had pleasures which the lords themselves could not enjoy. One was the theatre, another the very exquisite Japanese prints which were now being made in color.

The theatre was considered low class, therefore it was incorrect for the daimos and samurai to attend. The prints they simply failed to appreciate. Paintings to be correct must be done on silk scrolls, copied line for line from some approved pattern. These new drawings, printed in colored inks on flimsy sheets of rice or mulberry paper, were beneath their notice. To the common people, however, they were a great delight. It was a joy to be able to buy outside the theatre for a penny or two the picture of their favorite actor, or of the scene over which they had had the greatest pleasure shedding tears.

The prints showed not merely the theatre and the mountain, but all the common life of Japan as the people lived and knew it. Geisha girls with their beguiling smiles, cherry trees in blossom and in snow, children flying kites, ladies under tilted parasols or serving tea in their paper houses. "Passing World" pictures the Japanese people called them, because they showed the world as it passed before them, all the world, indeed, they knew about, in that secluded country of Japan.

Hokusai's drawings became more alive and beautiful with each year of his long life. One year he made a fine set of prints for a Dutch sea captain to take back with him to Holland. There they were greatly admired, and next year when he returned, as the Dutch were especially permitted to do once a year, he asked for more. Each succeeding year hundreds of the prints were taken to Holland, till the Shogun put a stop to it, sensing possible danger in even this indirect contact with the outer world. Let that outer world pass by! No evil influence must destroy the life pattern of Japan!

THE DUTCH WERE busy, energetic traders, and had long been rivals of the English in the harbors of the Far East and on the sea. Back in the 1600's, when Japan had closed her ports to all of Europe, she had made an exception of the Dutch, who were allowed to send two of their ships from Holland once a year. From then on the busy traders from the little land of dykes and windmills had made good use of their advantage in Japan. They had kept on building up their merchant fleet, till they were soon carrying most of the goods to and from England's ports and colonies as well as to and from their own. That was why, in 1651, the English Parliament had first passed the Acts of Navigation, which said that no foreign boats should carry any but their own goods into English harbors.

That had led to war between the two nations, but thereafter, the law had not been strictly enforced, and the smuggling had continued.

In 1660, the Dutch had first introduced tea into Europe. Now in 1770, a hundred years later, the Dutch East India Company was still smuggling tea into New York and Boston, while managers of the English East India Company bemoaned their tea, rotting in the warehouses.

So George III, needing money, had determined to enforce those old Acts of Navigation again, and put a complete stop to all smuggling, that carried on by the dauntless Dutch, as well as that carried on by the colonial merchants of Boston and other American ports, who brought in their cargoes of wine, rum, sugar and molasses from the West Indies.

That determination, which had already started trouble for him with his own American colonies, was to get George III into trouble also with the Dutch, and again bring Holland into war against England at a time when she already had more than enough enemies to face.

ALEXANDER HAMILTON, BOY OF THE WEST INDIES

THE WEST INDIES, those beautiful palm-covered islands dotted along the blue Caribbean, between North and South America, did not all belong to Spain, but were divided among the countries of Europe. And it was not all smuggling, but much legitimate shipping as well that was carried on between those tropical islands and the American colonies.

Seated on a high stool in the countinghouse of the busiest shipping merchant on the Island of St. Croix, one sultry day in 1770, there was a small bright-eyed boy of thirteen, named Alexander Hamilton.

Alexander was only twelve when he had first taken his place at the high sloping desk to learn accounting. Now, though he was still so young and small for his age, he was the best clerk his employer had.

Nevertheless, Alexander despised being a clerk, and found life

151

in the countinghouse very dull. He longed to do something bold and exciting—like going to war, perhaps, and becoming a great general.

"I wish there was a war," he wrote one day in a letter to his friend Ned. Ned had been sent away to New York to school, while he, Alexander, a far better scholar, had unhappily been left behind.

"All because," he said bitterly, "I have no father to send me."

The boy's face grew hot with shame as it always did at the thought of that roving Scotch father, who had deserted his family. Alexander could not forget how his mother had waited and watched for the man. His pretty French mother—how pale and white and ill she had grown before she had finally died and left him alone! Alone, that is, except for his uncles and aunts. They took good care of him, of course, but he was ashamed of having no father. So ashamed that whenever he felt people looking, he held his head very high and shut his lips tight.

"They shall see some day," he would say to himself, "that Alexander Hamilton is not a nobody. How I wish there was a war!"

But since there was no war, and no chance to leave the island, Alexander worked on three more years until suddenly his chance came in a most unexpected fashion. A terrific hurricane struck the island. One morning when he awoke, the air was very still and the moon filled with a sickly yellow light. By the time he reached the countinghouse there was a strong wind blowing and dark clouds raced across the sky. The clerks paid little attention. Wind was to be expected in August. But suddenly above the roar of the wind sounded the boom of guns! The hurricane warning! The men dropped their pens and sprang to the windows to bar the shutters. Already the air was full of flying shingles, sheets of rain, and branches torn from the palm trees.

The wind swept Alexander off his feet as he crossed to the stables for his horse. He flattened himself to the animal's back and raced down the long avenue of wind-torn palms to the plantation to help his aunt, who was there alone, except for the terrified Negroes.

Two days later Alexander rode back to town. Dead men and cattle and all kinds of birds and animals lay strewn on the barren fields. The harbor was full of wrecked ships and the shore heaped with decaying fish. The streets of the town were filled with rubbish, but the houses were still standing. Alexander sat down at his desk and began to write. His mind was full of the hurricane, and vivid words describing it rushed from his pen. Later he showed what he had written to his former teacher.

"A boy who can write like that," said the man, "must be given his chance."

The governor of the islands agreed and together the two men persuaded the boy's uncle and aunt to send their talented nephew to New York to college.

That was how Alexander Hamilton happened to arrive in New York City, just as war for which he had been wishing was about to start.

JOHN PAUL, AND THE HATED SLAVE TRADE

JAMAICA, the island directly south of Cuba, belonged to England. A line drawn from Jamaica across the Atlantic Ocean to the west coast of Africa marks the path of a very ugly trade. A line drawn from that west coast of Africa, back to Jamaica, from Jamaica to Boston and from Boston back again to Africa make a triangle, another path of the same ugly trade—the slave trade.

Sugar sent from Jamaica to Boston was there made into rum. A few barrels of rum, one hundred fifty gallons more or less, sent to Africa would buy a Negro from a native chief. The Negro, taken to the slave

153

market in Jamaica, would sell for eighty or one hundred dollars. Then the slave would be put to work on the sugar plantations to raise more sugar to make more rum to buy more slaves. Or he might be sent to the Spanish colonies in South America. Or to the English colonies.

African chieftains were only too ready to sell their subjects for the white traders' rum. They often sent men back in the jungle at night to set fire to the native villages, and capture the terrified creatures as they fled from the flames. Chained together, they would be driven to the sea-coast and the waiting ship. Still chained hand and foot, they were then crowded down into a stinking hold with only floor space one and a half foot square allowed to each. Before they were many days out at sea the wretched creatures packed in so close together, breathing the foul air, began to sicken and die. Every morning the men who went down to inspect them had to unchain the limp bodies of those who had died during the night and throw them overboard to the sharks.

It was a sickening business, one that John Paul had no taste for. As he paced the deck of the slave ship *King George,* carrying its cargo of black flesh back to Jamaica, he wondered why he had ever come aboard. It was the summer of 1766, and the Scotch lad was then but nineteen years old. He felt ill. There was no place on deck or in his cabin where he could not hear the groans of the miserable Negroes. When the hatch door was opened the rotten stench of disease and filth that filled his nostrils nauseated him.

He endured the slave trade just two years and quit. Being stranded in Jamaica without any money, he joined a company of Irish players and became an actor. In that way he added to his natural charm a polished manner, a cultured way of speaking, and also earned enough money to pay his way back home to Scotland.

There he became master of a merchant ship plying between London and the West Indies, and remained in that trade until he was twenty-six. Then occurred what he later called the "great misfortune of my life." In the harbor of Tobago, the ringleader of the surly, mutinous crew who had formerly been in the rum and slave trade defied John Paul and made a lunge for him with a club, at which John Paul, master of the ship, had run him through with the sword and killed him. It had been done in self-defense, but since the Commission was not there to try his case, friends declared that it was no longer safe for him on the island, got a horse for him and told him:

"Ride, disappear. Go to the continent of America, take a new name."

That is why it was John Paul Jones, and not John Paul who appeared in Virginia in 1775, and who later was to win fame as the bold commander in the great sea battle of the American Revolution.

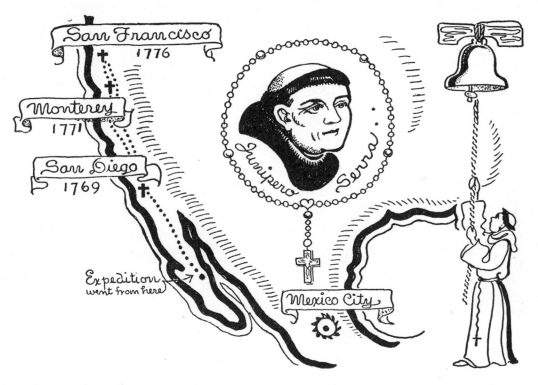

SPAIN'S NEW COLONY

"YOUR MAJESTY'S greatest problem," said his principal advisor to the King of Spain, "is how to protect your West Indian islands, and your possessions in the Americas from England." Carlos III was of the same opinion. Spain had already lost the colony of Florida to England, and now the King was apprehensive that George III might seek to annex still more of Spanish America.

The Viceroy of New Spain was also worried. He begged constantly that more troops be sent to Mexico for his protection. There was danger from the northwest, he reported. English fur traders from Hudson Bay were making their way to the Pacific. The Russians had again crossed Bering Strait to Al-ay-eska or New Russia, and were extending their fur-trading posts much too far down that western coast.

It appeared high time to the Spanish King that forts should be built along the shore of Alta California, whose coast line Spain had explored one hundred fifty years before, but never fortified.

In July, 1768, therefore, Galvez, a man of vim and energy, was sent to Mexico, as agent for the King of Spain, to take complete charge of building forts in California. He went first to that desert waste of rocks and thistles, the peninsula of Baja California. There he found as governor a generous-spirited man by the name of Portola, and as head of the missions a slim frail monk by the name of Junipero Serra, who immediately offered to accompany the expedition.

Galvez told him that they expected to establish two forts, one at San Diego and one at Monterey, a bay that had, he said, been described with great enthusiasm by the first explorer.

"But for our Father Saint Francis, is there to be no mission?" asked Fray Junipero Serra, to which Galvez replied:

"If Father San Francisco wants a mission let him cause his port to be found and it will be put there."

Satisfied, Fray Junipero threw himself eagerly into the work of enlisting the required missionaries and collecting and packing the church articles while Galvez took care of the other provisions for the expedition. Seven large bronze bells, two copper baptismal fonts, brass candlesticks, wax candles, incense burners, and images went on the first ship along with meat, sugar, raisins, chocolate, spices, red peppers and one hundred twenty-five pounds of garlic. Galvez had also brought seeds of flowers and vines from Spain, which he had thought might grow in the new land. Another ship was to follow the first ship and two expeditions were to go by land. After seeing them off, Galvez's work was over.

Portola was in charge of all four divisions and went in the second expedition by land, as did Fray Junipero. Knowing that the journey would be difficult even for those in perfect health, Portola had tried to persuade the feeble monk not to attempt it.

"I have faith," replied Fray Junipero, "that I will be given strength not only to arrive in San Diego to raise in that port the standard of the Holy Cross, but in Monterey as well. If it is God's will that I die on the road, then bury me there."

So they started, soldiers and priests. As they left the lower peninsula, they passed from rocks and thistles to more fertile country. The Indians they found friendly but timid. Most of them, too frightened to come near the curious strangers, watched them from the hills.

One day, however, several Indians met them with their usually bare brown bodies decked out in pieces of bright blue calico. Men on ships, they said, had given them the cloth.

At that good news, Fray Junipero, Portola and his men hastened eagerly over the few remaining miles. At last, rounding the top of a hill, they saw far below two ships at anchor on the clear blue water, and tents on the stretches of white sand.

"God be praised," cried Fray Junipero.

The soldiers fired their muskets. Full of joy, they descended to the harbor. There a dismal sight awaited them. Lines of men dying of scurvy lay before them. From the first shipload only one seaman and a cook remained alive. Mounds of sand marked where they had buried the others. Of the two hundred sixteen who had started, only one hundred twenty-six in all were left.

After a conference it was decided that one ship should return for more men and supplies. Fray Junipero and eight of the soldiers should remain at San Diego to care for the sick. Portola and his men should press on to find the harbor of Monterey, the real goal of the journey.

Monterey was a splendid harbor, according to the early explorer, but so over-advertised by him, that Portola and his men came to the

157

bay and failed to recognize it. They saw the "point of pines" and the other proper landmarks, but where, they asked, in this broad open bay was the landlocked harbor? Mystified, they continued farther north, until they looked down upon the finest harbor, the most beautiful bay on the Pacific coast line, the one which, it was later agreed, Father San Francisco had chosen for his own!

Looking back, Portola knew that they had gone too far, so they returned to Monterey, placing a huge wooden cross where they had stood, though still in a quandary as to where the harbor was. They had now been gone six months, and their food supply was exhausted. So they straggled back to San Diego, famished and discouraged, only to find that the ship which had gone back for more men and supplies had not yet returned! If the food ship did not come within a few more days there was no alternative, Portola said, but to return home.

"But I shall stay," said Fray Junipero. "What more do we need than a tortilla a day and the wild herbs of the field?"

Knowing well that it took more than tortillas and wild herbs to satisfy his soldiers, Portola took stock of what food remained.

"We will wait until March 19," said he, "then we will be obliged to leave if the supply ship is not here."

It was then March 10. Portola prepared to leave. Fray Junipero prayed and waited. To his great joy, on the last of the nine anxious days spent in prayer, he sighted the provision ship! God be praised! The settlement of California would not be abandoned.

By land and sea they all then returned to the Bay of Monterey where they found the wooden cross which Portola had left.

"It was surrounded with arrows stuck in the ground and sticks with many feathers, which they (Indians) had placed there: suspended from a pole beside the cross was a string of small fish all fairly fresh, while pieces of meat were deposited at the foot of the cross and a pile of mussels."

Near that cross, with the fresh clear air blowing from the bay, gulls soaring above it, and the sun on his shaven head, Fray Junipero Serra in his brown robes sprinkled holy water on the land, "to put to rout all infernal foes," then knelt to chant the Mass. The soldiers in their brown leathern jackets fired their muskets and the bay echoed with the roar of the cannon. Portola stepped forward, planted the flag of Spain and proclaimed in a loud voice that he took possession of the land in the name of his Majesty, King Carlos III of Spain, and was prepared to defend it against all comers.

Thus, on the third of June, 1770, the summer that England's flag was planted in the continent of Australia by James Cook, California was born and baptized.

Six years later England's colonies in America declared their independence, and that year, on his most beautiful harbor, facing the western ocean, the mission to Father San Francisco was built.

OVER THE MOUNTAIN WITH BOONE

THE YEAR that the Spaniards started for California, Daniel Boone shouldered his long black rifle and set out from his home in North Carolina on an exploring trip over the Alleghany Mountains into that part of the wilderness that later became Kentucky. Five men went with him, all lean, sunburned men with sharp eyes and sinewy muscles, all with their long rifles and long knives at their belts. One of them, a fur trader, knew of a gap or break in the mountain

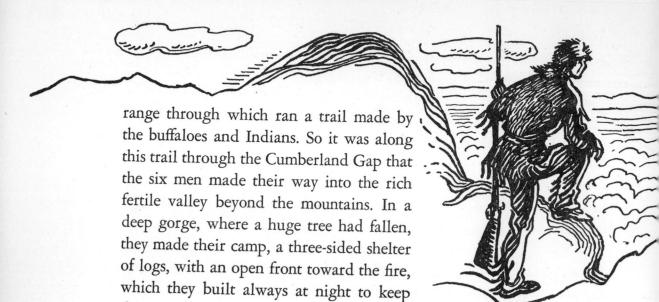

range through which ran a trail made by
the buffaloes and Indians. So it was along
this trail through the Cumberland Gap that
the six men made their way into the rich
fertile valley beyond the mountains. In a
deep gorge, where a huge tree had fallen,
they made their camp, a three-sided shelter
of logs, with an open front toward the fire,
which they built always at night to keep
the wolves away. Their days were spent
exploring the country, wandering through fields of cane that grew
higher than their heads, or hunting the buffaloes which came in great
numbers to feed in the lush fields of clover. For six months they did not
see an Indian. Then one day Daniel Boone and one other man followed
buffalo tracks deep into the forest. Without warning, Indians sprang
upon them, seized them and led them off, captives.

"Keep calm. Take it easy," said Boone in a low even tone to his
companion, who found it difficult to control his feelings.

For seven days they were led along through the cane-brakes, not
knowing what torture was in store for them at the journey's end. All
that time, though he behaved as if his mind were quite at ease, Daniel
Boone was watching his chance. One night it came. The whole party
was exhausted from a long day's trip. Boone lay awake staring up at
the stars and listening until he could tell by their deep breathing that
all the Indians were fast asleep. He sat up . . . rose silently to his feet
. . . touched his companion on the shoulder. In perfect silence they
stole away and slipped back into the forest. The stars gave them the
direction of their camp, but when they reached the spot they found the
camp wrecked and deserted. Their four friends were never seen again.

A few weeks later Daniel Boone's younger brother and a hunter from North Carolina surprised them and made the party four. It was soon reduced again to two: one of the men was shot and scalped, the other lost in the woods. Then the brother went home to fetch more ammunition and Daniel Boone was alone in the wilderness. There he was for three months, a lone man surrounded by wild beasts and savage Indians, without a horse or a dog, without salt or sugar or bread. And apparently the only reason that he stayed on was because life in the wilderness was the life he liked. He was a born pioneer. North Carolina, rough as it was, had already grown too civilized for him.

Too many people there, he thought. Too high taxes.

This fertile valley suited him, and he made up his mind to go home to sell his farm, and fetch his wife and family back to settle in "Kaintuckee." Even though it was against the law.

That was a law which could never be enforced, for what law was there that could make poor people stay in the eastern colonies where all the land was claimed by others, when just over the mountains there was land aplenty for any man who had courage enough to go out and take it? Many followed Daniel Boone into Kentucky through the pass in the mountains and along the great Wilderness Road that he marked out. Others put their belongings on flatboats and floated down the gray winding waters of the Ohio. It took brave men and brave women to go out to set up homes in this unknown land, for they knew that out where they were going there were no soldiers of the King to protect them from the savages. But they were shrewd, hardy, self-reliant people, those early pioneers.

"We don't ask help," they said, as they turned their faces toward the vast land beyond the mountains; "reckon we kin care for ourselves!"

161

REBELLION IN MASSACHUSETTS

T HE *Liberty,* a sloop belonging to John Hancock, sailed into Boston Harbor one pleasant night in June, 1768, docked at the Hancock wharf, and proceeded to unload a cargo of smuggled wine. Officers from an English ship which was on guard came to investigate the suspicious cargo.

"Go on. Get off," they told John Hancock, "you forfeit your ship."

John Hancock left the ship, but in the morning he returned and a mob came behind him. With sticks and stones and bottles and bricks, they drove the customs officers out of town and the sailors back to the warship in the harbor. The customs officers appealed for help to the

162

royal governor, and he in turn appealed to the King. The King sent over more soldiers to settle the trouble, which only made the trouble worse. They were not the best kind of English soldiers, but a rough noisy crew who swaggered about town in their red uniforms, jeering at the townspeople, and singing "Yankee Doodle" at them.

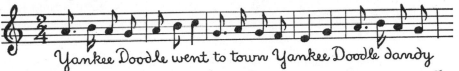

Yankee Doodle went to town Yankee Doodle dandy

In return, whenever a redcoat came in sight, the town ruffians would bawl out, "Hi there, lobster. Red lobsters for sale!"

Insults grew uglier till in 1770 there was a street fight and men were killed. Only a few men, but Samuel Adams called it a massacre.

Samuel Adams (second cousin of John) was a radical, one of those men whose ideas are so passionate and deep-rooted that they can never see any side of a question but their own. British soldiers, he cried aloud, had deliberately shot down innocent people in the streets! With such words he excited the mob. Then he rushed to Paul Revere, the copper- and silversmith, and had him make this engraving of the "Massacre." Let the world see what an outrage had occurred in Boston!

Samuel Adams
from a portrait by
Copley

John Hancock

Now John Adams also believed in liberty, but likewise in justice. The mob, he knew, had begun the fight, and when the soldiers were tried, he defended their case and secured the verdict "Not guilty."

One gray winter day in 1773, three English tea ships sailed into the harbor of Boston and dropped anchor.

"They can't bring that tea ashore here," said the people of Boston.

"We don't sail away till the tea's unloaded," the captain retorted.

Days went by while the ships with their chests of tea lay rocking in the harbor. The people became very much excited, but the most excited man of all was Samuel Adams. He sent a messenger to the royal governor asking him to send the ships away. Then he called a meeting to be held December 16 at the old South Meeting House. Seven thousand people came. They filled the meeting house and all the square outside, while they waited through the winter afternoon for the governor's answer. When it finally came, the word was "No."

"Then," said Samuel Adams, rising to address the people as the first candles were being lighted, "this meeting can do nothing more to save the country."

Suddenly, outside, they heard a wild Indian warwhoop, and saw a band of young men dressed like Indians race by down Milk Street toward the wharf, where the tea ships were anchored. These "Indians" went right to work with their hatchets, broke open two hundred sixty-four chests of tea and dumped the contents into the water where it floated and soaked till the crisp night air was full of the smell of wet tea leaves. A delightful, thrilling aroma for the excited audience to sniff as they went crunching homeward in the snow.

Many good citizens of Boston, however, thoroughly disapproved of such unruly measures, and news of that "Tea Party" naturally enraged the King. He ordered Boston harbor closed, and decreed that not a ship should go in or out until every chest of the ruined tea was paid for. Four more regiments of soldiers were sent to Boston, to be quartered in Faneuil Hall, and on the Commons. And if they caused more trouble, the ringleaders were to be sent to England to be tried.

The feeling in Boston now became more and more intense.

" 'Twould serve the Boston people right to have their town knocked down about their ears," the British soldiers blustered, while the hot-headed young radicals were yelling that "all stiff-necked Tories and royal governors ought'a be tarred and feathered." Nobody felt safe.

Many conservative people, fearful of being attacked by the unruly mob, began leaving for England. Samuel Adams and John Hancock, fearing arrest, took refuge in Lexington. All the small towns of Massachusetts now formed companies of Minute Men, ready to serve on a minute's notice. Muskets and ammunition were gathered together at the town of Concord.

Nothing happened until spring. Then one night in April, like the cold mist from the bay, a whisper spread through Boston that the British were planning to capture the guns and barrels of powder at Concord early the next morning. There was no time to waste! The people of Concord must be warned . . . and the Minute Men called to arms!

Paul Revere and William Dawes stood ready with their horses, watching the belfry of Old North Church for the signal as to whether the British were starting for Concord by land or by boat up the river. It was to be one flash if by land and two if by sea. Two flashes shone in the dark and the men were off. Riding wildly through the night, they carried the warning to the sleeping villages. A knock at the door, and the cry, "To arms! The soldiers are coming!" left behind them little houses suddenly become alive. Yellow candlelight shone from their windows. Inside men hurried into their clothes, caught up their three-cornered hats and their muskets and were off!

April 19, 1775

The chill gray dawn of the next morning found fifty Minute Men gathered on the village green at Lexington, ready for the British.

"Disperse, ye rebels!" shouted the British commander. Cheers followed shouts and shots. Who fired the first one no one knows, but with that first shot on Lexington green, the American Revolution began.

Then the British went on to Concord, destroyed as many guns and kegs of ammunition as they could find, and after a skirmish with more of the American militia gathered at the small wooden bridge in Concord, they turned and began a quick march back to Boston. But the quick march soon broke into a wild flight, for news of the morning had spread, and from all over the stony countryside farmers with their muskets came swarming out like angry bees, and from behind the stone walls, fences kept up a stinging fire at the redcoats all along the way.

When the exhausted soldiers were safe again in Boston they had no desire nor breath left to sing "Yankee Doodle." That day the Americans put new words to the old song and began to sing it themselves. So "Yankee Doodle" became the song of the American Revolution.

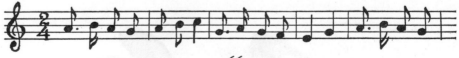

THE FIRST CONGRESS

T HE DIE IS NOW CAST," said George III; "the colonists must either triumph or submit."

"The Colonists" was a new idea. Up to this time kings of England had always dealt with each one of the colonies separately, as a small nation in itself. Now they were being treated as one, so it was only natural that they should decide to act as one.

Committees of Correspondence were established first, so that each colony might learn from the others the latest news from all parts of the continent, and act accordingly.

It was very fortunate now that the good post roads had been built.

The first news to reach Williamsburg, Virginia, in this way was that of the Boston Tea Party. Following soon came the word that the port of Boston had been closed and that Boston people who depended on their shipping business were suffering for want of food.

"An attack on any one colony should be considered as an attack upon the whole," said young Thomas Jefferson, at one of the meetings which now had to be held in the Raleigh Tavern.

"If necessary I will raise one thousand men," said George Washington, "support them and march at their head to the relief of Boston."

Though that seemed not yet necessary, no one knew how soon force would be needed. For who could tell what had happened since the last letters came? Merely writing to one another now began to seem inadequate, and it was decided that delegates from each of the colonies ought to meet in what one might call a Continental Congress. The meeting of this first Congress was set for September, 1774.

Some of the colonies were loth to elect or send delegates, for they were far from being united in their opinion. In North and South Carolina, the Tories far outnumbered the Whigs, and they were also very strong in Pennsylvania and New York. One half of the population of New York City, including the faculty of King's College, were Tories and two thirds of the property of New York belonged either to them or to the crown. At a big outdoor meeting held in New York City, to try to force the Assembly to send their delegates to the Congress, a slight young fellow pushed his way to the platform and made the best speech of the day. Those who knew him passed the word that he was a student at King's College named Alexander Hamilton.

Dry September days found delegates from all the colonies except Georgia on their way to Philadelphia. Most of them arrived three weeks ahead of time, curious to see what the strangers from the other colonies were like. John Adams and Samuel Adams with two other delegates from Boston came by stagecoach. It was the longest journey John had ever made, and the dustiest. Dust blew in and settled thick on Samuel Adams's new suit, for which the people of Boston out of self-respect had taken up a collection. Patrick Henry and George Washington, two of the five Virginia delegates, came on horseback. Every inn and lodging house in the city of Philadelphia was full.

Since the State House was still the headquarters of the royal governor it was not available for this unlawful assembly. The Carpenters' Union, fortunately, had just completed their new Guild Hall, and offered it for the meetings. John Adams said that the delegates were about one third Whigs, one third Tories and the rest "mongrels." They were alike, however, in thinking of themselves for the first time not as Virginians, or Pennsylvanians or New Yorkers, but as Americans, and in believing that as such they should act as one in settling their difficulties with Parliament and the King. But there they differed again. One side stressed the importance of keeping peace, the other side the importance of standing up for their rights. Finally it was decided to send a plea to the King that he acknowledge their rights as Englishmen, especially the right of making their own tax laws, and likewise to sign an agreement not to import any English goods until a satisfactory answer to their request had been received.

"Most excellent Majesty, Most gracious sovereign, We your Majesty's faithful subjects," was the way the letter began.

It was read with praise by all the friends of America in Parliament. Edmund Burke made an eloquent plea in behalf of the colonists, and so did William Pitt. "When your lordships look at the papers," Pitt exclaimed; "when you consider their decency, firmness and wisdom, you cannot but respect their cause and wish to make it your own."

Too many lordships, however, as well as the King, were still unable to consider any viewpoint except that Parliament had the right to make the laws, and the disobedient colonists must be forced into submission. Therefore, George III, most excellent Majesty, but most stubborn sovereign, treated this petition of his rebellious but still faithful subjects with contempt. And so gave another jolt to the diamond in his crown.

Benjamin Franklin, feeling that there was nothing more that he could do in England, after ten years spent there, sailed for home.

THE BATTLE OF BUNKER HILL

URGOYNE, CLINTON, HOWE were three British major generals who late in May of 1775 were sent with more troops to Massachusetts. Jeered at when they left by the Whigs of London, they were given a warm welcome by the Tories of Boston. Many of these people had been shamefully abused because of their opinions, and all were fearful of the future. Already on the stony hills surrounding Boston, American militia, Minute Men from the nearby villages and farmers from all of the neighboring colonies were trying to form themselves into some kind of makeshift army. The British generals, therefore, decided to fortify one of the nearby hills for their protection.

Just across the harbor from Boston was the little town of Charlestown, and just beyond there were two hills round and green and rather high. One was called Breed's Hill, the one farther away was Bunker Hill. It was Bunker Hill that the British decided upon, but before they had started their fortifications there, the Americans crept in one dark night, got to work and built a fort of their own on top of Breed's Hill.

Next morning at sunrise, one of the British generals was awakened by guns being fired from a battleship in the harbor. It was a fine day, a beautiful morning! He stepped out to see what was up, looked over the sparkling waters of the bay and saw to his amazement on the green top of Breed's Hill the brown mounds of fresh-turned earth which had been dug up during the night. With the American farmers on Breed's Hill, it was no longer a fine day for the British general.

All morning, while the three generals consulted how best to drive the farmers out, the ships kept up their firing. Most of their cannon-balls, however, didn't reach the hill, but exploded in Charlestown and set the small wooden houses of the village ablaze. The smoke of the fire could be seen ten miles away, at Braintree. There John Adams's eight-year-old son, John Quincy, and his mother Abigail watched it from the hill by the big rock. On the roofs of the houses in Boston, people watched the battle begin in the afternoon when the British soldiers rowed across the bay and made their attack.

Behind the earthworks, gruff old Israel Putnam was in command.

"Don't one of you fire," he shouted, "till they get near enough for you to see the whites of their eyes." So the farmers set their jaws and held their muskets ready till the shining bayonets of the British were just fifty feet away! Then they let loose such a burst of bullets that twice they drove the British soldiers back. But by the third advance, the Americans had run out of ammunition, and as they had no bayonets, they were driven from the hill. They fled, but General Howe gave no order to pursue them. Perhaps he did not wish to defeat them. Or perhaps he had no taste for more. Never, he said later, had he been in a hotter encounter than the Battle of Bunker Hill. Back in the stony pastures, the Americans were jubilant. 'Wish we could sell 'em another hill at the same price," they laughed.

"Yankee Doodle keep it up," they sang, "Yankee Doodle dandy."

Sir Wm Howe

JOHN ADAMS SELECTS A COMMANDER

THE SUN ROSE "with a superior luster," said Ethan Allen on the morning of May 10, 1775. To him that was a glorious morning, for just before dawn that young soldier from the Vermont section of New Hampshire and his little army of "Green Mountain" boys had surprised the commander of Fort Ticonderoga, on Lake Champlain, and demanded its surrender in the name of "the great Jehovah and the Continental Congress."

It was an exciting morning also in Philadelphia, for it was that of the opening meeting of the Second Continental Congress, which met this time in the east room of the State House. John Hancock, in the chairman's seat, looked genteel, as always, in a red velvet suit and lace-edged ruffles. It was George Washington, the Virginia planter, however, who attracted most attention, for he came dressed in military uniform, showing plainly that he was ready for action.

Less than a month it was since the battle at Lexington and Concord. All the delegates were excited. All believed that Congress should do something, but as to just what it was that congress ought to do, there were almost as many ideas as there were delegates.

Benjamin Franklin, now one of the representatives from Pennsylvania, wanted to write again to Parliament and the King, and try once more to settle the matter peaceably. John Adams and the Massachusetts delegates were ready to fight, while others wanted to do both—try to make peace and at the same time prepare for war.

"Of all the shillyshallying," grumbled John Adams irritably. "A sword in one hand and an olive branch in the other." Through the endless arguments and discussions he fidgeted nervously in his chair, slapped irritably at the flies that flew in from the livery stable next door. By the middle of June his patience was exhausted. He glanced over toward the Virginia gentlemen who had just taken their seats after a noon recess. There was the new delegate, with the sandy hair, Thomas Jefferson; beyond him Patrick Henry. Just inside the door, at the back of the hall, John Adams located the man he had in mind, the big man in the blue-and-buff uniform, sitting with one knee crossed over the other, and a tremendous sun-browned hand resting quietly on it. Then, since John Adams never lacked the courage to do what he thought was right, no matter how many enemies he made by doing it, he rose and addressed his old friend John Hancock, who occupied the chair.

"Mr. President," said John Adams, "I move that Congress should adopt the army outside of Boston, and appoint a general. I do not hesitate to declare that I have but one gentleman in mind for that important command and that man is . . ."

John Hancock listened so far with a smile of satisfaction, believing himself to be the gentleman in mind, but the smile soon faded from his face as his old friend John continued speaking:

"That man is a gentleman from Virginia, who is amongst us and very well known to all of us, a gentleman whose skill and experience as an officer, whose independent fortune, great talents and excellent character would command the approval of all America, and unite all of the colonies better than any other person in the whole thirteen."

By that time the Virginia gentleman's face was red with embarrassment. He rose hurriedly and disappeared through the door near by.

The next day, nominated by the delegate from Maryland, George Washington was appointed commander of the Continental army, part of which that very afternoon was engaged in the battle of Bunker Hill.

The newly appointed commander left for Boston immediately. Near by, in the village of Cambridge under the branches of a giant elm, George Washington formally took command of the "Continental Army." Since added to the New Englanders, there were soon troops from Maryland, Pennsylvania and Virginia, the group might be called "Continental" but it could scarcely be called an army. The men had no uniforms, no ammunition, and they needed months of training.

Not till the following spring could Washington make any attempt to drive the British out of Boston. Then he had no cannon, until one morning in March ox-teams lumbered into camp dragging the cannon that Ethan Allen and his Green Mountain boys had captured at Ticonderoga. They were set up immediately on the high ridge overlooking Boston. But they were never fired. General Howe caught sight of them through his spyglass and sent word not to fire, that he and his soldiers were willing to leave. So by the middle of March, 1776, the British and nine hundred Loyalist refugees with them boarded their warships and sailed out of Boston harbor headed for Nova Scotia.

(Among those refugees was a Scottish family from Rhode Island by the name of Stuart. Gilbert, their lusty young son, saw no future for him in Nova Scotia. Instead he wanted to study painting with Benjamin West, so he had borrowed passage money and gone to England.)

Three months after the British left Boston, the war of rebellion against England was over. From then on it was a war for Independence.

IV

WHEN GEORGE WASHINGTON WAS THE

Commander

Events in the American Revolution

THOMAS JEFFERSON
wrote the
DECLARATION OF INDEPENDENCE

1776

THOMAS PAINE
stirred the colonies to
declare independence.

BEAUMARCHAIS
sent secret supplies to
America from France

This Flag
was adopted
in
1777
★

After signing the
Declaration,

BENJAMIN FRANKLIN
went to make friends for America in France
& arranged a

TREATY WITH FRANCE
1778

BETSY ROSS
of Philadelphia was busy
making the new flags.

LAFAYETTE
served without pay in
the American army

1777
BURGOYNE
surrendered at
Saratoga

LOUIS XVI was forced
by his ministers to join
America against England

and what other People were doing

while Washington was Commander

1779

Spain declared war on England and laid seige to Gibraltar.

JOHN ADAMS went to Holland to borrow money.

CATHERINE II opposed England with a League of armed Neutrality

JAMES COOK looking for a Northwest passage, was killed by natives in Hawaii

SIMON BOLIVAR the "George Washington" of South America was born July 24, 1783

JOHN PAUL JONES raised stars + stripes for the first time on an American man-of-war

GEORGE ROGERS CLARK won forts in Northwest and gave U.S. claim to territory

THE PEACE TREATY

RUSSIA
ENGLAND
SPAIN
USA.

1781 CORNWALLIS surrendered at Yorktown,

NORTH AMERICA was again divided,

1783 John Adams B Franklin John Jay — signed the treaty of Peace with England

between the Years 1776 and 1783

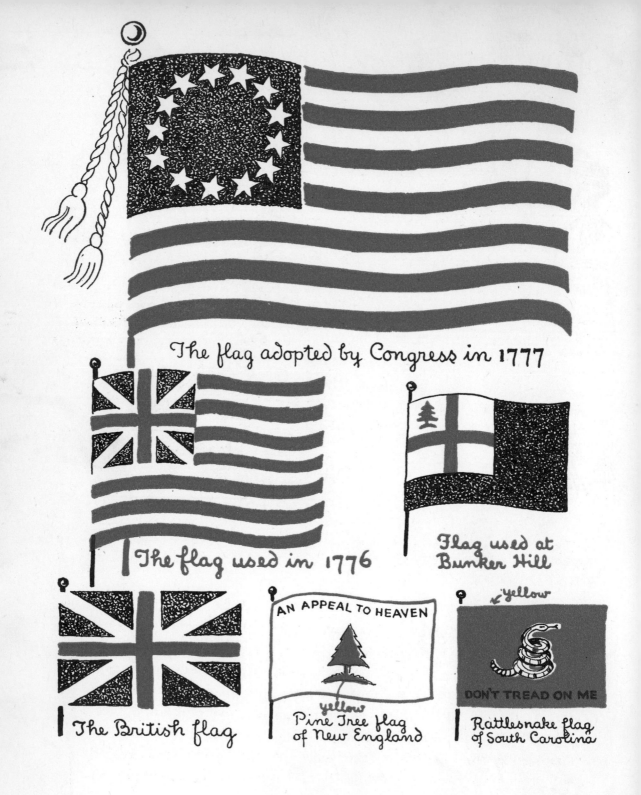

The flag adopted by Congress in 1777

The flag used in 1776

Flag used at Bunker Hill

The British flag

AN APPEAL TO HEAVEN

Yellow

Pine Tree flag of New England

DON'T TREAD ON ME

Rattlesnake flag of South Carolina

Th. Jefferson

DECLARATION OF INDEPENDENCE

THE NEW WORD, Independence, came with the year 1776, broadcast through the American colonies by a pamphlet called _Common Sense._ "O ye that love mankind," rang its challenging words, words that went echoing from one end of the continent to the other, "ye that dare not only to oppose tyranny but the tyrant, stand forth! Every spot in the old world is overrun with oppression. The birthday of a new world is at hand! Independence in America should date from the first musket that was fired against her." People were roused by the ringing words. In the taverns, on the plantations, on

179

street corners and on the wharfs, in the backwoods settlements, wherever people gathered in the colonies they argued about independence.

Thomas Paine had started them talking. For the author of *Common Sense* was that Jack-of-all-trades but master of ideas, who had come with Benjamin Franklin's introduction to America.

"I am charmed with the sentiments of *Common Sense,* wrote Abigail Adams from Braintree to her husband John, in Philadelphia. "I dare say there would be no difficulty in procuring a vote from all the Assemblies of New England for Independency."

There was no difficulty in Virginia either. Virginia delegates to the Continental Congress were instructed to vote for Independence.

Except for those instructions, Thomas Jefferson was downcast as he drove from Monticello in his two-wheel gig. His young wife was very ill, and little four-year-old Martha waved a pitiful good-bye.

But it was a great satisfaction as he resumed his seat in the hall facing John Hancock, to be one of the Virginia delegates who early in June proposed the motion "That these united colonies are and of a right ought to be free and independent."

"I second the motion," snapped John Adams with no hesitation.

Massachusetts and Virginia were ready for independence, but Pennsylvania and New York were not, and many other colonies were most uncertain. There were conservative law-abiding people in all the colonies, people of education and property, to whom the idea of being disloyal to their King was inconceivable.

Others were afraid of the future. "With independence established," they said, "we are in danger of being ruled by a riotous mob. If you vote for independence," they warned their friends in Congress, "you will be hanged." George III had denounced all rebels in America as traitors and the punishment for treason was hanging.

Not merely the colonies, but even members of the same family were split apart by their convictions. Thomas Jefferson and Benjamin Franklin stood for independence, but Thomas Jefferson's cousin John Randolph was a staunch Loyalist and had gone to England, leaving

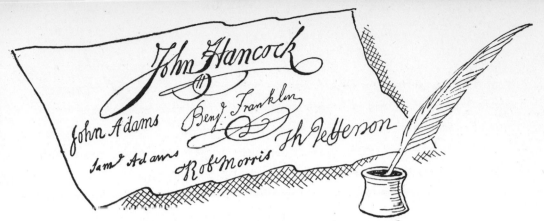

Tom his fine violin. Benjamin Franklin's son William, now governor of New Jersey, was also a Loyalist, and later was to act as President of the Associated Loyalists of New York City.

Endless debates and arguments filled the days of the Congress. The sound reasoning on both sides kept many delegates undecided, but gradually, John Adams said, "one after another became convinced of the truth of Independence."

A committee of five was appointed to put into writing a declaration. The three most active members were Benjamin Franklin, John Adams and Thomas Jefferson.

"You, sir," said Thomas Jefferson, turning to John Adams, "will of course draw up the declaration."

"I will not," replied the older man. "You shall do it, and I'll tell you why. You are a Virginian and a Virginian ought to head this business. I am unpopular, you are very much otherwise. Reason three . . . you can write ten times better than I can."

So Thomas Jefferson went to his lodgings and for eighteen days worked faithfully on what he had been set to write. When he had finished, crossed out and reworded a few sentences, and laid by his quill, he had written The Declaration of Independence.

Several days were taken up in discussing and changing some of the phrases, during which Benjamin Franklin with his homely humor kept the sensitive young author from becoming too disconsolate.

At last, on the fourth of July, Thomas Jefferson heard the final draft of his declaration read, voted upon and accepted.

"Thus was decided the greatest question which was ever debated in America," John Adams wrote his wife. "The second of July, 1776, will be celebrated by succeeding generations as the greatest anniversary festival—with guns, bells, bonfires and illuminations from one end of the continent to the other."

The great bronze Liberty Bell that hung in the belfry called the people of Philadelphia four days later to hear the Declaration read aloud in the square outside the State House. As a strong-voiced man stepped to the front of the small wooden platform and began to read, the last echoes of the bell caught the now well-known words:

"WHEN IN THE COURSE OF HUMAN EVENTS," he began. Silence fell as he continued: "WE HOLD THESE TRUTHS TO BE SELF-EVIDENT, THAT ALL MEN ARE CREATED EQUAL. THAT THEY ARE ENDOWED BY THEIR CREATOR WITH CERTAIN INALIENABLE RIGHTS. THAT AMONG THESE ARE LIFE, LIBERTY AND THE PURSUIT OF HAPPINESS. . . ."

As he ended with the last word "honor," the people cheered and the Liberty Bell rang out once more.

When the copy was complete on parchment, John Hancock, as President of Congress, was the first to sign. He took his quill in hand, writing the letters larger than ever before, turning the end of the *k* with a more determined flourish, and with a couple of graceful scrolls he finished this, his most famous signature!

"There!" said he, "King George will have no trouble in reading that without his spectacles."

"Gentlemen, we must all hang together now," said Benjamin Franklin as he took up the quill, then added with a quirk of a smile, "or we will all hang separately."

Spoken in jest, there was sober truth behind those words. Signers of the Declaration had taken a daring step.

"I am well aware," wrote John Adams again, "of the toil and blood and treasure that it will cost us to maintain this declaration."

All knew that there was many a crisis ahead that would call for more than brave words, cheers and bell-ringing, times when only in patience, perseverance and self-sacrifice could their faith be measured.

ECHOES IN EUROPE

THE DECLARATION OF INDEPENDENCE was translated into every language and copies of it sent to all the countries of Europe. George III vowed, when he had read it, that he would never recognize the independence of his American colonies. On the contrary, said he stubbornly:

"I shall resort to every means in my power of forcing the Americans to unconditional surrender."

George III had received his first news of the Declaration one afternoon when he was sitting to have his portrait painted by Benjamin West. It was a trying moment, for the painter's sympathies were with

183

his native land. Their difference of opinion, however, did not lessen the King's regard for his friend, but rather increased it.

"I honour you for it, West," he said. "A man who did not love his native land could not be a faithful subject of another, or a true friend."

The English people were still divided in their sympathies, as they had been when the rebellion in America started. Most of the Whigs definitely opposed the war. Some even went so far as to say that England had best grant American independence at once, or else France would be drawn in, and then the war would indeed be ruinous.

The Whigs also feared that if the King should by any chance triumph over the colonies it would be the death of liberty in England too, and the King would indeed establish himself as a despot. Many officers gave up their commissions in the army rather than go to America to fight and the common people held the war "in such abhorrence" that George III could not get enough English soldiers to enlist. He had to hire foreign soldiers. Catherine II of Russia refused to furnish any. Holland also refused. So in February, 1776, he arranged with the princes of some small German states (one of them was Hesse), to hire their soldiers for thirty-four dollars and fifty cents apiece.

Frederick the Great, it is said, was so disgusted, that he charged the German princes the same tax per head for marching their soldiers across his territory, as if they had been driving cattle.

"Now I trust the rebel army will soon be dispersed," said George III, not realizing that in hiring foreign soldiers to fight his own people, he only increased their determination to resist.

"It is intolerable," said Fox, one of the Whigs, "that it should be in the power of one blockhead to do so much mischief."

But so far it seemed to be within that so-called royal "blockhead's" power and he stubbornly repeated that he would resort to every means of forcing the Americans to unconditional surrender.

England had good reason to fear France. Not a little pleased at seeing her old enemy in trouble, a month before the Declaration of Independence had been signed, France had already begun secretly sending guns, ammunition and all kinds of war supplies to the Americans.

On June 19, 1776, Vergennes, the French foreign minister, made the final arrangements with Pierre Caron de Beaumarchais, who was to act as the government's secret agent.

"I am sure you understand," the French minister said to him emphatically, "that there is need for absolute secrecy. Take every precaution that our motives, our intentions, and as far as possible our proceedings, be hidden from the British."

Pierre Caron de Beaumarchais signified that he understood perfectly as he laid down his pen, having signed a receipt for a million livres received from the French government. Spain, he was told, had also agreed to put up the same amount. All was to be spent on war materials for the Americans and he was to do the spending. But he was not to use his own name. According to the scheme, everything that was shipped was to go as if sent by a private Spanish firm named Roderigue Hortalez and Co. Beaumarchais was elated. A great international mystery play was about to begin in which he was the chief actor. It was an exciting rôle which suited him to perfection and set him to work with boundless enthusiasm. Another and worthier incentive for his work came when he read the Declaration of Independence.

"All men are created equal," he read in the great document, and the words arrested his attention. "All men are created equal?" He queried. And suddenly he realized that here were people who had done away with the very thing that he himself had been fighting against ever since he had first found out that he had not been born a nobleman.

If those Americans won the war then and established their government, there would be at least one country in the world where a person could not be "born wrong!" For the first time in his life Beaumarchais had an incentive not wholly selfish. He doubled his energy.

He scouted around for French officers willing to go to America. One day he was approached by a Prussian officer named Von Steuben who wished to go. Beaumarchais paid his passage and sent him.

In spite of all precautions, it was but natural that English spies in

Paris and at the seaports soon reported that munitions of all kinds, large and small, had been leaving the country. The English ambassador suspected that the French government had a hand in the matter and consulted the French minister Vergennes. That clever diplomat soothed the excited Englishman, blandly assuring him that the French government, far from encouraging the Americans, actually was profoundly alarmed over the sympathy that some of their people felt for the rebels.

"The sympathy which the French feel for the Americans is a great and serious danger," said Vergennes and his tone was most convincing. "And do not think that this sympathy is based on a love of America or a hatred of England. No," he added, and this time truly in earnest, "the roots are far deeper than that."

from a French statuette

BENJAMIN FRANKLIN IN FRANCE

LIBERTÉ . . . AMITÉ," said Benjamin Franklin as he paced the deck, his coattails flying and his bright old face ruddy and wind-burned beneath his brown fur cap.

"Lee-bear-tay—am-me-tay," repeated the two boys, keeping

step with their grandfather, while the ship that was carrying them to Europe rolled and tossed on the rough winter waves of the Atlantic.

It was November, 1776, Benjamin Franklin was on his way to France to try to persuade the French government not only to send secret help but openly to join the Americans and declare war on England.

The old philosopher was then past seventy years.

"I am old and good for nothing," he had told the Congress when they appointed him, "but if I can still be of any use, do with me what you like." So here he was on his way, charged "To negotiate a treaty of amity and commerce" with the French, and trying to drill his young grandsons in the foreign language during the voyage over.

Their teeth chattered in the cold, and the spray dashed high. The old gentleman, after trying in vain to pull his fur cap down more snugly, suddenly stopped. He removed it, and the wig beneath it, replaced the cap, threw the wig overboard, and then with a little grunt of great satisfaction continued his constitutional around the deck.

No sooner had his boat docked at the French seaport than news that the great Doctor Franklin was on his way travelled ahead of him to Paris. So the people were expecting him, and when they saw him, a famous man as he was, but dressed so plainly, they went wild with joy.

"Vive, vive!" they cried. "Long live Benjamin Franklin."

"Le Bon Homme Richard," they called him affectionately, for they had long read the sayings of Poor Richard, translated into French. Every one wanted to see him. They admired him because he did not wear a powdered wig, nor carry any defense except a "walking stick in his hand." They admired his square-rimmed spectacles, and the women were so pleased with his fur cap, that they dressed their hair to look like it and called it "the hair dress à la Franklin!" So instead of being good for nothing, Benjamin Franklin soon found himself the idol of Paris. He saw pictures of himself in every print-shop window, and on all kinds of articles, even on snuff boxes, ladies' fans and handkerchiefs.

"Over here," he wrote home, "my face has become as common as that of the moon," and that therefore he would have to behave himself.

That wise and kindly face not merely touched the hearts of the people of France but in their minds Franklin also represented America. When they cheered him, they cheered also the Americans, brave people who had dared to defy the tax collectors. "Vive l'Américain," they cried, "cheers for the land of Liberté!"—a land, they had been told, where justice was to rule, and all people, rich or poor, share equal rights.

The bourgeoisie were his friends. Benjamin thought that if he also made enough friends among the noblemen at Versailles, he might be able with their help to persuade their government to join the colonies in war. It was no task for that friendly person to make friends; it had always been his greatest pleasure. He went about becoming acquainted with everybody, so charming them all with his gracious simple manner that he was invited everywhere, and entertained by some of the most important noble families. Because of his experiment with electricity, French scientists also knew of him and were glad to welcome him.

The second year that he was there, Benjamin Franklin heard that the great Voltaire, who was then eighty-three, was coming to visit Paris just once more before he died. Franklin took one of his grandsons and went to see him. The aged man was frail and delicate, but his eyes were still bright as steel. He laid his thin, almost transparent fingers on the head of Franklin's grandson, and bade him dedicate himself "To God and Liberty." So the two met, the brilliant, sparkling philosopher of the Old World, and the kindly, homespun philosopher of the New.

As to the mission on which he had come to Paris. That was not so easily arranged. However friendly the French felt toward the American ambassador personally, they were not ready to join the Americans openly or declare war on England.

First of all, the Americans must show themselves able to win at least one victory alone. News that came from America during 1776 and the spring and summer of the following year was most dismal and discouraging. Benjamin Franklin had patience and faith that the fight for liberty would succeed.

"It will go," he kept saying staunchly, "Ça ira,"—"it will go."

MARIE ANTOINETTE AND LOUIS XVI

Louis XV was no longer King of France when Benjamin Franklin arrived in Paris. He had died two years before of smallpox. Louis XVI had now become the King of France and Marie Antoinette its queen.

Queen! Free at last to do as she pleased, to have every joy and pleasure that her heart desired. And why not? she thought. Was not that the privilege of a queen?

"Isn't it marvelous," she had written her mother, "for me, the youngest of your children, to be Queen over the finest realm in Europe!"

It was Louis XVI who was the King. It was his kingdom, but it was on gay and graceful Marie Antoinette his Queen that the spotlight fell.

189

As for being King and Queen, the only thing that the two had in common was that they were both too young to rule; and both out of step with the formality and fussy etiquette of the old court life. Otherwise Marie Antoinette and Louis XVI were as unlike and as ill paired as a ballet dancer and a ploughboy set to do a minuet, the one always eager to be on her toes, the other just content to plod, though at the same time embarrassed that his clumsy feet were not made for dancing.

"It seems as though the whole universe had fallen on my head," Louis XVI had said solemnly when he heard that the time had come when he must follow his grandfather on the throne.

For good, honest, clumsy Louis XVI was another boy in France who had been "born wrong." He realized that himself. But though he knew that he was slow at thinking, and never meant to be a king, he was determined he would do his best. He gave up making locks, to have more time for his new duties. He also decided to spend no money foolishly and even spoke to the Queen about economizing.

"Economize?" mocked Marie in ripples of laughter. "Why should I bother to think things over and economize? Let me enjoy myself!"

And so she did. He could deny her nothing, she was so pretty, so much cleverer than he was. When she bought diamond necklaces, he made no complaint. When she wanted a little palace of her own to play in, he gave her the Petite Trianon, a miniature palace in marble, where she might entertain her friends and live life as she liked it.

He went his way and she went hers. He plodded off to bed every evening at eleven just when she might be starting out with her gay friends for a masked ball in Paris, not to return till four or five in the morning. Over the gambling tables, the horse races, and other exciting amusements she whirled away days and nights, leaving no minute that might be boring, no pleasure untried that money could buy.

The King said nothing, but the aunts and the old court gossiped and disapproved of the frivolous Queen, men on the streets repeated unpleasant stories about her, and the common people of France blamed her because they were starving. They spoke of her now as an intruder, and called her "that Austrian woman." But it made no difference to her.

Marie Antoinette laughed and paid as little heed to what they said as she did to her own mother's continual letters of warning.

"I am distressed," wrote Maria Theresa; "the newspaper leaflets which used to delight me because they had so much to say about my daughter's kindness of heart have changed their tone, so that I can no longer bear to look at them. You are so light-minded, so heedless. I hope I shall not live until misfortune overtakes you. I, who love my little Queen and watch her every footstep."

"Poof!" said Marie Antoinette one morning, and tossed one of these tiresome letters lightly aside to give attention to the hairdresser.

"Today, I have an exquisite conception for your Majesty," announced that ingenious man, holding his comb like the baton of an orchestra leader about to produce a symphony. "La coiffure de la Liberté! a hairdress in honor of this American revolution!"

"Headdress of Liberty?" repeated Marie Antoinette. "I like that. It's amusing! Coiffure de la Liberté!" She gave a gay little laugh.

tres chic

a la mode....

(from an old cartoon)

"cur non?"

LA FAYETTE SAILS FOR AMERICA

ADRIENNE LA FAYETTE woke up one March morning in 1777 to find that her young husband had gone off to America, without even bidding her or his little daughter good-bye. Her father, the Duc de Noailles, was in a temper, shaking the farewell letter from his young son-in-law as furiously as if it were the collar of that impetuous young man himself. Adrienne's mother did not cross her irate husband, but in her gentle manner bade Adrienne have faith in La Fayette and pray with her for his success in America and his safe return.

The previous summer at Metz, La Fayette had heard the Declaration of Independence read aloud by the Duke of Gloucester, brother of the King of England. At once his heart had "been enrolled" in the cause of Liberty, and immediately his mind filled with but the one thought of leaving for America to join the revolution. But he soon found all efforts to carry out his desire blocked at every turn.

The commander at Metz refused to help him in any way.

The French Prime Minister showed him a letter de cachet signed by Louis XVI and warned him that if he persisted in his foolhardy notion he might find himself cooling his heels in the Bastille. With bad news coming from America those days, the French government dared run no further risk of antagonizing the English by allowing a young man from so important a family as the Noailles to go to America.

Even Benjamin Franklin and the other American representatives, not wishing to offend the French government, raised all kinds of objections to discourage La Fayette. But the eager young man met every objection. When they said that they had no money, he said that he intended to serve without pay.

"We have no credit," they said, "therefore we cannot so much as charter a ship to send you."

"I will buy a ship of my own," replied La Fayette, "for I wish more than ever to go now that your cause is in great danger."

So he won them over and bought his ship, and, while it was being put in shape for the voyage, he took the greatest precaution that not a hint of what he was doing should reach the French minister or his own father-in-law. When he finally received the long-looked-for word that his ship, now christened the *Victory,* was ready to sail, he dashed through Paris under cover of night, stopping only to rush into a friend's bedroom with the words "I'm off!" and rush out again.

A few days later at the seaport he joined the eleven other young French officers who were going with him, only to find that the *Victory* was, after all, not quite ready to sail.

"Three days more it will take," said the captain.

"Impossible!" cried La Fayette. His secret was out. His farewell letter in the hands of his father-in-law. With a handful of gold coins he persuaded the captain that he could just as well finish taking aboard the necessary provisions in a port in Spain.

No sooner, however, had they cast anchor in the Spanish harbor and gone ashore, than they were met on the dock by a messenger with a letter signed by the King positively forbidding the expedition. There was then nothing for La Fayette to do but have his trunks removed from the ship and return with the messenger to the city of Bordeaux.

There, however, he found that the orders from the King were not for his arrest, but merely bade him meet his father-in-law at Marseilles and go with him on a pleasure trip to Italy.

Hiring a post chaise, La Fayette had his new trunks bearing his bright coat-of-arms piled high on the trunk rack, and apparently set out at once most obediently. Very shortly, however, only the trunks and a servant dressed in La Fayette's clothes were rattling over the road to Marseilles, while red-headed La Fayette, disguised with a black wig and a post-boy's uniform, was riding at top speed back to Spain.

Next day he was back on his ship, and that night of April 17, 1777, the *Victory* let out her sails to the wind and was off for America. For three weeks there was a raging storm at sea. When the rough waves had calmed down enough for the young passengers to be untied from their hammocks and to venture on deck, La Fayette set himself to learning the English language and to writing letters home. These are a few sentences from his letters to Adrienne:

"My dear Heart: "On board *La Victoire*

"It is from far away that I am writing, and added to this cruel distance is the still worse uncertainty as to when I shall have news of you. . . . What fears and worries I have joined to my grief . . . at leaving all that is most dear to me! How will you have taken my going? Do you love me less? Have you forgiven me? . . . I shan't send you a diary of the voyage; days follow each other and are all alike; always sea and sky and the next day just the same. . . . As for the service in store for me, you will surely agree yourself, dear heart, that it will be quite different from idling and pleasure-going in France. . . . As a defender of Liberty which I adore . . . coming to offer my services to this interesting republic, I am bringing nothing but my genuine good will. In working for my glory I am working for their happiness. . . . Adieu. It grows dark and I cannot go on for I have strictly forbidden any light on board since birds have brought us the promise that we are nearing shore."

de Lafayette

194

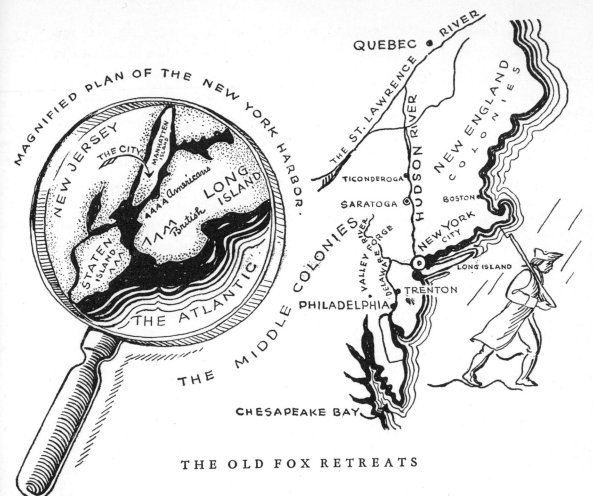

THE OLD FOX RETREATS

EORGE WASHINGTON was in New York City when he read the Declaration of Independence. Believing it to be the town that the British would next try to occupy, as soon as he saw Howe sail out of Boston, George Washington moved his ragged army from Boston to New York.

There the American soldiers heard the Declaration read aloud to them by their battalion commanders, just two days before they saw British ships sail into New York harbor, and troops disembark and go into camp on Staten Island. It was General Howe back from Nova Scotia. The next month his brother Lord Howe, the Admiral, also arrived with his great fleet of ships and anchored in the busy harbor,

Lord Howe, as well as his brother, found war against the Americans distasteful. Still hoping for a peaceful agreement, he arranged to meet Benjamin Franklin, John Adams and a third member of Congress on Staten Island. But now unfortunately it was too late to negotiate without acknowledging American independence. He rejoined his fleet.

The Americans of course had no fleet at all, only about a third as many men, and those few men, unfortunately, were divided. One division was in the city, the other on Long Island, completely cut off by water from the mainland. Even the poorest checker player can see that all General Howe had to do was to ship his troops to Long Island, come up behind the American lines and have them in a trap. That, of course, was exactly what he did. On a hot morning in late August the Battle of Long Island began. By midday, when Washington arrived with more troops on flatboats from the city, the situation looked utterly hopeless, as if the war for independence might end right there and then. But suddenly great drops of rain began to fall. The firing ceased. The British generals, for some unknown reason, retired to their tents, and the battle was over.

All the next day it rained. All that gloomy day, while the soldiers contemplated what would happen to them when the battle began again, George Washington kept his head and laid his plans for their escape. That night in the fog, while the moon fitfully slipped in and out behind the breaking clouds, a long line of shadowy forms stole silently down to the water's edge and pushed off in leaky fishing boats for the town on the opposite shore. Washington himself was the last to leave.

Though safely there, he dared not stop in New York but withdrew to the north of the city. And General Howe moved in.

To secure further information of the British plans, a young man, Nathan Hale, offered to go back as a spy. He was caught and sentenced to death, but so great was his devotion to his country's cause that he said that it was his regret that he had "but one life to give."

In the next months of discouragement and retreat, if all of his soldiers had had but half as much devotion to the cause as Nathan Hale,

Washington's task would not have been so difficult. But when he had desertion, disobedience, treachery to contend with, on top of lack of food and clothing and ammunition, it is remarkable that he even kept the little ragged army together at all.

Howe and his men drove them out of the fortifications north of the city, up along the Hudson River, and across into New Jersey.

Then Howe returned to New York City and sent Lord Cornwallis, newly arrived from London, and companies of Hessians to carry on.

"I'll bag the old fox," said Cornwallis, confident that he could trap Washington into a pitched battle.

There Washington was wise. He knew that his ragged soldiers could no more face the well-trained Hessians than one lone fox could battle a pack of hounds. So he kept on retreating, and retreating, and retreating, with the Hessians following close upon his heels.

So October came and went. . . . November came and went . . . more than half of December, before the chase came to an abrupt halt at the town of Trenton and the Delaware River.

Though it was filled with treacherous ice cakes, Washington crossed the river to the Pennsylvania side, but the Hessians, whom Cornwallis had sent on ahead, stopped to rest in the town of Trenton. They expected, naturally, that Washington and his exhausted men, safe at last on the other side, would do the same.

On the contrary, for Washington saw his chance to make one desperate effort to take them by surprise. On Christmas night, when of all nights he knew the Hessians would be least expecting them, Washington took twenty-five hundred men with him back across the Delaware

River. After battling their way in small boats among the floating ice cakes, almost blinded by the freezing sleet, they landed on the Jersey shore. There in Trenton, quite sure that they were safe, the Germans had been feasting and celebrating Christmas as they did back home. With their swords unbuckled and laid by, they were still drinking, singing songs of the "Heimat" when all of a sudden on the edge of morning, in a whirl of snow, the Americans were upon them. "Der Feind; heraus, heraus!" they cried and, in the wildest scramble for their swords, were captured.

Washington was still there on the Jersey side with his back to the river when Cornwallis caught up with him.

"We'll bag the old fox on the morrow," said Cornwallis confidently as he went to bed one night.

But while he slept, Washington, leaving campfires burning to deceive the enemy sentries, stole away and at sun-up Cornwallis discovered that the "old fox" had been too sly and he still "held the bag."

It was then the first of January. As the weather was growing colder every day, Lord Cornwallis gave up the chase and went back to spend the winter with General Howe and the Loyalists in New York.

Washington spent that winter not far from New York at Morristown. There Martha joined him, and she and the other officers' wives busied themselves sewing and knitting for the soldiers. Many of the ragged men deserted. Those who were there Washington wisely kept busy through the long winter months, building fortifications out of logs and stones. "Fort Nonsense" some of the officers called it, and put their share together in a sloppy fashion. In contrast, some of the earthworks were built uncommonly well, and caught Washington's attention as he went his rounds one day.

"What officer was in charge of building these?" he asked, and upon being told, requested that he be sent to report at headquarters. When the young captain appeared Washington offered him his well-earned promotion. So Alexander Hamilton one year after becoming a captain was a lieutenant colonel, adjutant to General Washington.

MISADVENTURES OF 1777

SEVEN WAS A MYSTIC NUMBER, so a year with the three sevens must be an ominous one, said superstitious people, making dire prophecies. No foretold event, however, but an unforeseen American victory was to make 1777 an extraordinary year.

With spring, the British began the new Hudson River plan for conquering the colonies. All winter while Howe was in New York, Burgoyne ("Gentleman Johnny" was his nickname) had been in London. There he had spent many hours going over his brilliant new plan with George III and getting his Majesty's approval of it. On the map it looked very simple. While he, Burgoyne, started from Canada, and came down along the Hudson, General Howe was to start out from New York City and march up the river till they met. So, controlling the Hudson, they would separate the New England from the middle colonies, weaken them both and in that way force them to surrender.

"The war is won!" chortled George III. Burgoyne, he said, should go right back to Canada to put his plan in action. The minister of war should notify William Howe at once of all details.

In May, "Gentleman Johnny" Burgoyne arrived in Canada and by July the King received word that he had captured Fort Ticonderoga.

"I have beat 'em! Beat all the Americans!" shouted George III, bursting in on Queen Charlotte's afternoon nap, to tell her the good news. The sturdy man danced about absurdly. He did not seem to realize that Ticonderoga was just an empty fort. Nor did he know that General Howe was *not* on his way to meet Burgoyne!

Howe had known in a general way about the Hudson River plan, but by June, having received no details from the minister of war (who had neglected carelessly to send them), Howe thought that he would probably have time first to go down and capture Philadelphia.

George Washington was still in camp where he had spent the winter. Still patiently carrying on! Still writing endless letters to Congress begging them to secure food and clothing for his soldiers and advancing money from his own pocket to keep them from deserting for at least another month. Those who didn't join the British had a tormenting habit of going home for a spell to milk the cows, or put the hay in, or take care of the spring plowing.

Also tormenting to the commander were the swarms of useless young adventurers who now arrived with almost every boat from Europe, looking for excitement. Washington implored Congress not to give any more of them commissions in the army.

But when he went to Philadelphia himself in the middle of summer to confer with Congress, with what should he be confronted, in spite of all he had said, but another young foreigner. A boy of nineteen whom Congress had made not merely an officer but a Major General.

They met at a dinner, those two, the big quiet Commander, and his enthusiastic young Major General, the Marquis de La Fayette, who said later that he had recognized the great man at once.

La Fayette was thrilled by his first sight of Washington, and Washington was charmed with the boy in spite of himself, and courteously invited him to visit camp, although adding that he hesitated to show an officer of the French army his poor ragged soldiers.

"I am here, monsieur, to learn and not to teach," was La Fayette's answer, and that modest answer opened the door to Washington's heart.

Washington knew no French, and La Fayette's English was still vague, but there at camp to help them was the new adjutant, Alexander Hamilton, to whom French was as much his mother tongue as English.

It was then the first of August. Word had been received that Howe had sailed the week before from New York harbor. Where he was going remained a matter of guesswork but of great concern, until, two weeks later, scouts reported that British ships were in Chesapeake Bay. There was no doubt then that Howe was headed for Philadelphia.

Washington prepared as best he could to hold the city. He had Alexander Hamilton send a warning to Congress, whereupon Congress, much alarmed, gathered up its papers and fled to Annapolis, Maryland. The "rebels" in Philadelphia were terrified. To try and calm their fears, Washington decided to break camp and march his whole army, such as it was, through the streets of Philadelphia. To brighten up their ragged appearance, the soldiers stuck sprigs of fresh green leaves in their dilapidated caps. At their head, on his white horse, rode their devoted leader. On one side of him the young Lieutenant Colonel from the West Indies, and on the other, in his new uniform, the young Major General, the nobleman from France. Down Chestnut Street they marched, past the State House where the Declaration of Independence had been signed the year before, past the Carpenters Guild Hall where the first Congress had met, down to the Delaware River and the harbor, where, the previous November, Benjamin Franklin had sailed for France.

To the people cheering in the streets, that was a brave though ragged army marching by. Many other people, however, looking out of their windows could see but a motley crew of rebels, and looked forward hopefully to the time when General Howe and soldiers of their king would once more bring law and order to the city. Quaker merchants also looked forward eagerly to seeing good English gold pieces being spent again in Philadelphia.

They had not long to wait. In September, the following month, the British defeated the Americans in the battles of Brandywine and Germantown and took Philadelphia with little difficulty.

The delighted Loyalists opened wide their doors and gave "Sir Billy" Howe and Lord Cornwallis a most cordial welcome!

And now what about "Gentleman Johnny" Burgoyne? And what of the Hudson River plan that had started out with such good omen?

Three weeks after the British captured Philadelphia, General John Burgoyne surrendered. Discouraged he was, puzzled as to what on earth had happened to his friend Howe, and worn down by months of hardships in the wilderness. His plan that had looked so simple on the map had miscarried. But on maps great distances look short. Maps don't show underbrush, bogs, swamps or crooked backwoods trails too narrow for lumbering baggage wagons. British and Hessian soldiers were not trained to chop down trees to make roads nor hunt for game for food, nor fight against enemies hidden in the trees who shot them down like sparrows. Those hardships of the wilderness had worn down the British till they were no match for the hardy pioneer sharpshooters armed with their matchless American rifles.

After two dreadful battles, Burgoyne had drawn up what were left of his soldiers in two long lines on the battlefield at Saratoga. There they stood gaunt and half starved in their bedraggled scarlet coats while their general handed his sword to General Gates, in surrender. General Gates, who had taken but small part in the battle, stepped forward brazenly. The victory belonged to Benedict Arnold, largely, and his bold leadership; to Kosciusko, to Morgan, to any number of officers more than Gates, but in a letter to Congress, Gates took all the credit for Burgoyne's defeat.

That defeat meant a serious turn in affairs for England, because it was the American victory for which France had long been waiting.

Historians say that there have been but seven truly decisive battles in the history of the world, and that this battle of Saratoga is one of them, for without that victory the French would not have entered the war, the war might not have been won, and there might have been no United States of America!

And, incidentally, about number 7. Saratoga, one of those seven decisive battles, took place on the 7th of October, and the surrender was on October 17, 1777.

"TO CARRY THE NEWS!"

NEWS OF BURGOYNE'S SURRENDER was sent by special messenger to France on the fastest ship out of Boston harbor. But since the sea was full of British battleships, that important news might never have reached France, entrusted to one messenger. So Captain John Paul Jones was also to carry it on his new battleship the *Ranger*. John Paul was the happiest of men at the appointment; his three-cornered hat sat cocked on his head at a merry angle as he prepared the ship and gave the orders to sail.

"Heigh-ho, carry the news!" sang the sailors lustily as the stiff breeze swelled the sails. Over the waves of the stormy Atlantic they flung the rollicking song of the *Ranger* like a banner in the wind:

"So now we had him hard and fast,
Burgoyne laid down his arms at last,
And that is why we brave the blast
To carry the news to . . . Paris,
Heigh-ho, carry the news! Heigh-ho, ca-r-r-ee-ee the news!"

Sailing night and day, head in the wind, John Paul Jones made a record crossing. He left Portsmouth, Maine, October 31 and laid the despatches in the hand of Benjamin Franklin on December 5. Then he saw at once by the expression on the old gentleman's kindly face that he had arrived too late. The messenger who had left Boston a whole day earlier had beaten him by half a day!

The messenger from Boston had indeed reached Benjamin Franklin at his home in Passy, just outside of Paris, on December 4.

That December day had been mild enough for him to find Doctor Franklin, with other Americans and a number of important Frenchmen, waiting impatiently in the garden. They had heard that a messenger was on the way, and were fearful that it was more bad news he brought. Beaumarchais paced nervously. Benjamin Franklin was trembling with anxiety. His lips quivered as he seized the man's hand.

"Sir," he asked, "is Philadelphia taken?"

"Yes, sir," the messenger replied. "But, sir, I have greater news than that: *General Burgoyne and his whole army are prisoners of war!*"

At those words, mists clouded Benjamin Franklin's square-rimmed spectacles, and tears of relief rolled down his tired, kind old face. His first thought was that now perhaps there would be peace.

Beaumarchais, in a frenzy of excitement, dashed for his coach, eager to be the first to carry the glorious news to Paris. But, as Poor Richard would say, "haste makes waste." The coach upset and that over-eager messenger found himself upside down in the ditch.

"I'm ruined," he said to himself when he was on his way once more. "If the Americans make peace with England, I will be ruined! France will be ruined. England will take revenge on her for the secret help already given!" Only one way out: *France must join the war!*

VALLEY FORGE

"Camp near Valley Forge
January 6, 1778

"Dear Heart:

WHAT A DATE! And what a place to write from in the month of January! I am in camp, in the middle of woods, fifteen hundred leagues from you, imprisoned in the middle of winter . . . and it is here that the American army will pass the winter in little huts that are about as gay as a prison cell."

La Fayette had recovered from the wound which he had received at the battle of Brandywine and could walk without a limp when he wrote this letter to Adrienne.

The American soldiers had been at Valley Forge since the middle of December. It was a dreary place. Just a few houses huddled around a small iron forge, a narrow frozen creek, and high wind-swept hills.

There on those bleak hills in cruel wind that left their bare hands raw and bleeding, the soldiers had set to work as soon as they arrived to build themselves log huts to live in. As they tramped back and forth, their feet, wrapped in rags for lack of shoes, left tracks of blood on the white snow. Until the huts were finished Washington had stayed in a tent close to the men and ate and lived as they did. That willingness to share their hardships won him their unbounded admiration and increased if possible the love and affection of La Fayette.

By Christmas, when the huts were finished and the officers were quartered in the tiny village, Washington moved into a small four-roomed stone house overlooking the little frozen creek. The front room served well enough as his headquarters, but a log dining-room had to be built on long enough to accommodate the nine generals who made up what Washington affectionately called his "family," as well as their wives, who joined them for the winter.

Washington had now come to rely greatly on his brilliant young aide-de-camp, Alexander Hamilton. He was able to put so perfectly into words the facts and thoughts that Washington wished to have expressed, that he now wrote all of the General's letters. To be a secretary, however, was not the young man's ambition. More to his liking had been the duty assigned to him earlier in the winter. For then Washington had sent him on a difficult mission to General Gates.

It had been shortly after the victory at Saratoga. Though Howe had already moved into Philadelphia, Washington saw a chance to attack the British base of supplies before they were moved to safety, provided Gates would send him the necessary reinforcements. Gates, being Gates, had refused. His own glory shone brighter against Washington's defeat. So all that winter while Congress heaped their praises upon Gates, Alexander Hamilton, back again at Valley Forge, had to answer letters from Congress filled with nothing but denouncements of Washington.

Congress had even formed a War Board and put Gates at its head. A plot had also been formed by jealous generals (among them a man named Conway) to ruin Washington and put Gates in his place.

Washington met the criticism with courage, saying that in so great a contest one must "not expect to meet with nothing but sunshine."

One day late in January, Washington folded a letter from Congress that he had finished reading, and sent an orderly with a summons to La Fayette. While he waited for the young man to come, he walked to the window and looked out grimly over the bleak hills and frozen stream. His gaze did not waver, his face was calm, but a muscle tensed on the side of his jaw as if he were biting back violent, angry words.

What a letter! he thought. Instructions sent out by General Gates as President of the War Board, saying that Congress had resolved to send an army to invade Canada . . . and La Fayette was to be given the command.

Washington knew that no expedition to Canada could be undertaken at this time. It would fail just as the daring expedition against Quebec undertaken by Benedict Arnold had failed three years before. That year Congress had also tried in vain to persuade the French people in the Quebec colony to join them against England. But the Quebec Act passed by Parliament in 1774 had guaranteed to them their own religion, and their old French laws and customs. Therefore they had no reason to rebel, but felt grateful and loyal to England.

Talk of invasion into Canada, Washington recognized as merely part of the plot to ruin him, first by winning away the young La Fayette and then discrediting him, by giving him an impossible task.

Still it was a decree from Congress, whose authority Washington never questioned. His sense of honor forbade him to influence La Fayette, so when the boy entered, fresh and windblown, Washington gave him the letter and left him to make his own decision.

"To invade Canada!" Those were thrilling words to La Fayette. "To make Canada New France again! What a glorious undertaking!"

Only one thing troubled him. There was no mention of General Washington as his superior. In his reply he agreed to undertake the expedition, only if he was to be considered one of Washington's subordinates. That understood, he set out at once, writing Adrienne, the night he left, to tell her of his high hopes and "dazzling" prospect.

The letter was dated February 3, 1778. That month of February was the worst of all at Valley Forge. More than three thousand men were unable to leave the huts for lack of food and clothing. More than a thousand had deserted to join the British, and Washington knew that more than three times as many would be gone by spring, if no help came from Congress.

Before February was much more than half over, La Fayette reached Albany, New York, halfway up the Hudson River, and discovered no preparations whatever made to invade Canada, and that, to his great chagrin, he had been made a fool of. Humiliated, he returned.

Spring had come when he again reached Valley Forge. It was April and the dreadful winter was over. The ice in the little frozen creek had thawed. The bitter winter winds no longer swept the hills. Best of all, the plot against Washington was a thing of the past, to be forgotten. Like one of the wind-swept hills himself, the big man had stood firm, while intrigue and jealousy had whirled about him, lashed themselves out and died away. The soldiers, too, were in much better spirits. They had food to eat. Congress, he found, had at last given Washington free hand to do as he thought best. He had sent his generals out over the countryside to bring in food.

The soldiers also looked much better. Their hair was combed, their clothes, such as they were, clean. Baron von Steuben, La Fayette was told, was responsible for that. He was an officer, from the army of Frederick the Great, who had arrived in March. Every spring morning the big blue-eyed man had the soldiers out on the parade ground shortly after sunrise, putting them through their manœuvres, and, to their great amusement, blustering away at them in all the oaths he knew in French and German.

Washington's joy at having La Fayette back was only exceeded by that due to this great good news he brought—Congress, he said, was soon to receive official word that a treaty had been signed with France. France, in other words, had also declared war on England.

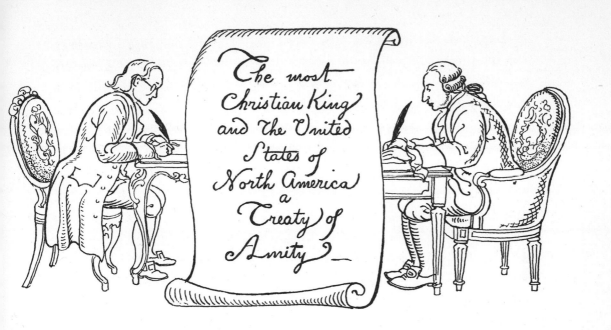

The illustration shows text on a scroll reading: "The most Christian King and the United States of North America a Treaty of Amity"

THE FRENCH ALLIANCE

THAT FEBRUARY OF 1778, John Quincy Adams, eleven years old, accompanied his father to Paris. John Adams had been appointed to assist Benjamin Franklin in arranging the treaty, but before he arrived, he heard from a French pilot who boarded their boat, that the treaty had already been signed. And at Bordeaux, as envoy of the now allied nation, he was greeted with cheers, speeches, thirteen-gun salutes and a lighted sign which read: "God Save Congress, Liberty and Adams."

So John Adams, who had come as brisk as a new broom and as ready for duty, found the work already accomplished. The treaty had been signed on the sixth of February.

Pierre Caron Beaumarchais had written it. Like any good salesman, he had had the agreement drawn up ready for Louis XVI to sign the moment that the foreign minister had persuaded the King to do so.

Louis XVI had not wished to involve his country in another costly war. But Vergennes and his ministers had felt that war was imperative.

"If England and America now make peace," they argued, "England will send her forces no longer needed in America to seize our islands in the West Indies. If the war continues and England loses, she will try to make up for that loss by seizing them."

The ministers had talked fast and brilliantly. Their phrases, "protecting the West Indies!" . . . "breaking England's naval supremacy!" . . . "regaining India" . . . had gone whirling about Louis XVI's head, till hopelessly outwitted he had finally written the large scrawly capital L that stood for the signature of the King of France.

Then on February 6, 1788, Benjamin Franklin had also placed his name on the important treaty. Never before in the history of the world had there been a treaty signed by people of such unequal birth as the son of a candlemaker and a king.

John Quincy Adams and his father went to live with Benjamin Franklin, at his home in Passy, a suburb between Paris and Versailles.

There on a most significant day in March, a wigmaker arrived to deliver an order. It was the day of the King's reception when the delegates of the new nation were to be received for the first time. Wigs being the rule at court, Benjamin Franklin had thought he ought to wear one, and sat very patiently while the wigmaker pulled and twisted the wig this way and that.

"What's the matter?" asked Benjamin Franklin placidly. "Is the wig too small?"

"The wig too small?" repeated the exasperated man. "Non, monsieur, the head—it ees too big!"

Since it was then too late to have another made, Benjamin Franklin, dressed in his plain brown velvet suit, appeared at court without one.

"What, no wig?" gasped the other Americans, who were there, attired in the height of fashion. "What will people say?"

They were distinctly worried as the doors of the King's apartments were opened and the voice of the guard boomed forth:

"The Ambassadors of the Thirteen United Provinces."

All heads were turned but instead of a murmur of disapproval one of delight ran through the assembled company as, leaning on the arm of the French foreign minister, Benjamin Franklin advanced down the length of the apartment toward the King.

His simplicity and charm put even Louis XVI at ease. Taking Doctor Franklin by the hand, the King thus addressed the envoys:

"Gentlemen, I wish that you would assure Congress of my friendship. I also pray of you to make it known that I have been most satisfied with your conduct during your sojourn in my realms."

So it was that the oldest kingdom in Europe first recognized and introduced the youngest republic to the world.

That alliance was bad news for England. In Parliament it raised a great discussion. One of the Whigs moved that, before disastrous war with France actually got under way, the British soldiers be withdrawn from America and its independence be recognized.

"What! Fall prostrate, shall we, before the throne of France?" cried William Pitt, as he rose to protest strenuously against England's losing that great part of her empire. Ill, he was swathed in blankets and on crutches. At those last words, William Pitt fell, and as a dying man was carried from the House of Commons.

George III still stood out for unconditional submission of the colonies, but this time Parliament prevailed. Five commissioners were sent to America to try and arrange peace, on any terms except independence. Congress flatly refused to confer with them until the British forces were withdrawn from the United States and their independence acknowledged. So the war went on.

General Howe now sent in his resignation and returned to London, where some months before Burgoyne had already arrived in chagrin.

That left Clinton in command. General Clinton, the only one remaining of that confident trio of Major Generals: Burgoyne, Clinton, Howe, who had come to America in 1775 to quell a slight rebellion.

In 1776, that slight rebellion had become a war for independence, and now in 1778 it was about to become a world war.

GEORGE ROGERS CLARK

T HE FRENCH ALLIANCE was proclaimed in America in May and
then celebrated in a frenzy of joy by the American army and
all the friends of the revolution in the thirteen United States.
That May, George Rogers Clark set out with a little band of
soldiers to attack the British in the old forts along the Ohio and the
Mississippi rivers that had once belonged to France.

Northwest of the Ohio was a section of land known at this time as
the Northwest Territory. That territory was even wilder than Kentucky,
for by the time the first shots had been fired at Lexington and Concord
several small settlements had been established in Kentucky and Daniel
Boone had a log fort built at Boonesborough. That fort had been much
needed. Even before it was finished one man at work on the roof had

been shot down by the savages, and in the following year, had it not been for Daniel Boone's quick thinking, the whole settlement would probably have been wiped out. After 1776, the Indian attacks constantly grew fiercer and more frequent.

"That's the work of the 'Hair buying' general," said the settlers bitterly. "That devil pays the Injuns fer every scalp they bring him."

Hamilton was this British general's name, and he was stationed at Fort Detroit, to guard and govern this wild western territory. If he had asked the Indians for help, he was but following an old and common custom. The people of Massachusetts, it was also said, had called upon the Mohawks to "whet the hatchet for war against the British." It is most unlikely, however, that any white man ever paid the Indian for scalps. Once on the war path, the Indians were beyond control. They needed no urging to massacre the wives and children of those hated "Long Knives" who destroyed the Indian hunting grounds. It was a pleasure to scalp them, cut off their arms and legs or roast them alive in their blockhouses! So up and down the border the savages swept, spreading bloodshed and terror.

One day, late in the winter of 1777 (the winter of Valley Forge), Patrick Henry, governor of Virginia, looked up over his spectacles into the bright black eyes of a young stranger with an extremely high, sun-bronzed forehead, who had just entered his office.

"My name, sir," said the young man, "is George Rogers Clark. I have come to get help for Kentucky," and he told the extreme need.

"Kentucky must be defended, sir," he insisted. "If the people of Kentucky are wiped out, Virginia will no longer be safe."

Convinced, Patrick Henry lent ear to the bold plan which the young man had in mind. What George Rogers Clark proposed to do was to go west himself—to take an army and attempt to capture the British forts in the Northwest Territory. The governor gave his help. Two hundred fifty men were enlisted and money, guns, and ammunition for the expedition were sent to Fort Pitt.

There in May, 1778, when spring came, Clark put the men and

supplies on flatboats and floated off toward the west down the gray, winding Ohio. After two months on the water, they left the boats and threading the forest in single file they padded along in their deerskin shoes over the remaining miles to Kaskaskia.

A rough, dirty, unshaven crew of men they were, when, after dark one night in July, they crossed the river to the Kaskaskia fort. All the windows of the fort were lighted, and the sound of music and shuffling feet floated out over the water, for, as the story goes, there was a ball being held at the fort that night. At the landing the men divided; half went up to the little town, while Clark climbed the log steps to the door of the ballroom. Leaning against a post with his arms folded, he watched the dancers, French voyageurs in bright sashes and caps, Indian women with long black braids and beaded trousers, dark-eyed French girls, all whirling and swaying to the wild high strains of the fiddles. Not one of them noticed the stranger until an Indian lying on the floor looked up. Drunk though he was, he could never mistake a chief of the "Long Knives." He leaped to his feet and his warwhoop curdled the blood of the dancers. The music stopped; women screamed and fainted; officers rushed to the door. Then with a smile of triumph George Rogers Clark stepped calmly forward. Light from the torches flared over his high bronzed forehead and his dirty, unshaven face.

"On with your dance," said he, "but remember you're no longer dancing under the British flag, but under the banner of Virginia."

General Hamilton was alarmed when news of what had happened reached Detroit, and with his own men and about three hundred red men set out for Kaskaskia.

When he got as far as Fort Vincennes, however, it was winter, and it seemed too cold to venture farther. So he let the Indians go back home. Spring would be time enough, he thought, to settle with that young upstart, George Rogers Clark.

George Rogers Clark, however, was not the man to sit still at Kaskaskia and wait to be attacked. As soon as scouts brought word to him that Hamilton with only a small force was stationed at Vincennes, he planned to start for that fort at once. He dared not go by the river for fear of being discovered. Going overland at his time of year would be like wading through one great swamp. But go he would. There had been a February thaw; the swollen rivers had overflowed their banks and flooded much of the country. Vincennes was almost two hundred miles away. Day after day the men sloshed in and out of muddy water, which was in places up to the shoulders of the tallest. Night after night they lay down to rest on some soggy hillock, wet to the skin, tired to death and also hungry, for the water had driven away the game. The last six days before they reached Vincennes they did not have one regular meal. Their arrival was a complete surprise, and unbelievable as it may seem, after about two hours of fighting on February 25, 1779, the fort was theirs. From then to the end of the war, George Rogers Clark remained on guard in the forts of the Northwest Territory.

from a portrait

"A HERO IN TWO WORLDS"

ON JANUARY 11, 1779, not quite a year from the time the French had acknowledged the independence of what they called the "Thirteen United Provinces," the young Marquis de La Fayette, with a letter in his pocket expressing the heartfelt gratitude of Congress, sailed for home! He was dressed again

215

in his French captain's uniform, for he had been discharged with honor from his duties as an American major general, in order that for the rest of the war he might serve with his countrymen of France.

Less than two years from the night he had been obliged to slip away in secret to America, on his own ship the *Victoire,* the runaway returned to France on the American warship christened fittingly the *Alliance,* and found himself welcomed as a hero. For while he had been gone, everything had changed! France had signed the treaty with America and was now openly America's friend.

La Fayette's father-in-law, the Duc de Noailles, who had once been angry enough to have had his rash young son-in-law put in the Bastille, now threw his arms about the splendid boy and kissed him on both cheeks. Adrienne's mother, who had always been his loyal champion, was overjoyed to see him, and darling Adrienne, loving and faithful, melted into his arms, assuring him again and again that he was forgiven for leaving her—that nothing mattered now except that, safe and unharmed, he had returned to her. And then the nurse brought in the baby daughter who had been born while he was gone.

Notified of his arrival, Louis XVI summoned him to Versailles and welcoming him as best he could in his awkward fashion, asked him questions about America and Washington. Then because he seemed to think he ought to do something in the way of punishment, he sentenced La Fayette to stay at home in his father-in-law's palace for one week. All week the house was thronged with visitors. At the end of it Marie Antoinette invited him to open the Court Ball with her. There the ladies flocked around him and none of them seemed to mind having her toes stepped on by a hero.

When he appeared at the theatre with Adrienne one night, the performance was stopped, while the leading player presented him with a laurel wreath and recited verses in honor of "The hero of two worlds."

From the audience he received enthusiastic and repeated applause so that fame and glory were his, which, only ten years before, he had been merely dreaming of in the forests of Auvergne.

"I've not yet begun to fight!"

The flag flown by the Bon Homme Richard

THE "BON HOMME RICHARD"

"THE AMERICAN FLAG and I are twins!" John Paul Jones always said with pride and referred those who questioned to the strange double resolution that Congress had passed on June 14, 1777, adopting the flag and appointing him Commander of the *Ranger*. "So," said he, "the flag and I are twins; born the same hour, we cannot be parted in life or death. So long as we can float we shall float together. If we must sink, we shall go down as one!"

After his disappointment at not being the first to bring Benjamin Franklin the news of Burgoyne's surrender, John Paul Jones had returned to the harbor most dejected. But presently his bubbling spirits rose again and as soon as he received permission, he set out to attack the English coast, and after six months returned to France, proud of his successful venture. Then Congress ordered his *Ranger* taken home by some one else, which left John Paul Jones without a ship, and so again dejected. The French had promised him a ship, but it did not come.

"Where is my ship?" he kept writing every one he knew in Paris.

Too impatient to wait longer, he set out for Paris himself, bent on seeing Louis XVI in person. And so he did, spent an hour with him and secured his ship. An old East India trading ship it was, an ancient affair, no longer sound, but when its old weatherbeaten sides had been freshly painted, John Paul was delighted. He named her the *Bon Homme Richard* in honor of his friend Benjamin Franklin.

About sunset on September 23, 1779, the captain of the British battleship the *Serapis* saw the old India trader, with its new coat of paint, and strange new flag, sailing down the east coast of England.

"Who goes there?" he cried.

For answer the *Bon Homme Richard* sent a cannonball. The *Serapis* returned the fire, and the battle was on. Now John Paul Jones was bold and young but his ship was old. With the first shot one of her guns burst, killing some of the crew, and tearing a huge hole in her side. The water rushed in; the pumps refused to work; fire burst out on deck; the crew were in panic. A shot broke the flagstaff.

"Do you give up?" yelled the British captain through his megaphone, thinking he saw the stars and stripes pulled down.

"No," howled John Paul Jones. "I've not yet begun to fight."

So the battle waged on, until the British commander raised the white flag of surrender. Just in time. The water was pouring into the torn sides of the *Bon Homme Richard* and she had to be abandoned. The crew went aboard the *Serapis*. There from the deck of the captured ship, John Paul Jones watched the old but victorious *Bon Homme Richard* slide beneath the surface of the sea. From the broken flagstaff, the flag of stars and stripes was still flying as it touched the water.

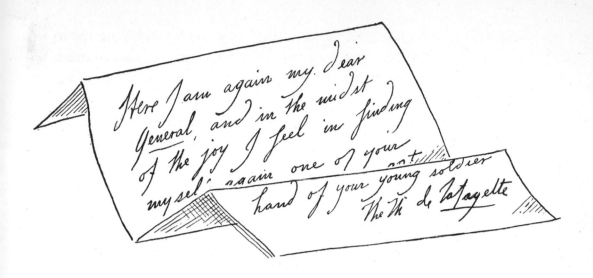

Here I am again my dear General, and in the midst of the joy I feel in finding myself again one of your ... hand of your young soldier
The M^l de Lafayette

LA FAYETTE, HERALD OF THE FRENCH EXPEDITION

A FRENCH FLEET had been sent to America, the summer follow-ing the treaty, but had accomplished nothing. Late in 1779, after much indecision, France finally decided to try another expedition, La Fayette, irked by idleness, had long been besieging the foreign minister to assign him to some task. Now with an expedition to America in prospect, La Fayette's great hope was that he would be given command. But the command was given instead to Count Rochambeau, a man thirty years older, who had been fighting in the Seven Years' War when La Fayette was in his cradle.

"You are too young," said Vergennes to the disappointed boy.

It had been arranged, however, he said, that La Fayette was to go on ahead to announce to General Washington that the French expedi-tion was on the way, and also to tell the General that this time the whole expedition, both army and navy, were to be under his command.

Christmas Eve, 1779, three months before La Fayette left again, a baby son was born and christened George Washington La Fayette, in honor of his illustrious father's beloved general. Bidding a fond farewell this time to his little family, La Fayette returned to America, wearing once more an American major general's uniform. As his ship sailed into the Boston harbor he was finishing a letter to George Washington, which, with its first words, "Here I am again, dear General," was to fill the eyes of that weary man with tears of happiness.

At the wharf it was as if all Boston had turned out to welcome the young French hero. A shouting, cheering, joyful crowd with flaming torches escorted his carriage to the home of the Massachusetts governor, John Hancock. The bells of old North Church rang till midnight.

SPAIN BESIEGES GIBRALTAR

SPAIN HAD HESITATED. Carlos III and the Spanish ministers had not been so sure that if the American colonies gained their independence, the ambitious young nation might not be more of a menace than England to the Spanish colonies. Also, the possible success of the English colonies in breaking away from their mother country might encourage the Spanish colonies in South America to make a similar attempt.

But that was only a possibility. The naval supremacy of England on the seas was a real danger, and the English smuggling trade with the Spanish colonies a long-endured annoyance and a source of loss.

In addition there was the great desire to regain Gibraltar, which had been in England's possession for more than fifty years. So Spain joined the war against England in June, 1779, after having signed an agreement with France that no peace was to be made until Gibraltar had been won back from England and restored to Spain.

The siege of the fort began immediately. By the end of June all communication between the great rock and the mainland was cut off, and in the following month a complete blockade was put in force. The siege, carried on by both France and Spain, was to last four years.

NAPOLEON BUONAPARTE

IN A MILITARY SCHOOL for young nobles in Brienne, France, there was enrolled in the year 1779 a small, morose, lonely ten-year-old boy from Corsica. A silent boy he was, sullen and suspicious of his schoolmates whom he sized up with a judgment keen beyond his years. He hated them, because they mocked him and poked fun at his queer clothes, his Italian accent, and his peculiar foreign name.

Occasionally to their amazement he burst into violent fits of rage, and fought off every one who came near him.

"He is made of granite, that little Corsican," said one of the schoolmasters after some such explosion. "But he has a volcano inside!"

HOLLAND DEFENDS HER TRADE

THE WINTER OF 1780 John Quincy Adams, who was then thirteen, went to school in Amsterdam, Holland.

For some time past his father had been writing Congress expressing his opinion that they might borrow money in Holland. Then, impatient of delay, John Adams went there himself.

He found Holland in a turmoil of discussion as to what stand to take toward England. Many Dutch felt friendly to the English, but on the other hand, British ships on the high seas were seizing and searching the Dutch merchant vessels.

France and Spain were both urging the Dutch to join them. Early in 1780 it was also learned in Holland that Catherine II of Russia had formed an organization called the League of Armed Neutrality. The league declared the right, and their intention to defend the right, of all ships of neutral nations to trade freely with nations at war, and to carry all goods except arms and ammunition. Prussia, Austria, Sweden and Denmark had all joined Russia in the league.

Holland's ministers finally decided to join also. That meant that Holland stood ready to fight if England searched any more Dutch merchant ships or blockaded any Dutch port.

In answer to that, England declared "general reprisals against ships, goods and subjects of Holland"—in other words, she declared *war*.

222

BENEDICT ARNOLD, TRAITOR

THAT YEAR, 1780, was the blackest of the war for Washington. No victories gained, food and supplies reduced to almost nothing, soldiers deserting constantly, and worst of all, a trusted officer turned traitor.

The scene of war had shifted back again to New York City. The summer that he had replaced Howe, Clinton had marched the British army out of Philadelphia and, dragging behind him a train of baggage wagons twelve miles long, had succeeded after the battle at Monmouth and other skirmishes with the Americans in reaching New York City.

Washington had then moved his army to a spot in New Jersey where he could keep close watch over General Clinton. It was there that La Fayette, just returned from France, delivered his good news that French soldiers under General Rochambeau were on the way.

Later in the summer when Rochambeau landed with his army of fine French noblemen, Washington naturally sent the young Major General La Fayette to carry the respects of the American commander to the French general. "Old Papa" Rochambeau received La Fayette in his kind, fatherly manner, but brushed him aside as too young to be bothered with when plans for carrying on the war were to be considered.

"For that," said he, "I must insist upon a personal interview with General Washington himself."

It was fortunate that Rochambeau happened to insist on a meeting with Washington just when he did. Otherwise the plot between General Clinton and Benedict Arnold might not have been discovered till too late to prevent serious harm being done to the American cause.

So far, the record of Benedict Arnold had been that of a bold and gallant soldier. He had fought bravely since the beginning of the war but now believed that he had been slighted and misused by Congress.

Washington still trusted in Benedict Arnold, not knowing that resentment and jealousy had poisoned the man's mind and destroyed his sense of honor. So at his request, Washington gave him command of the fortifications at West Point, about fifty miles north of New York City on the Hudson River. West Point was a most important fort because it blocked the British from sending supplies down the river from Canada to the army in New York.

Once there, Benedict Arnold immediately resumed his correspondence, begun some months before, with General Clinton in New York, their letters being carried back and forth by spies. Together they perfected a plan whereby Clinton was to go up the Hudson River as if to attack West Point, and Benedict Arnold was to surrender the fort.

One night in September, the final arrangements were completed. Early next morning, after his meeting with Arnold, Major André, the British spy, was on his way back to Clinton with papers showing the plans and details of the fort. That same morning, as it happened, Washington, La Fayette and Hamilton, returning from the meeting with General Rochambeau, were riding toward West Point. The American headquarters being a few miles farther north, they were planning to take breakfast with Benedict Arnold.

Almost there, Washington turned aside to inspect certain new fortifications. La Fayette went with him, while Alexander Hamilton rode on ahead to say that the others would follow shortly.

Hamilton found Arnold and his pretty wife at the breakfast table and joined them. Before they had finished, a letter was handed to Arnold which he read immediately. His face gave no indication of this disastrous news which the letter contained: Major André had been captured. The papers had been found in his boots and were being forwarded to Washington!

Arnold excused himself at once and left the room. A few moments later Mrs. Arnold rose and followed him upstairs. Neither returned.

Before long Alexander Hamilton knew the truth, for the messenger had arrived bringing the packet of papers found in the boots of the spy. With a posse of soldiers he dashed after Arnold, but too late. The traitor had rowed out into the river and taken refuge on a British boat.

When he arrived, Washington opened the packet of papers laid in his hands, and saw before him the carefully drawn plans of the fortifications at West Point—full explanations and directions written and signed by—Benedict Arnold. Benedict *Arnold? Benedict Arnold a traitor!* As his mind fully grasped the almost unbelievable truth, Washington's face looked suddenly very old and careworn, and his voice was gray, as he said:

"Who then is there that we still *can* trust?"

When would the French fleet arrive? was another question, also unanswered. Rochambeau did not know, but both he and Washington were of the opinion that they must wait for it.

They had also agreed, that their next move must be to attack General Clinton and try to drive the British from New York, but that it would be foolhardy to attempt to do it until the French fleet should arrive. In the meantime, therefore, there was nothing to do but keep themselves in readiness and wait. That was all for Rochambeau—Washington had to try to keep his soldiers from starving to death while they waited.

But while the Americans and French waited to attack the British at New York, another division of the British army was trying to conquer all the southern states, beginning with Georgia and South Carolina. Lord Cornwallis was the commander of that British army of the south.

To hear that Savannah, Georgia, and then Charleston, South Carolina, the largest seaports in the south, had surrendered, was disheartening news for Washington. Disheartening also the word that Cornwallis, aided by the Loyalists, was marching through those states, hunting out the patriots, burning their homes and destroying their property. But with such bad news the black year of 1780 wore on, nor was the prospect any brighter with the beginning of the new year.

CORNWALLIS SURRENDERS

IN JANUARY, Thomas Jefferson, who was governor of Virginia, sent word to Washington that the patriots were in danger of losing all the war supplies stored in that state. Benedict Arnold, now in command of British troops, had landed in Virginia and was laying waste the country, burning tobacco warehouses, searching out storehouses of food, rum, and ammunition to be used by the British. The very name of Benedict Arnold made Washington's blood boil. He sent La Fayette to Virginia with orders to capture the scoundrel dead or alive. Before leaving, La Fayette used his own money to buy uniforms for his men to wear, for they were destitute.

Soon after he reached Virginia in April, Arnold was recalled. But Cornwallis came marching up from South Carolina. He had had a difficult time in the southern states. Though the Loyalists were strong in the eastern part along the coast, in the mountains along the frontier there were many patriots, fearless woodsmen, perfect riflemen. Gathering in small bands of less than a hundred men, they had made sudden and continual raids by night on the British camps. Hiding by day in some swamp or thicket, they had been as impossible for the British to fight against as Indians.

In Virginia, Cornwallis set out to capture La Fayette. "The boy cannot escape me," he said confidently. But the "boy" did escape him, and it was not long before it was Cornwallis himself who could not escape. He had retired to Yorktown the end of August, and in so doing had stepped into a trap of his own making.

At Yorktown, Cornwallis was cut off from all help except that which came by sea, because the Americans, commanded by La Fayette, joined by the other divisions under Von Steuben and Wayne, came up behind him. From then on everything worked out neatly for the allies.

The long-looked-for French fleet was sighted in the West Indies, and from there set out for Chesapeake Bay. The English fleet, also on the way to Chesapeake Bay, met the French fleet and was so badly damaged that it was obliged to return to New York City for repairs.

Meanwhile Washington and Rochambeau gave up the plan to attack New York and set off instead to meet the French fleet in Virginia. Before leaving, however, Washington made great show of building an encampment across the Hudson River. General Clinton, thus fooled into believing that Washington's plan was still to attack New York, thought that there was no need to hurry reinforcements to Cornwallis. So Cornwallis waited desperately in Yorktown, while his soldiers sickened and died, and the French fleet, with thirty thousand men aboard, came sailing into Chesapeake Bay.

The French commander urged La Fayette to begin the bombardment of Yorktown at once and have it over, but La Fayette, who might so easily have consented and taken the glory, thought of Washington. He begged them to wait, meanwhile writing frantic letters imploring the American commander and Rochambeau to hurry.

When Washington arrived at last, and stepped from the French flagship where he had gone to meet the admiral De Grasse, his grave face was lighted with a smile. After six long heartbreaking years, the victory that he had waited for so long was now at hand.

On October 9 he touched off the first cannon and the bombardment of Yorktown began. After ten days Cornwallis raised the white flag of surrender. That afternoon the British troops in their red uniforms marched slowly out of Yorktown while their bands played a popular English tune, "The World Upside Down." The American bands played "Yankee Doodle." The British troops passed between lines of French and American troops who stood in respectful silence in obedience to Washington's command.

"My brave fellows," he had told them, "let no feeling of triumph induce you to insult your fallen enemy. No shouting or huzzaing."

Washington was a good winner, and George III, though a stubborn fighter, took his defeat with equally good sportsmanship. Two years later John Adams happened to be in London on a visit and heard the King acknowledge American independence in the House of Lords.

"Religion," said George III, "language and affections will I hope yet prove a bond of permanent union between the two countries; to this end no attention on my part will be wanting."

One hundred years later, at the celebration in Yorktown, representatives from England were present to express good will toward the United States. Today more than half of another century has passed and the respect and friendship between the two great nations still continues.

WASHINGTON REFUSES ABSOLUTE POWER

YOU SAY GEORGE WASHINGTON will not make himself the king?" asked George III. It seemed incredible that any revolution could end without having the military leader seize the power. He could think of none in history that had ended otherwise. He asked the question again.

"No," repeated Benjamin West. "He will return to private life."

"If so," said George III solemnly, "Washington will be the greatest man in the world today."

After Cornwallis surrendered, the fighting in America ceased, but until peace was actually declared, the American soldiers could not be disbanded. With every idle day they grew more restless and angry. They blamed Congress bitterly for having let them go half clothed and half starved throughout the war. With peace in sight, they grew terrified as to what would happen when they were turned loose without a cent to live on until they found work to do.

"Washington ought to seize the power," they said. "He ought to get rid of Congress and run things himself the way they ought to be run."

One of the older officers wrote to Washington, and though he did not say it in so many words, he suggested very plainly that Washington should make himself a military dictator. The great man was shocked.

"What have I done?" he asked himself, "how have I conducted myself that they even dare make such a suggestion to me?"

In his answer he rebuked the officer most severely. "Be assured, sir," were his words, "nothing in the course of the war has given me more pain. If you have any regard for your country or respect for me, banish these thoughts from your mind. No one wishes more than I do to see justice done to the army, and as far as my powers go in a *constitutional* way I shall do my utmost to secure it."

"Washington will do his utmost, that's certain," said the soldiers. "But what if he fails? Shall we just go off to starve and be forgotten?"

As they talked, their distrust and hatred of Congress grew to such a pitch that they swore not to lay down their arms until they had a promise of being paid, even if they had to seize the government and break open the Treasury! So Washington received another letter, written this time by his former adjutant, Alexander Hamilton.

This letter was not a suggestion, but a cleverly worded threat that if Washington didn't seize control himself, somebody else would.

Faced with such a choice, many a man might have become confused into taking the step as the lesser of two evils. Washington kept his head, as always, and also showed that he knew how to manage men.

He called a meeting of all the officers. He appointed General Gates, one of the chief agitators, as chairman, so that he would not be able to take part in the discussion. When the meeting was assembled he appeared before them. The faces of the men were set and stubborn as Washington unrolled his manuscript and began to read. His voice, calm and low at first, grew stronger as he continued. He begged them as they valued their honor to do nothing to overturn the liberties of their country or to dull the glory which they had gained. As he read, the words on the page apparently seemed indistinct, for he paused a moment, then reached in his pocket for his spectacles. As he slipped them on, he looked up with a smile and said, half apologetically:

"You have seen me grow gray in your service, now you see me growing blind."

Up to that time the men had listened in stony silence, but at those words their eyes filled with tears. Those words spoken so simply had touched their hearts, and dispelled all feeling but that of devotion and loyalty to their beloved commander. When he had finished Washington left the room, and the men passed a unanimous vote to follow his judgment, to trust in him and the established government, to see justice done.

MONEY

WARS COST MONEY, a great deal of money, and Congress had none and no power to raise any. That was why the soldiers had gone without clothes and food, the army without supplies and the officers without pay, all through the war. Congress could ask the colonies if they would please raise some by taxing the people and send it to help the cause, but that was as far as the powers of Congress went. Sometimes the colonies sent help and sometimes they didn't. When they did, it wasn't money in pieces of gold or silver, but tobacco or grain or furs, whatever product each particular colony had been accustomed to use for money.

Those products were difficult to handle. Congress needed actual money. So, early in the war, they had decided to print some on paper. Continental money, backed by the Continental Congress, was to be good all over the continent. The money went all right at first, but not for long. People soon realized that it was worthless. A paper dollar to have value must represent a dollar's worth of gold laid away in the national treasury. But the Continental dollars represented nothing laid away, and as soon as the people realized that, the value of the paper money sank so low that a Continental dollar wouldn't buy twelve cents' worth of goods. In 1779 shoes cost $125 (paper dollars) a pair, and Samuel Adams paid $400 for a hat. It got to such a point that if anybody

231

called a thing no good, he said "it wasn't worth a continental!"

Congress had borrowed money from France and then from Holland. Both of these countries sent large sums, but not in actual pieces of gold and silver, which might have been sunk on the way over to the bottom of the sea, but in bills of exchange. These had actual value, because they were backed by gold. So they could be sold to raise money, or used to buy supplies, but that required some one to do it who knew how.

Congress needed a treasurer the moment the war started, but it was 1781, the year that Cornwallis surrendered, before Robert Morris was finally appointed to superintend the money affairs for the government. By then, continentals weren't worth anything. Men used them when they were shaving to wipe the soap off their razors.

The first thing Robert Morris did after he opened his office was to buy two thousand barrels of flour with his own money.

Then he called in the brokers of Philadelphia to help him sell the colonial products and the foreign bills of exchange. But most of these brokers, supposed to be loyal Americans, were so much more eager to help themselves than the government that they charged the outrageous price of two or three cents for each dollar they handled. Robert Morris had to look for some one else. It was then he found the nation's "little friend on Front Street near the river."

For two years Robert Morris had read advertisements of Haym Salomon, the broker, in the Philadelphia newspaper. Now he put down his newspaper and sent for the stranger. Punctually at the hour appointed a small, quiet, dark-eyed man appeared. He said very little and coughed slightly as he spoke. Morris asked him what he would charge for handling money for the government.

"Not over a quarter of one per cent," the little man replied.

Less than one eighth as much as the others had demanded! From that morning on, Robert Morris relied more and more on Haym Salomon, who could not only manage dollars as other men manage soldiers, words or ideas, but was also devoted to the cause of freedom.

He sold the foreign bills of exchange. He took the products from

232

the colonies: tobacco, deerskins, grain, linen, indigo, potash, beeswax, anything they sent, and turned it into money. If, at times, these did not sell quickly enough, he loaned or gave of his own money to the government or the officers if they were in need. As long as he had money left, Haym Salomon never refused to lend or give. He never asked to be repaid: he never mentioned what he had given. He died two years after the war was over and the United States owed him more than half a million dollars. The life of this immigrant from Poland was short in his adopted country, but while he lived, he gave generously in service and money toward the war fought for its freedom and independence.

From his first day in office, Robert Morris talked of establishing a mint to coin United States money. But nothing ever was done about that till after the war. Then Thomas Jefferson was again a delegate to Congress and helped decide what kind of coins to use.

There were at that time all kinds of different European coins floating around the colonies: English shillings, guineas and pounds, Dutch guilders, French francs, and Spanish pistareen, half jos, pieces of eight, and, most commonly seen of all, the Spanish dollars.

"Let us begin with the commonest coin we know, the Spanish dollar," suggested Thomas Jefferson, when they had decided to devise a new, simple, sensible system for the new nation's money. So a dollar became the standard unit. One tenth of a dollar became a *dime* from the Latin word meaning ten; one one hundredth of a dollar became a *cent* from the Latin word meaning hundred.

This is the "Franklin Penny," the first United States coin made in the new mint. On one side is a chain with thirteen links. On the other the sun and the maxim of Poor Richard: *Mind Your Business.*

front   *back*

PEASANTS OF RUSSIA

IN THE SUMMER of his fourteenth year, John Quincy Adams went as secretary to the American Ambassador to Russia, a Mr. Dana. These are parts of some letters he wrote to his parents describing what he saw of people's life and liberty in the lands he visited:

To JOHN ADAMS

"St. Petersburg, August 21, 1781 (O.S.)

"Honour'd Sir:

"We arrived here on Monday the 16/27 inst. having left Amsterdam the 7th of July (N.S.) and rode the greatest part of the way day and night. The distance is about 2400 English miles.

"The first place of any consequence we stopped at was Berlin, the capital of the King of Prussia's dominions. . . . He is not beloved in Berlin and everybody says publicly what he pleases against the king. . . . They have great reason to complain of him, for he certainly treats them like slaves. Among other things, if a farmer has two or more sons, the eldest inherits all the land, and all of the others (when of age) are soldiers for life at a gros[chen] and a half which is about two pence sterling per day, and they must with that find their own provisions. In peace time the troops are disbanded nine months in a year, and in all that time their pay ceases and they must get their living as they can.

"We pass'd through Courland, a province which does, strictly speaking, belong to Poland. But Russia has much more influence there than Poland itself. In that province all the Farmers are in the most abject slavery, and are sometimes even changed for dogs or horses. Their masters have even the right of life and death over them, and if they kill one of them they are only obliged to pay a trifling fine.

"Just before we got to Berlin, by the carelessness of a postilion our carriage overset and broke, so that Mr. Dana was obliged to buy another there; but luckily nobody was hurt by the fall.

"This is not a very good place for learning the Latin or Greek languages, as there is no academy or school here. . . . There is nobody here but Princes and Slaves, the Slaves cannot have their children instructed and the nobility that chuse to have their's send them into foreign countries. There is not one school to be found in the whole city."

"Hague, July 23rd, 1783.

"Honoured Mamma:

"It is indeed a long time since I have received any letters from my friends in America.

"I set off from St. Petersburg the 19/30 of last October, in company with Count Greco, an Italian gentleman, with whom I was acquainted at that place; and on account of the badness of the roads and weather, and of our having a great number of considerable water passages, which began to freeze over, did not arrive in Stockholm, the capital of Sweden, until the 25th of November. . . .

"Sweden is the country in Europe which pleases me the most, that is, of those I have seen, because their manners resemble more those of my own country than any I have seen. The King is a man of great ability. He is extremely popular, and has persuaded his people that they are free and that he has only restored them their ancient constitution. They think they are free and are therefore happy.

"Last night at about 11 o'clock Pappa arrived here from Paris all alone, only accompanied by a servant. He intends to return to Paris in about three weeks."

(John Adams was working at that time with the other peace commissioners in Paris, to draw up the treaty of peace. When he returned to Paris John Quincy went with him to act as another secretary.)

"Paris, September 10th, 1783.

"Honoured Mamma:

"As you have ordered me in a letter, which I have lately received, to give you my observations in the countries through which I have travelled, the following are some upon Russia:

"The government of Russia is entirely despotical; the sovereign is absolute in all the extent of the word. And the nobility have the same power over the people that the sovereign has over them. The nation is wholly composed of nobles and serfs, or in other words masters and slaves. The countryman is attached to the land in which he is born; if the land is sold he is sold with it . . . and he is obliged to give his landlord the portion of his time which he chooses to demand. It is commonly two days in the week I think. . . . Some of the nobles have an amazing quantity of serfs. Out of each five hundred they are obliged to furnish one to the empress every year and this forms her army. I have been assured from good authority that there is one nobleman who furnishes 1300 men a year to the Empress. According to that the number of his slaves would be 650,000.

"Some of the serfs are immensely rich, but they are not free and therefore they are despised. The richer they are the more the nobles prize them. Thus a common man costs but 80 or 100 rubles at most; (N. B. that a ruble is four shillings sterling or thereabouts) but I have seen a man who gave his landlord for his liberty, and that of his descendants, 450,000 rubles. This proves the esteem they have for liberty even where one would think that they should not know that such a thing exists.

"As I am a little pressed for time, and as my letter has already run to a considerable length I must for the present subscribe myself,
"Your most dutiful son,
"John Quincy Adams."

an unfinished painting Peace Commissioners *by Benjamin West*

Done at Paris this third Day of September,
In the Year of our Lord one thousand seven hundred
and Eighty three.

THE PEACE TREATY

THE PEACE TREATY had been signed just a week when John Quincy Adams wrote that last letter, for the next day, September 11, Benjamin Franklin wrote these words to a friend in Boston, Mr. Josiah Quincy:

"The Definitive Treaty was signed the third instant. We are now Friends with England and with all Mankind. May we never see another War! For in my opinion there never was a Good War or a Bad Peace!"

237

Benjamin Franklin, John Adams and a man named John Jay were the three representatives of the United States of America who signed that treaty of peace which ended the American Revolution. It had taken months of arguing, discussing and debating before all the points had been agreed upon. Through it all John Adams had been on his guard, suspicious of being outwitted by the foreign representatives. One day the British peace commissioner spoke to him about his apparent distrust, which John Adams describes in his diary:

" 'You are afraid of being made the tools of the powers of Europe,' says he.

" 'Indeed I am,' says I. 'What powers?' said he. 'All of them,' said I. 'It is obvious that all the powers of Europe will be continually manœuvring with us, to work us into their real or imaginary balances of power. Indeed, it is not surprising; for we shall very often, if not always, be able to turn the scale. But I think it ought to be our rule not to meddle; and that of all the powers of Europe, not to desire us, or perhaps even to permit us, to interfere if they can help it.' "

In the case of this treaty, John Adams must, however, have felt that the ambassadors of the United States had reason to congratulate themselves. It would seem that they had been granted everything they had asked for.

First of all, Independence. Second, all the land to which they laid claim between the Atlantic Ocean and the Mississippi River. The land east of the Alleghanies would naturally have been theirs, but the fact that their claim to the land west of the mountains was recognized is due to the fact that the hardy pioneers of Kentucky had been brave enough to stand their ground, and George Rogers Clark had been bold enough to seize and hold some of the forts in the Northwest Territory. If there had been no settlers west of the Alleghany Mountains; if all the forts had been held by the British, the great prairies west to the Mississippi might never have become a part of the United States.

In return the United States agreed to pay all debts which they had owed England before the war began. They also promised to urge each state to give back to the Loyalists any property which had been taken from them. Also all Loyalist refugees who had fled the country, but now wished to return, were to be allowed to do so.

Spain recovered Florida, but not Gibraltar. That great rock fortress guarding the Mediterranean was still held by England.

France got very little, an island in the West Indies, a piece of Africa, but on the whole little or nothing, except the satisfaction of seeing England defeated, which was a most expensive pleasure. By those five years of war, France had sunk herself so deep in debt that there was no way of pulling out. And also the ideas of liberty and equality which the French soldiers brought back from America were the very ideas which, only a few years later, were to turn the "world upside down" in France, and send poor Louis XVI's head rolling from the guillotine!

Almost a year before the final treaty was signed, an agreement had been drawn up by the English and American commissioners. Therefore in April the proclamation was read aloud to the American soldiers telling them that the war was over. That occurred on the nineteenth of April, 1783, eight years to the very day since the first shot had been fired at Lexington and Concord.

It was not until late in December, however, that the last British soldiers left the country and Washington bade farewell to his officers, at the old Fraunces Tavern in New York City. "With a heart full of gratitude," he said, "I now take leave of you, most devoutly wishing that your later days may be as happy and prosperous as your former ones have been glorious and honorable."

From Paris, Benjamin Franklin wrote again, this time to a friend in London: "I join with you in rejoicing at the return of Peace. I hope it will be lasting, and that Mankind will at length . . . have Reason and Sense enough to settle their Differences without cutting Throats; What Conveniences and Comforts of Living might Mankind have acquired by spending those Millions in doing good which in the last war have been spent in doing Mischief! For in my opinion" and here he repeated himself, "there never was a good war or a bad peace."

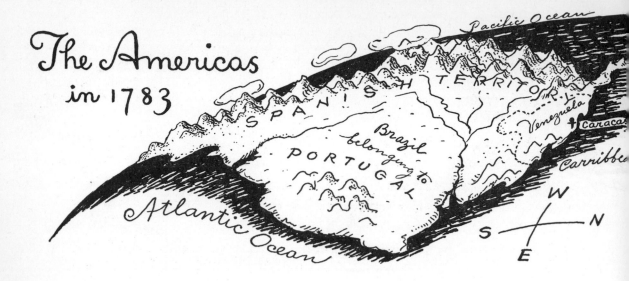

The Americas in 1783

SPANISH TERRITORY

Pacific Ocean

Venezuela · Caracas

Carribbea

Brazil belonging to PORTUGAL

Atlantic Ocean

W
S — N
E

EMPIRES OLD AND NEW

S O ONCE MORE the continent of North America had been divided. Of the two rivals, Spain and England, the one had lost her finest possession, while the other had regained all of her old empire. But that empire was not to be Spain's for long.

In July of that very year, 1783, when the American colonies gained their independence, "the Liberator" of South America was born. He came of a noble Spanish family, and his birthplace was Caracas, the capital city of Venezuela, on the old Spanish Main.

"Let us christen the little one Santiago," said his father, "in honor of the patron saint of Spain, on whose name day he was born."

"No, my son," said the priest. "Rather should we call him Simon. It was Simon Maccabaeus, the Israelite, who led his nation to freedom, and I feel that one day this child of yours will do the same."

And so the future proved. Standing today on the square of Caracas there is a monument to that Spanish hero, "Simon Bolívar, Liberator of Venezuela, New Granada, Ecuador and Peru and founder of Bolivia."

In 1783, Spain's was an old and dying empire. But England was strong and, in the wilderness to the north of the possessions she had lost, began at once to build another empire. By 1784, forty thousand

240

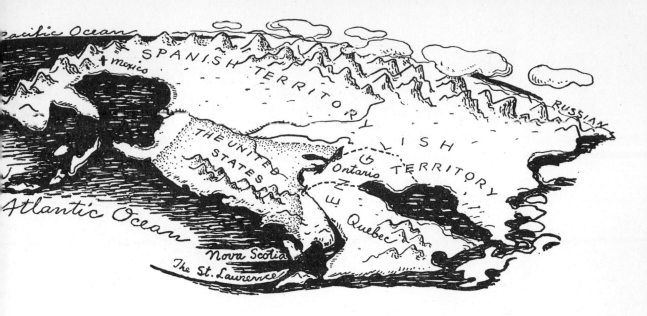

loyal subjects of the King had left the United States to settle in Nova Scotia, in New Brunswick, in Quebec, and especially in the province of Ontario. Most of them came from homes of comfort and luxury, but there in those Canadian forests they courageously started life again as pioneers. Plowing fields, building log houses, establishing villages, they laid the foundation of the Dominion of Canada. Later, in appreciation of their loyalty, the English government allowed them to affix the letters U. E. to their names. United Empire Loyalists, a distinction which their descendants are still proud to claim.

Not only in America, but all around the world, the British Empire soon grew stronger. In 1786, Lord Cornwallis, sent to Bengal as governor general, was to give such distinguished service, as firmly to establish English authority over India. The following year, 1787, seven hundred fifty immigrants landed and broke ground for the first English settlement in far-off Australia.

These English-speaking colonies, given increasing liberties as the years went on, have been held to the mother country by that close affection which, as William Pitt had said, "grows from common names, from kindred blood, from similar privileges and equal protection . . . ties which though light as air are strong as links of iron."

STARS AND STRIPES IN CHINA

THE YOUNGEST MEMBER in the family of nations now introduced itself to the most ancient one. In 1783, a trading ship from the United States set out for its first trip to China. But it did not arrive. Near Cape Good Hope it was met by a ship of the British East India Trading Company bringing home a load of tea. The captain of the British ship, alarmed to see Americans already competing for the valuable Chinese trade, offered the captain of the sloop twice as much as his cargo of ginseng was worth. The American, with an eye to business, accepted the offer and returned home.

On Washington's birthday, February 22, 1784, however, another American ship, the *Empress of China,* left New York harbor bound for Canton. This time the ship arrived, and the Americans exchanged their ginseng roots for the desired tea, porcelain, nankeens or silk.

At first the people from this newest nation in the world were called merely "New People" by the inhabitants of the ancient empire. But after their new flag of Stars and Stripes was raised above the American hong, they were known as "Hwa-Chi"—People of the "Flowery Flag."

242

V

WHEN GEORGE WASHINGTON WAS JUST A

Citizen

What other people were doing

CANADA
was settled by Loyalists
from the United States

AUSTRALIA
received its first ship
load of English settlers

AVIATION
Man's first voyage in the air was made in a balloon,
after the test flight taken by a cock, a sheep and a duck.

BEAUMARCHAIS
defied the King with his play
"The Marriage of Figaro"

THOMAS JEFFERSON
went to Paris to arrange for
United States trade with Europe.

FRANKLIN
bade farewell to France

JOHN ADAMS accompanied
by **ABIGAIL** went to England
to represent the United States

and what happened in the World

when Washington was just a Citizen

In France

ROUSSEAU's
ideas of simplicity became popular.

MARIE ANTOINETTE
played at being a peasant while the real peasants were starving

her farmhouse.

POTEMKIN
was Russia's War Minister

They made War on Turkey

FREDERICK II
a lonely old man of Prussia died in 1786.

CATHERINE II
was now called "the Great"

JOSEPH II
was Emperor of Austria
His mother Maria Theresa died, 1780

The Constitution of the United States was written 1787

JAMES MADISON
"the Father of the Constitution" did most of the writing of it,
He also recorded the meetings

MADISON, JOHN JAY & ALEXANDER HAMILTON
wrote articles on the Constitution and persuaded the states to ratify it.

between the Years 1783 and 1789

BACK TO HIS GOOD LAND

CHRISTMAS EVE, George Washington was on his way home at last, happy that he was free to return to the life he liked best, the peaceful life of a farmer.

The day was unusually cold for Virginia; the fields were powdered with snow and the horses' hooves rang on the frosty road as they sped along. Washington watched with pleasure for each familiar landmark, as the horses clipped off the last few miles that lay between them and Mount Vernon. Martha, cozy, plump and cheerful as ever, sat beside him in the coach. She had spent each summer at home, but

Washington himself had seen Mount Vernon only once in the eight years that he had been gone. All afternoon he had hoped they might arrive while it was still daylight and that the young French officers who followed in the coach behind them might enjoy the view of the Potomac before the sun had set. But they had still several miles to go, when the red sun dropped behind the hills, and dusk had fallen by the time they neared the boundaries of the plantation.

Far down the road they could just make out the shadowy figure of an old Negro standing before the first little cabin. It was Old Bishop. They could almost tell from the way he stood how proud he was to be the first man, black or white, to welcome home the General. As the carriage pulled up, he drew himself erect and saluted, and Washington noticed that in honor of the occasion he had dressed himself in his old soldier's uniform. It was the one he had worn when Washington had first brought him to Mount Vernon after his former master, General Braddock, had died in the French and Indian War.

"Old Bishop" must be well over eighty, thought Martha. He was an old man when I came to Mount Vernon as a bride, and that will be twenty-five years ago in January. Her eyes clouded with tears as she thought of the two little children who had then been with her. Now those two, Patsy and Jacky, were both gone. Hastily she brushed her tears away, as they rode up the gravel driveway to the house, for the front door stood open wide, and there in its great square of yellow light she saw two other children waiting to greet her. They were Nelly Custis and baby Washington, Jacky's own little son and daughter. Washington, holding on to his mammy's hand, bobbed up and down on his small unsteady feet, as his adoring grandmama held out her arms to him. Nelly, who was five, curtsied and looked up with shining eyes into the handsome face of her big, soldier grandfather.

Gathered in a circle around the open doorway, the house servants shouted their welcome to the Master and Mistress, and inside the house were guests and relatives from Alexandria and Fredericksburg, who had come to spend the holidays. The hall was hung with ropes of cedar,

248

and sweet with the smell of pine. Mistletoe and holly were in every doorway. A great fire of hickory logs was blazing in the fireplace, and from the dining room came the delicious odor of fried chicken, Virginia ham, hot beaten biscuits, coffee, and all the good food which was ready for the travellers and their guests. For days the cooks had been preparing the Master's favorite dishes, the house servants had cleaned and polished as the Mistress would have had them, while outside there was a pile of hickory logs which would more than last till Twelfth Night, the end of the Christmas holidays. Christmas was always a great festivity at Mount Vernon, but when Christmas and the Master's homecoming day were one, it meant a doubly joyous celebration!

During the long winter days, after the holidays were over and the guests were gone, Nelly became acquainted with her grandfather and the two grew to be great friends. She was happy that this wonderful grandfather of hers had adopted her and her little brother and that they were to live there always at Mount Vernon. Nelly followed the big man about like a small shadow, often with her slim hand clasped about one of his huge fingers. He never seemed to tire of his small companion, and enjoyed having her stand quietly beside him while he wrote or drew.

"These are plans to make this house we are living in larger," he told her one day. "When spring comes, masons and carpenters will follow these plans to do the building."

He showed her the wide veranda, where she and grandmama could serve tea, where the new spinning house and smokehouse were to be, the kitchen house, the gardens and the serpentine drive.

"When spring comes," he told her, "you can help me plant the trees and bushes."

But when spring came, though Nelly helped him, she found that she could not be her grandfather's only companion. As soon as it was warm enough for the carpenters to begin to saw and hammer, her grandfather became a very busy man. When the fields were ready to be plowed and planted, he was up every daybreak for an early breakfast and then off on horseback to spend the morning with the overseers of the various farms. At three o'clock, of course, he was back again for dinner, but then there were always guests to be entertained.

It had been an unusually cold winter, and the snowy roads had made it impossible for many guests to reach Mount Vernon, but when the snow melted, a perfect flood of visitors came pouring in. Nelly then discovered that her grandfather was a very famous man. All kinds of people came from everywhere—east, west, north and south—to see him. Authors brought manuscripts for him to read, inventors brought models for him to inspect, painters came to paint his portrait, and many others, Nelly decided, came just to gaze at him, as if grandfather were a mountain or an especially big horse! Some of them even acted as if he were a man to be afraid of; they got red behind the ears and stuttered. But no matter who they were or where they came from, grandfather was equally courteous to every one, until in August a guest arrived from France. As soon as he had stepped from his coach there had been an expression of joy on her grandfather's face that Nelly had not seen before.

"You are now to meet the Marquis de La Fayette," Washington told her when it was her time to be introduced, "my little granddaughter, Eleanor Custis," he added as she made her curtsey. She smiled up at the delightful stranger as he told her about his own little daughter, home in France; his son, George Washington La Fayette, who was, they found, just Nelly's age and named for her own grandfather; and the baby sister, named Virginie.

One day toward sundown they planted a tree in the garden in honor of their French guest. All the family had stood about in a circle on the grass, while La Fayette with his own hands set a small magnolia tree in the hole which had been dug for it, and then placed the first shovelful of earth upon its roots. It is still standing at Mount Vernon.

It was hard for Washington to say good-bye to La Fayette when the time came for "his boy" to leave. He went with him on horseback part way along the road. They were never to see each other again.

LONELY THOMAS JEFFERSON AT MONTICELLO

ROBABLY NOW I shall never cross the ocean. I shall never visit the Old World," thought Thomas Jefferson gloomily as he stood one afternoon in September, 1783, looking off from his mountain top over the woods and countryside to the far horizon.

The previous winter he had been appointed to go to Europe to help arrange the peace treaty, but soon the word that negotiations were almost completed had made sending another ambassador unnecessary.

"I lost my opportunity," he said, "the only one I ever had and perhaps ever will have."

He felt sad and listless. His fingers turned the smooth tape in his pocket over and over but he felt no inclination to measure any more of the new road which he was laying out around the mountain. The sumac vines, he noticed, were touched with early frost but he felt no desire to jot it down in the notebook in which, all the past years, he had faithfully recorded almost every bud and blossom on the whole plantation. Now he was no longer interested. Waves of sadness welled up from his heart and submerged all thoughts except those of the unhappy changes which had taken place since he had built his home there on his beloved mountain, which he now called by the Italian name for "little mountain," "Monticello."

There, almost beside him underneath the oak tree, was the grave of his best friend, Dabney Carr, the boy with whom he had first climbed the mountain, and who had later married Jefferson's sister, Martha. True to their boyhood promise, Thomas Jefferson had buried him there, had brought the six fatherless children to live at Monticello, and had tried as best he could to take the place of the father they had lost.

Now for the past year he had had an even harder and sadder task, to try and be mother as well as father to his own three little daughters, for it was just a year ago that Martha, his wife, had been laid there also beneath a green mound on the hill slope.

The lonely man turned and walked slowly back in the direction of the small red-brick building where he and Martha had come in the snowstorm on their wedding night. They had called it "Honeymoon Lodge" and set up housekeeping there. How many evenings she had sung while he played the violin, and with what interest from that little house they had watched the big house being built!

His glance travelled on to that house itself. In the late sun, the tall white columns cast long even purplish shadows against the soft red brick. The air was very quiet.

Suddenly the door burst open. Out popped a little girl of nine or ten, in a full pink skirt with a flouncing ruffle on it. She tilted a second on the edge of the step to look this way and that, then, catching sight of her father, came skipping toward him across the lawn, her brown curls blown back over the small bottle-green cape she had tied about her shoulders.

"Father," she said breathlessly, "have you any cornmeal in your pocket? Cæsar says that the doe with the two fawns is under the clump of beech trees in the hollow. Let's hurry before she takes the babies away again into the thicket."

The two crossed the lawn, and followed down the winding path to the deer park. All but the shyest of the older deer were tame enough to take the corn which their master held out to them, and even the mother of the twins left her fawns for the moment to put her soft nose in Patsy's hand.

"Who will feed the deer while we are away?" the little girl said, looking up at her father. "And who," she laughed, "who will name all the pigs while you are gone? . . . And how many weeks will it be before we go to Philadelphia?"

"Not many now," her father answered. "I am obliged to be in Congress by November, and we must first have time to place you in your boarding school."

The weeks before they left passed so quickly that it seemed to Patsy almost too soon that the day was there when she and her father had to say good-bye to the family and ride off down the mountain. Aunt Eppes and Aunt Martha said they would take good care of little Polly and the baby, and promised to send word about all the other children.

"It will not be for long," her father said as he laid his violin case in the seat between them. "We shall soon be back to live here on our lovely mountain, always."

As their carriage wound down the road beneath the trees, the leaves already turning color, Thomas Jefferson had no other thought but that he was going to Congress for a short session and would soon return. He had no idea that in less than a year he and his small daughter would be on board the boat for Europe, making the other half of his boyhood dream come true, a dream he had almost despaired of realizing.

253

AVIATION IS BORN

BALLOONS WERE THE MAIN TOPIC of conversation in Paris the winter of 1783. In September three unsuspecting barnyard animals, a cock, a sheep and a duck, had been sent up in a balloon into what was supposed to be the "dangerous upper air," and to every one's amazement had come down again quite unharmed by their strange experience. Since that day, Paris and Versailles had talked of almost nothing but balloons.

No one was more interested in the subject than the old philosopher, Benjamin Franklin. Some one lacking imagination asked him why.

"Of what use is a balloon?" inquired the literal-minded gentleman.

"Of what use is a newborn baby?" answered Benjamin Franklin, who could see that, as surely as a baby grows to be a man, these first balloon experiments would develop into the great science of aviation.

"Yet I fear," said he, for he was nearly seventy-eight years old, "I fear that it will hardly be a common carriage in my time."

He could not help thinking how much more comfortable it would be than bumping over the cobblestones in a coach. That was so painful to him now that to his great disappointment he had not been able to make the trip to Versailles the day the animals went up, but he never missed any of the following balloon ascensions when he was well enough to go. He was also very much interested in hearing of how the two brothers had come to make their first balloon.

Joseph and Stephen Montgolfier, the inventors of the balloon, had grown up in a small town in southern France.

Looking up into the summer sky one day, the younger brother had said, "I believe that if one of those clouds could be captured in a paper bag it would carry the bag up and an extra weight besides." Later, the idea had occurred to the brothers that they might make a paper bag rise by filling it with hot air and smoke. They made several trial balloons and then in June, 1783, announced a public demonstration in the market place of their home town. The curious crowd, gathered from far and wide, saw a huge blue paper bag, hanging over an open fire, swell to its full spherical size, break the ropes which held it and before their astonished eyes rise into the air and sail away! Like a thing bewitched! News of the experiment spread like wildfire. Scientists wrote and invited the Montgolfiers to come to Paris, after which Louis XVI summoned them to bring the balloon to Versailles that he too and his court also might see this interesting invention.

One afternoon in November, Benjamin Franklin set out in his coach, for a balloon ascension, in as great excitement as an old gentleman could possibly be, for he was about to witness the first voyage in the air ever taken by man. A daring young fellow, by name of de Rozier, had volunteered to make the flight and a friend had offered to go with him. This is part of the account of it which Benjamin Franklin sent to the Royal Society of London:

"Dear Sir: Nov. 21, 1783.

"Enclosed is a copy of the Experiment made yesterday in the Garden of the Palace where the Dauphin now resides, which being near my House, I was present. The Balloon was larger than that which carried the Sheep Etc. Its Bottom was open and in the middle of the Opening was fixed a kind of Basket Crate in which Faggots and Sheaves of Straw were burnt. When it went over our Heads we could see the Fire which was very considerable. There was a vast Concourse of Gentry in the Garden, who had great Pleasure in seeing the Adventurers go off so cheerfully, & applauded them by Clapping etc., but there was at the same time a good deal of Anxiety for their Safety. Multitudes in Paris saw the Balloon passing, but did not know that there were Men with it, it being then so high that they could not see them. One of these coura- geous Philosophers did me the honor to call upon me in the Evening after the Experiment with Mr. Montgolfier, the very ingenious Inventor. I was happy to see him safe. Improvement in the management of Bal- loons has already made a rapid progress and one cannot say how far it may go. A few months since the idea of witches riding through the air upon a broomstick and that of Philosophers upon a bag of smoke would have appeared equally impossible and ridiculous. This Experiment is by no means a trifling one. With great and sincere esteem, I am, sir, your most obedient and humble servant."

B Franklin

"I begin to be almost sorry I was born so soon," he remarked to himself as he dusted what he had written with sand, laid down his quill and removed his spectacles, "since I cannot have the Happiness of Knowing what will be known a hundred years from now."

256

"THE MARRIAGE OF FIGARO"

PIERRE CARON BEAUMARCHAIS had now completed his very famous and very witty comedy, "The Marriage of Figaro." It was ready to be produced, and waited only for the King's permission. On an afternoon, in the small apartment of the Petit Trianon, with the manuscript spread on a delicate table before her, Marie Antoinette's lady-in-waiting read it aloud to the King and Queen.

"That's horrible," shouted Louis XVI, interrupting her, full of determination for once in his life.

"Then it will not be played?" asked Marie Antoinette.

"Certainly not! You may rely upon that!" replied the King.

Figaro, the hero of the comedy, was a character from a previous play by Beaumarchais, "The Barber of Seville." He was a servant, an impudent fellow but a likable rascal, who always had something pointed to say on any topic. He poked fun at the rich, scoffed at the nobility, ridiculed the government, and in the last act was sarcastic about that injustice by which he, who had no money, could be put into prison for merely talking about it.

"That's going too far," exclaimed the King when they came to that part. "That man Figaro scoffs at everything in the state that should be respected. We might as well tear down the Bastille as let that play go on.

"So the King says 'The Marriage of Figaro' is not to be given, eh?" scoffed Beaumarchais when he heard what the King had said. "I, on the other hand, promise that it will be shown, even if I have to produce it in Notre Dame Cathedral!"

Then he, who had always lived by his wits, set about making good his boast. He distributed the most catchy songs in the play, and soon every one was singing them, talking about the play and wondering why the King would not let it be acted. Finally a duchess engaged a theatre and set the night for a private performance. A gay occasion it was, attended by all the fashionable. The theatre was full, the curtains just on the point of being drawn, when in marched an officer of the King, and holding aloft a paper, announced:

"The play must not go on. The King has forbidden it."

Lights were snuffed out. The people, cheated of their fun, drove home in a rage. Such an order, they said, was tyranny and oppression. They were more than ever determined to see the play.

Petitions were sent to the King. Beaumarchais promised to cut out all speeches that the King objected to, and so with every one against him, poor befuddled Louis XVI gave in, as usual, and the play went on, without a word changed that any one could discover.

Except for the King himself, almost everybody who was anybody in Versailles or Paris was there on the gala night of the opening performance, April, 1784. It was a great success. The nobility went night after night and laughed with delight at hearing themselves derided. . . . It was all so witty, so gay, so clever and ridiculous!

Beaumarchais watched the audience with amusement and laughed at them as they laughed at themselves being laughed at. For he was keen.

"There is just one thing more ridiculous than my piece," he remarked to himself, "and that is its success."

And it was ridiculous. For while the nobility laughed, they were laughing away the very form of government that gave them their privileges and kept them where they were, and which they should, instead, have guarded with their lives. For that government was crumbling.

When Beaumarchais, the son of a bourgeois, could defy and defeat the will of Louis XVI, the King, the absolute monarch of France, the day when that monarch's throne would come crashing down about his ears was not far off. Revolution was beginning.

THREE AMERICANS MEET IN FRANCE

ON JULY 5, 1784, the day after the Declaration of Independence had been read in Faneuil Hall, to celebrate its eighth anniversary, Thomas Jefferson, the man who wrote it, and little Mistress Jefferson sailed out of Boston Harbor, bound for France. They had a rapid voyage, and just one month later, *Patsy* took off her bonnet and shawl in Paris. Her father kept her with him until some of the strangeness of the new surroundings had worn off, and then put her in a convent school near by where he could visit her.

Thomas Jefferson had been sent to France by Congress to help arrange treaties whereby the United States might trade with the countries of Europe. The new country had such products as tobacco, rice, wheat, lumber, fish, and furs to sell, which had formerly all gone to England. Now customers must be found among the other countries.

Benjamin Franklin was, of course, the first man Thomas Jefferson went to see. The old gentleman had been expecting him for some weeks. John Adams, he said, had written from The Hague in Holland that he would also come to Paris as soon as Jefferson arrived. That night Benjamin Franklin wrote to John Adams:

"Passy 6, August 1784.

"Sir: I enclose herewith some new instructions. You will see that a good deal of business is cut out for us—treaties to be made with I think twenty powers in two years—so that we are not likely to eat the bread of idleness; and that we may not surfeit by eating too much our masters (in Congress) have diminished our allowance. For my own part if I could sit down to dinner on a piece of excellent (New England) salt pork and pumpkin I would not give a farthing for all the luxuries of Paris. I am glad to hear that your family are safely arrived at London and that you propose to bring them here with you."

A few days later, John Adams and his family arrived in Paris. So Adams, Jefferson and Franklin, the three members of that committee appointed in 1776 to draft the Declaration of Independence, were reunited in Paris, and set to work on the new commercial treaties. The three men spent many long hours working over the first draft of the treaty. However, when copies of the original had been struck off on Benjamin Franklin's small private printing press and one presented to the French foreign minister, that gentleman showed no particular interest in the document. Neither did the other countries seem at all eager to sign any treaties with the new United States.

"It appears," said Thomas Jefferson, "that the other countries know little about us except as rebels who have been successful in throwing off the yoke of the mother country. They are ignorant of our commerce which has been monopolized by England."

Frederick "the Great" of Prussia, for some reason or other (for no one could ever be quite sure of what was going on in that crafty old head) was the first to sign the treaty of commerce with the United States. But he was only one out of twenty. At best it would be slow, tedious work for the three Americans to peddle their wares.

Benjamin Franklin was too old and tired and feeble to work longer. For months past he had been begging Congress to allow him to return home. When permission finally came for him to leave, a whole nation of friends turned out to bid him farewell. He rode away in a travelling litter, one of her own which Marie Antoinette had loaned him in order that his journey might be more comfortable than if made by coach. Cheering crowds followed him to the outskirts of the city and all along the way to the seacoast the people opened their homes to him, inviting him to dine with them or spend the night. To them all he was still their beloved Bon Homme Richard. Thomas Jefferson had been made ambassador in his place, but he knew that in the hearts of the French people no one could take the place of Benjamin Franklin.

"You replace Doctor Franklin," Vergennes, the French foreign minister, said to the new ambassador at their first meeting.

"I succeed; no one can replace him," answered Jefferson.

That well-turned answer gained for Thomas Jefferson the immediate approval of the French diplomats and put him on easy terms with them at once. His many accomplishments and fine mind won the admiration of the French scholars.

"No object has escaped Mr. Jefferson," said one of them who had also visited him in America. "He is an American who, without ever before quitting his own country, is at once a musician, skilled in drawing, an astronomer, a scientist, a legislator and a statesman. 'Twould seem as if from his youth he had placed his mind as he placed his house on a mountain top, from which to contemplate the entire universe."

from a painting by
Fragonard

ROUSSEAU AND SILVER SHEEP SHEARS

THOMAS JEFFERSON was also welcomed by the people of France as the author of the Declaration of Independence.

All the young soldiers who had returned from America had brought back enthusiastic reports of that land where there were no poor, no hollow-eyed peasants, no officers collecting toll at every bridge, no forests where only the king could hunt. It was a land, they said, where all were brothers, free and equal. Liberty, equality, those were the words that had been written by Thomas Jefferson. Those words, "Liberté, Equalité," when would those words be heard in France?

262

But those words had long been heard in France. When Thomas Jefferson was a small boy, Jean Jacques Rousseau had been writing that liberty, equality, and brotherhood should be established among men.

Rousseau was a Swiss philosopher, who was born the same year as Frederick the Great and died in 1778, the same year as Voltaire. Rousseau and Voltaire had agreed about the evils in society, but their remedies for curing those evils were exactly opposite. Voltaire had believed that people needed to be taught to think, that they should become more educated and civilized. Rousseau said that the whole trouble lay in the fact that people had become *too* civilized. People were good at heart, he said. All they needed was to go back to the simple way of living. The life of a farmer in the country was far better than that of a citizen of Paris. Better still was the simple life of primitive people living in the wilderness like the American Indian. There among such people could the true nobleman be found. Voltaire had laughed at Rousseau's romantic ideas, but they had appealed to the French people. As Voltaire stirred their minds and intellect, Rousseau stirred their emotions.

The common people who had been "born wrong" welcomed the idea of equality and brotherhood. Noblemen who had become bored with useless form and etiquette welcomed the idea of simplicity.

The Queen, who from the first had rebelled at the etiquette of the court, caught the fever also. She had probably never given the American Revolution a serious thought, but she spoke of the people as "my dear republicans." She probably had never read a book that Rousseau had written, but she built a "farm" and played at being a peasant.

In a simple white muslin dress, she went skipping about her "farm" with her hair in curls, under a broad-brimmed straw hat trimmed with a wreath of roses and tied on with a blue ribbon to match her eyes.

Ladies who wished to be in fashion followed the Queen, took down their towering headdresses. They discarded their brocaded gowns for ones of muslin, and tied over their curls broad-brimmed straw hats with streamers of blue ribbon. Noblemen left off their red heels and embroidered coats and lace ruffles and tramped about in thick-soled shoes, carrying "knotty cudgels" in their hands instead of lace handkerchiefs.

Marie Antoinette's "farm" had grown, naturally, out of the informal gardens she had decided to have laid out about the Petit Trianon, to replace the stiff clipped hedges and exact flower beds. In their place she had wanted an informal garden, a lovely one with little hills and winding paths, trickling brooks with pools and wooded nooks.

"And it must look as natural," she had said, "as if a piece of lovely countryside had been transplanted near my door."

So she had called in artists and architects, painters and sculptors, and they had drawn, designed, painted, and modelled until they had brought forth a perfect dream of a garden. It had cost thousands and thousands of livres, but why worry?

"It is such a lovely place!" said Marie Antoinette, entranced. "With just a few peasants about it would look perfectly natural."

How gay it would be to play at being a peasant, herself, she thought. Her friends, too! They would all be peasants! But for that they really needed a small thatched farmhouse, one with roses growing over the door . . . and a barn or two . . . and a dairy . . . even a mill.

So the artists and architects and painters and sculptors came back and when they were through they had built a perfect dream of a farm. A little farm on whose miniature meadows sheep with wool as white as snow could be led to pasture with blue ribbons, and sheared in spring with silver sheep shears. The most famous painter of the day designed small barns, all perfect, with lovely old cracks painted in the plaster, and where stood Brunette and Blanchette, the cows, on polished hooves.

There Marie Antoinette and her "farmer" friends caught the foaming streams of milk in porcelain vases, made pats of butter in the dairy, fed the doves, picked the flowers, danced on the green, and did all the gay and delightful things carefree peasants were supposed to do.

Only on Sundays for an hour or so was the Queen obliged to lay by her play, and hold court with his Majesty. That was a great bore.

"Peasants don't appreciate how happy they are," said Marie Antoinette; "they don't know what trouble and worry it is to be a Queen!"

JOHN ADAMS & GEORGE III

THE SUMMER that Benjamin Franklin left for America and Thomas Jefferson was made ambassador to France, John Adams was appointed ambassador to England, and the Adams family went to live in London.

Three years before, John Adams had taken a short sightseeing trip to London. At that time full of curiosity, he said he had gone "trotting about the city as fast as good horses would carry him," to see Westminster Abbey, the Tower of London, and all the places he had always heard of. He had paid a visit to Mr. Josiah Wedgwood's factory to see his new porcelain and pottery, and also his fine collection brought back from the buried city of Pompeii. He had gone through Buckingham Palace escorted by his friend Benjamin West, who had received permission from their Majesties to show John Adams his paintings which were there, and also to take him on a tour of the "whole house."

A pupil of Benjamin West's from Boston, by the name of Copeley, had procured a card for him to attend the King's speech in the House of Lords. There on a foggy day he had heard George III acknowledge the independence of the United States. So that visit had been gratifying.

In 1785, however, he was going to London not as a visitor, but as the first ambassador from those lately acknowledged United States. It was a rather uncertain position especially for a man named Adams.

Newspaper announcements could scarcely be called encouraging, as for example this one which appeared in *The Public Advertiser:*

"An ambassador from America! Good Heavens, what a sound! *The Gazette* surely never announced anything so extraordinary before."

His presentation, however, to King George III turned out far better than John Adams had anticipated. The King received him in his private apartment in St. James's Palace. John Adams was ushered in alone, and the two very blunt but very honest men stood face to face. Mr. Adams bowed and then standing squarely on both feet spoke with a firm voice, though inside he was quivering with emotion.

"Sir," said he, "the United States of America have appointed me their minister plenipotentiary to your Majesty and have directed me to deliver to your Majesty this letter which contains the evidence of it."

The King took the letter and, with his face growing very red, listened as John Adams continued:

"I think myself more fortunate than all of my fellow citizens in having the distinguished honor to be first to stand in your Majesty's royal presence in a diplomatic character . . . and I shall esteem myself the happiest of men, if I can be instrumental in restoring the old good humor between people who, though separated by an ocean and under different governments, have the same language, a similar religion and kindred blood."

The King grew redder, tried to clear his throat to answer, but no words came. When he did speak, his voice shook and he hesitated.

"Sir: The circumstances . . . of this audience are so extraordinary . . . the language you have now held is so extremely proper . . . that I must say . . . that I not only will receive with pleasure the friendly assurances of the . . . United . . . States . . . but I am very glad that the choice has fallen on you to be their minister. I wish you, sir, to believe that I have done nothing in the late contest but what I thought myself bound to do. I was the last to consent to a separation, but the separation having been made, I have always said that I would be the first to meet the friendship of the United States as an independent power."

Those were the ceremonial speeches. Then said the King:

"And did you come here directly from France, Mr. Adams?"

"From France, your Majesty," replied John Adams.

"There is an opinion," laughed the King, "among some people that you are not very much attached to France."

"That opinion, sir, is not mistaken, I must avow to your Majesty, I have no attachment but to my own country."

"An honest man will have no other," replied the King, and so ended the meeting pleasantly.

But members of the King's court, said John Adams, treated him with the most haughty and studied indifference.

HISSES FOR MARIE ANTOINETTE

MARIE ANTOINETTE laughed with delight over "The Marriage of Figaro," and was humming one of the songs from the play as she took her place one morning to have her portrait painted. She paused with the gayest little laugh. "Sing it with me," she said, beginning the merry tune again.

At these words, the lively elfin face of Mme. Vigée Lebrun peeped from around the side of the canvas. She joined in the song with a clear sweet voice, and then turned back to her painting.

"Of all your costumes, your Majesty," she said, "there is none I think more lovely or becoming than this simple muslin frock."

The portrait, when it was finished, was beautiful, but when it was put on exhibition in the art gallery at Paris, the common people sniggered and sneered.

"Look," they pointed, "the Queen's been painted in her underwear." A queen wearing a plain white dress was no queen to them.

The old nobility felt the same. "In our day," said one of the old duchesses who clung to her elegance, "no Queen of France would have allowed herself to be painted dressed like a common dairymaid." Too fat to look well in muslin, the duchess bitterly bemoaned the good old days when silks and satins were the fashion.

"In my day," snapped another, "queens also behaved like queens and not like dairymaids, or worse."

"Foreigner . . . Austrian . . ." sneered the three old aunts. "She spends her days in a cowshed and her nights over a gambling table. Swindlers, gamblers, and low-class bad women are her friends."

Tradesmen also had complaints to make. Silk manufacturers blamed the Queen because this fad for muslin was ruining their business. Jewelers said the Queen's new style was driving them bankrupt.

That came to a climax in what was known as the Affair of the Diamond Necklace. "We are ruined," declared a firm of diamond merchants. "We delivered a diamond necklace which the Queen had ordered, worth 1,600,000 livres, and she refused to pay for it."

Though this was a plot of a gang of swindlers who had forged the order and stolen the necklace, people refused to believe the truth.

"See," said the taxpayers, pointing to the huge sum asked for the necklace, "that's where our money has been going. The Queen throws it away. It's not the King, but the Queen who's ruining France."

Marie Antoinette gave no heed to the criticism until one evening

Malbrough
a nursery song
Marie Antoinette
sang her children

Louis
Charles
the baby became
the "lost Dauphin"

the older brother
died in 1789

when she appeared in Paris and, instead of the applause with which she was accustomed to being greeted, there was a silence, then a hiss rose from the crowd. The next day the police officer sent word that in the future it would be wise for her Majesty not to come to the city.

Too late Marie Antoinette was awake at last to her mistakes. She closed her gambling rooms, cut off many of her good-for-nothing friends and spent much of her time with her children.

Her face was grave and she did not laugh or sing as she sat with them for this last portrait which Madame Lebrun painted of her. By the time it was finished, the artist scarcely dared send it to the exhibition in Paris, for people had made the threat:

"If we have to look at another portrait of that Austrian woman we'll smash it up!"

The portrait, fortunately, was not damaged. The people were not quite ready yet to carry out their threats. But the time was coming.

OLD FREDERICK'S LAST REVIEW

FREDERICK THE GREAT, a dirty, wizened old man of seventy-four, curious to set eyes on the young French hero, invited La Fayette to visit him in 1786 and see a review of Prussian troops in Silesia. La Fayette was flattered. He accepted, and gave the old tyrant an enthusiastic report of the American Revolution, and of the new government by the people. Frederick the Great believed in government by kings, not people, and dropped the young enthusiast a word of warning.

"I once knew a young man that talked the way you do," said old Frederick dryly, with his head on one side, fixing his great blue eyes on La Fayette. "Do you know what became of him?"

"No, your Majesty, what?" replied La Fayette, vaguely uneasy.

"He was hanged," said Frederick the Great, helping himself to a pinch of snuff.

George Washington received a letter from La Fayette about his visit, in which he described Frederick as "an old broken, dirty corporal, covered all over with Spanish snuff, with his head leaning on one shoulder and his fingers almost distorted by gout.

"But what surprised me much more," La Fayette continued, "was the fire and sometimes the softness of the most beautiful eyes I ever saw.

I went to Silesia, where he reviewed an army of thirty thousand men. For eight days I made dinners of three hours with him, which gave me an opportunity to admire his wit, the endearing charms of his manner, so that I did see that people could forget what a tyrannic hard-hearted and selfish man he is."

In August, Frederick the Great, most famous ruler in Europe, died with no friend to mourn for him but his greyhounds. His old heart stopped beating Thursday morning, August 17, 1786, at exactly twenty minutes past two, and at that very instant, the story goes, his clock at Potsdam also stopped ticking, "never to go again."

Maria Theresa had died six years before. Her son Joseph II, Marie Antoinette's oldest brother, was now Emperor of Austria.

The following October, La Fayette wrote Washington again:

"The Russians and Turks are quarrelling. The Empress is going to the Crimea, where it is said she will meet the Emperor of Austria. She has given me polite hints that I should go to St. Petersburg; I have answered with a demand to go to the Crimea, which has been granted. So I think I will set out for the Crimea, and return by Constantinople."

CATHERINE'S TURKISH FAIRY TALE

S O FREDERICK "the Great," long the terror of Europe, was dead. Catherine II of Russia, now also called "the Great," had taken his place as the most powerful ruler in Europe, and therefore the one most watched with fear and distrust by all the others.

In 1787 Catherine was again ready to go to war with the Turks. Four years before she had acquired the Crimea by forcing its independent ruler to turn over his peninsula in the Black Sea to Russia. Now she was determined to force the Turks completely out of Europe, sweep their ships from the Black Sea, and capture Constantinople.

She wanted only the help of Austria. Joseph II, the Austrian Emperor, was also eager enough to see the Turks driven out of the land along the Danube which he wanted, but he was timid about starting the war. To egg him on, Catherine had the bright idea of inviting him to visit the Crimea and admire with her the newly acquired territory.

"That will make his mouth water," she predicted.

Catherine had never seen the land herself, but she had heard about it from Potemkin, her war minister, who was there. Actually the Crimea was little better than a wasteland, but according to his letters it was a fairyland on earth.

But that Potemkin was a man of great imagination and probably the strangest man on earth. Like Russia itself, he was a giant. Like Russia, too, he was half Asiatic and half European, half civilized and half barbarian. One day, dressed in perfect elegance, he would dine with guests on the rarest and most delicate of foods. The next day he might be lying with rough Cossacks in a dirty hut, munching onions and raw turnips, or asleep in a corner with his unwashed hairy legs half covered by a mangy fur. He had but one eye in his head. One of the Orlov brothers had poked out the other in a little argument.

That was Potemkin, who was now faced with the job of turning the wasteland, which Catherine had invited her celebrated guests to visit, into some semblance of the fairyland he had led her to expect. He bit his nails to the quick, but he produced a gorgeous spectacle.

Catherine met her foreign guests at Kiev on the Dnieper. From there eighty-seven ships, some like golden palaces afloat, carrying three thousand people, sailed off down the river.

And as they glided along, what a scene unrolled before their eyes! Charming villages appeared upon the river bank, triumphal arches hung with flowers, peasants in gay-colored costumes, cattle grazing in the fields, great companies of soldiers in new uniforms. The royal sightseers were entranced. The whole scene, however, vanished as soon as their

boats passed out of sight. The village was a stage set. The houses had no roofs, the trees had no roots, and the merry peasants were just poor serfs who had been forced to dance. At sunset, cattle, trees, houses, peasants, all were bundled into carts and hustled down the river to be set up at another spot. At Sevastopol the journey ended in a boom of cannons and a view of the Russian Black Sea fleet lying at anchor in the harbor. And the show was over!

It had achieved the desired effect. Joseph II, though still hesitating a little, signed the secret treaty. Catherine was keener than ever to capture Constantinople from the Turks.

Potemkin also. "A hundred thousand men," he boasted, "are waiting for me to say the word 'go.'"

But no one quite wanted to say the word. Russia wanted the war but wanted to dodge declaring it. So by stirring up trouble in the Turkish colonies, she aggravated the Sultan of Turkey into declaring it himself. At the desired declaration of war, Potemkin was elated. Russian armies and ships were sent toward the Mediterranean. Eighty thousand Austrians marched off toward the mouth of the Danube River.

Then began one of those tangles of diplomatic intrigue, of making and breaking treaties, in which the nations of Europe have so often been involved. First of all, Catherine sent to England, France, and Holland for more seamen. They refused to send any. As a substitute, Louis XVI suggested the name of John Paul Jones, that audacious fellow who had made such success in the war against England. So John Paul Jones set out with bubbling spirits for St. Petersburg, but after a few engagements against the Turkish fleet, in which he received no credit for his part in the victories, he went back to St. Petersburg, whence he returned to Paris, most disconsolate.

In the meantime the King of Sweden had seized the golden opportunity, while the Russian troops were busy with the Turks, to march into Finland and attack the old enemy, Russia. He tried to get Denmark to help him. The Danes, however, refused because of a treaty with Russia. Instead, they sent a fleet to Norway (which also then belonged to Denmark), attacked the western province of Sweden and laid siege to the town of Gothenberg. Meanwhile the Russians had come up against the Swedes on the eastern front. So it looked very bad for Sweden—until England stepped in.

England, Prussia and Holland had an alliance to maintain the balance of power, and were not at all sure that they wanted Russia to get control of Turkey.

Therefore England rushed to Denmark and demanded that they raise the siege of Gothenberg and so leave the Swedes free to fight the Russians. That was bad for Russia. Since it was not easy to fight two so widely separated enemies at once, Catherine made peace with Sweden, and wrote Potemkin to hurry up and end the war with Turkey.

In two years' time that war also ended, with the Treaty of Jassey, which gave the Russians control of the north shore of the Black Sea, but left the Turks still holding Constantinople. By that time, however, all the eyes of Europe had turned to the more exciting events that were taking place in France, the first events in the French Revolution.

THE ASSEMBLY OF THE NOTABLES

L A FAYETTE had missed Potemkin's great show in the Crimea. Before he was able to set out to meet the Empress Catherine, things began to happen at home. Money matters of the kingdom were by this time in such a muddle that the French Minister of Finance had finally thrown up his hands in despair, and told the King that he'd better call an Assembly of the Notables and see what advice they had to offer. Accordingly, one hundred and forty-four noblemen were summoned to come and talk things over at Versailles, and the young Marquis de La Fayette was one of them. Since talking was about all they could do, having no actual power to make any laws or changes, some people considering the meeting perfectly useless, sarcastically dubbed it an Assembly of the "Not-Ables" rather than of the Notables.

275

The capable Minister of Finance, however, had in mind one thing that these so-called Not-Ables *would* be able to do, and that was to agree to let their lands be taxed. Was not nine-tenths of the land of France free from tax, because it belonged to noblemen? So after the King had opened the meeting, the Minister of Finance made his speech. The national debt, he told them, had now reached eighty million francs. To raise more money he proposed that not merely one tenth but all the land of France be taxed.

"What!" exclaimed the noblemen. "Upset all of the old traditions? No indeed! Beside, we of this Assembly have no power to levy taxes."

Then La Fayette spoke up. "First, before we consider how to raise *more* money," said he, "I propose that we look into how those eighty millions of francs have been squandered by the Minister of Finance and the court." That was a startling proposal and a daring one to make. But he signed his name to it and made a still more startling proposal at a committee meeting held a few days later.

"It seems to me," he said, "that this is an appropriate time for us to supplicate to his Majesty to bring all these matters to a happy issue by calling together a National Assembly."

"What, sir," exclaimed the Count d'Artois, the King's younger brother, in complete amazement. "Are you asking for the Convocation of the States-General?" He was astounded. Nobody could remember when a States-General or a National Assembly had ever been called.

"You wish me," the Count repeated, "to carry to the King the words: M. de La Fayette proposes a motion to convoke the States-General?"

"Yes, Monseigneur," said La Fayette, "I do."

By chance, this Assembly of Notables had met on February 22, 1787, George Washington's birthday. La Fayette wrote him what was going on in France. "Ideas of Liberty have spread rapidly here since the American Revolution," he wrote. "We have at least succeeded in putting into everybody's head that the King has no right to tax the nation without consulting and receiving the consent of a National Assembly."

Washington was always glad to hear from La Fayette, but at that moment he was concerned far less with what was happening in France than with what was going on in America, for if ever there was an assembly of "Not-Ables" in need of power it was the American Congress.

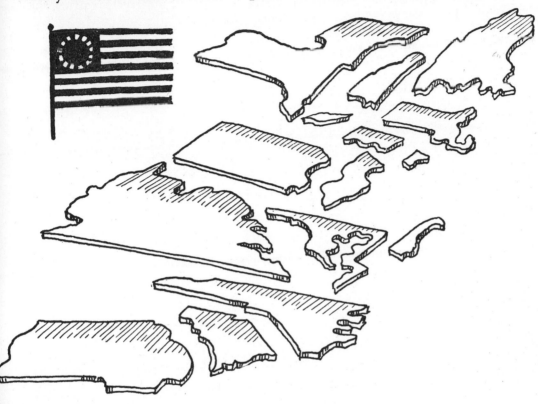

THE NOT-YET-UNITED STATES

IN 1787, THE NEW NATION was still having a desperate struggle to stand alone, and as George Washington said, it "was tottering at every step." Congress, the central government of the United States, was so weak that it was given no respect either at home or abroad. Over in England John Adams' honest face was red with shame because Congress had not been able to get the states to pay their debts.

"Our country has been dishonest," he was forced to admit. "She has broke faith with other nations." He was humiliated, and baffled.

England would not sign a treaty of commerce, continued to attack American trading ships, and refused to give up Fort Detroit and other forts in the Northwest Territory along the Canadian border until the United States fulfilled their part of the treaty. Since John Adams could offer no excuse for his country, he was glad to return home in the spring of 1788, when his term of office was over.

"We are the lowest of the whole diplomatic tribe," Thomas Jefferson wrote dismally from France. The European nations still showed no interest in his treaties of commerce.

"By the way," they asked, "these so-called United States of yours . . . are they one nation or thirteen?"

And actually which were they? The Confederation was, after all, just a "League of Friendship" between the thirteen states. Congress had no real power to make them act as one. During the war they had been united because they were fighting a common enemy, but now they were beginning to make enemies of each other.

Trade arguments between the northern states had come to such a pass that a New Jersey farmer hauling a load of wood or a cart full of cabbages into New York would be halted at the state line by a New York sheriff and made to pay a tax.

Resentment of the poor against the rich broke out in rebellion. Farmers in western Massachusetts, who could barely scratch a living because taxes and prices were so high, saw many people of Boston enjoying great war fortunes made out of profiteering and privateering (that is, selling goods at exorbitant prices, or seizing enemy ships and selling the cargo). They grew furious at being thrown into prison for not being able to pay their debts, by those people who had sat back and made money out of the war, while they had grown poor fighting to win it. Where now, they asked, was this "Life, Liberty and Happiness" they had fought for? Under a captain by the name of Shays they joined together and rebelled. They stormed the governor's mansion and demanded an accounting.

Now joined to these honest, hardworking farmers there were also

278

worthless troublemakers, and the government of Massachusetts stamped out the rebellion, but that uprising alarmed all people of property. John Hancock, re-elected governor, was himself a very wealthy man, although his was no new ill-gained fortune, and he had given his share generously in wartime. But what if the rebellion had gone on? Would the angry men have stopped to consider when and how each rich man made his fortune? George Washington was also a wealthy man. He had property to protect and news of Shays' Rebellion alarmed him.

"This country needs," he said, "a good strong central government."

Settlers west of the Alleghanies, who were still being scalped by savages, also felt none too kindly toward the folks back east. "With all that money to spend," they said, "why in God's name don't Congress make them pay the debts to England they had before the war?" Perhaps then the English would give up the forts in the Northwest Territory and the Indians would leave the settlements alone.

Beside the Indians to scalp them, there were also the land sharks from the East. Right and left, the unsuspecting settlers were being robbed and cheated of their land. Daniel Boone had now drifted sadly out of Kentucky without an acre of ground left to his name.

"Cain't blame folks much fur going over t' Spanish territory," he thought. "Leastways they kin ship their furs to market down the river."

That was another trouble. Spain refused to let people of the United States use the Mississippi, and Congress was able to do nothing about it. It was plainly impossible for the settlers of Kentucky to drag their goods back across the mountains. So some of them had accepted Spain's invitation to come and homestead farther west. Others who remained behind wanted to make Kentucky into a nation by itself.

"No use stayin' jined up to them easterners," they said. "They don't know or care what goes on west of the mountains."

So in 1787, with such lack of sympathy between the people, such a weak central government, it looked as though the United States might indeed break up once more into thirteen little no-account nations ready to be gobbled up by any of the larger nations who might care to do so.

James Madison

THE CONSTITUTION

ONE EARLY FALL day, when the leaves were turning yellow, George Washington left Mount Vernon to make a journey on horseback with a friend up into the Northwest country, to see about the many acres of land he owned. Squatters had settled on his land and were paying him no rent, dishonest speculators had laid claim to much of it and were offering it for sale. His troubles, in fact, were similar to those which had worried his old friend Lord Fairfax, thirty-five years ago.

The path Washington took to the Northwest was that which he had taken on his first surveying trip, and also the one over which he had gone as a messenger to the French commander. It led past the

Great Meadows and Fort Necessity, and over the road where Braddock had been buried, and over which three years later Washington had returned after the final capture of Fort Pitt. It was the same old road to the Northwest, but the country had changed.

Crude settlements had sprung up where there had once been unbroken wilderness. Along the rough roads where he had once been alert for skulking Indians, Washington now saw wagon trains of pioneers making their way still farther westward, and flatboats floating down the rivers loaded with rude furniture and supplies.

In that land to the west lay the future wealth of America, thought Washington, and the rivers were the natural highways by which to connect the states lying east of the Alleghany Mountains with this new western land. All the way home he was planning how the Potomac River, which rose in the Alleghany Mountains and flowed east, might be joined by a canal to the Ohio River, which also rose in the mountains and flowed west. That would form an unbroken waterway, and a ship might sail from the Atlantic, through Chesapeake Bay, the Potomac, the canal, the Ohio, the Mississippi, and down to the Gulf of Mexico.

Washington talked to his friends and neighbors about the idea when he reached home. Sometime later he invited men from Maryland to come to Mount Vernon to talk with the Virginians about these plans for increasing trade on the Potomac. They found that people of Pennsylvania and Delaware were also interested and wanted to have their say. So it was decided to call a meeting of delegates from all the states to talk over trade relations. The meeting was held at Annapolis, but not enough delegates came to accomplish anything.

"But after all," said those who were there, "what good would it do to make trade regulations, when Congress could not enforce them?"

"Far better," said Alexander Hamilton, "to call another meeting and first add to the powers of Congress."

All agreed, and the meeting was set for May, 1787, in Philadelphia. That meeting was called to order in the same room in the State House in which the members of Congress had met to sign the Declaration of Independence eleven years before, and was to be known thereafter as the Constitutional Convention. For, instead of adding to the powers of Congress, the delegates were to do away with it altogether, and establish a new form of government based on a new Constitution, whose first words stated their reasons for so doing:

"We the people of the United States, in order to form a more perfect Union, establish justice, insure domestic Tranquility, provide for the common defense, promote the general Welfare and secure the Blessings of Liberty to ourselves and our Posterity, do ordain and establish this Constitution for the United States of America."

James Madison was to go down in history as the "father of the Constitution." In spite of certain changes, the finished document followed closely a plan which that young Virginian had painstakingly worked out. A little man was James Madison, with a small face, and the nearsighted eyes of a typical bookworm peering through his glasses. When he spoke, however, it was not long before the other delegates discovered that this unimportant-looking little man had more knowledge of political science than any one else among them.

The sessions were held in absolute secrecy. When he wasn't speaking Madison was bent over, taking down quantities of notes as to what went on in the meetings. If it had not been for Madison's record, we could not know of the hours of debate, the many compromises, the steadfast patience that it took to draft a document that would be acceptable at least in part to all the states, so varied as they were in population.

George Washington presided, and in hours when the debate grew bitter, his presence alone kept the meeting together.

On September 17 the Constitution was finally complete.

Benjamin Franklin, then eighty-one, was the oldest delegate to put his name to this last of the four great documents he had signed.

"I confess I do not entirely approve of this Constitution at present," said the old gentleman as he carefully traced the quivering letters.

That was not strange. No one approved entirely. Every person and every state had been obliged to sacrifice certain pet ideas for the good of the whole country.

"But," said George Washington, "there are as few defects in it as could well be expected. As a door is opened for future amendments and alterations, I think it would be wise in the people to accept what is offered to them."

Nine states were necessary to approve or ratify it, and it was no easy task to bring those nine states into line. Brilliant articles written by Alexander Hamilton in a pamphlet called the *Federalist* had great influence. Delaware was the first, New Hampshire the ninth, to ratify it. Then Congress notified the people that the new Constitution was in effect, and the new government would begin its work in March, 1789.

Thomas Jefferson received a copy of the Constitution in leaflet form in France. He read how there was to be a President elected for four years, a Senate and House of Representatives to make the laws, and a Supreme Court to administer justice.

"A strong central government," he mused. "People of property will be well protected. But where are the rights of the common citizen guaranteed against oppression from the government? The poor man's right to Life, Liberty and the Pursuit of Happiness must also be protected," he insisted. And so, largely because Thomas Jefferson insisted, the first ten amendments, called the Bill of Rights, were added, and with that addition, the Constitution stood complete.

"It will be the pattern for all future Constitutions," said young William Pitt, son of the great Commoner, with admiration.

Benjamin Franklin was less optimistic. He made a remark which sounded like a note of warning:

"I agree to this Constitution, with all its faults," he said, "if they are such; because I think a general Government necessary for us. I believe that this is likely to be well administered for a course of years and can only end in despotism, when the people shall become so corrupted as to need despotic Government, being incapable of any other."

from a portrait by Gilbert Stuart,

G Washington

MR. PRESIDENT

ON A FRESH April morning in 1789, George Washington rode off, as usual, to look after the spring work on the plantation. When he returned from the fields at noon, he was told that a messenger was waiting. To hear the important message the family gathered in the dining-room. There, standing in that small silent group, George Washington received the announcement that his countrymen had unanimously chosen him to be the first President of the United States. For a moment he was silent. Then he bowed and spoke. He said that he was touched by this proof of his country's trust in him, that he hoped they would have no reason to regret their choice, but that all he could promise was to do his best. But even as he spoke he was filled with fear—a deadly fear that here was a task that was too big for him. In the days that followed, the fear increased. While Martha bustled busily about seeing that his satin breeches, his ruffled shirts and his long white stockings were all packed in perfect order, George Washington paced back and forth or stood in gloomy silence gazing out over the Potomac. With each day his anxiety grew greater, until the night before he left he wrote these words: "I approach the chair of government with feelings not unlike those of a culprit who is going to his place of execution."

John Adams, on the contrary, felt perfectly capable of filling his new office when the messenger arrived in Braintree with the announcement that he was to be Vice-President. He would have felt the same had his countrymen seen fit to elect him President. He was well versed in the law and he had served his country well. He left Braintree and after a triumphant journey, arrived in New York in good season, well ahead of Washington. He proceeded to the new Federal Hall just recently completed, and passing under its arches and between its stately Doric columns, he walked briskly over the shining marble floors to the new Senate Chamber, took his place under the crimson velvet canopy, and, as President of the Senate, brought the meeting to order. A short stout man, chairs he occupied were always large for him, but this one was *very* large, he thought, large enough for two! Indeed, on second thought, it was obviously designed for two! What did that signify, exactly? Did it mean that he and President Washington were supposed to sit together? He put the question to the Senate. Also he was President of the Senate, was he not, but when President Washington should come in, who would be President then? And about this title President. "Mr. President," was that any way, he asked, to address the head of a nation? That question of the President's title was not a new one. It had been puzzling the worthy senators for some time before John Adams brought it up. They wished for some fine high-sounding name, but what? "Your Majesty" was too regal; "Your Excellency" too much like the army. "Mr. President" was too common. It sounded like the head of a "fire company or a cricket club," said John Adams.

"How about 'His Serene Highness,'" some one suggested, "or

285

would 'His High Mightiness' be better still?" The excitement had reached quite a pitch, what with one suggestion and another, by the time the question came to the House of Representatives. There James Madison quietly ended the matter. He announced that the Constitution had already given the head of the government a title: it was simply "President of the United States."

And so it stood. But though they might be obliged to address George Washington as "Mr. President," that was not going to prevent those senators and their wives who loved their pomp and ceremony from making preparations to receive him, much as if he were a king and they were members of a royal court.

These members of the so-called court were all a-tingle and the whole town of New York was a-flutter with excitement on the thirtieth of April, the day set for the President to arrive. Flags flew, bells rang, flowers and wreaths hung in the windows; throngs of people laughing and cheering crowded the narrow streets. In the early afternoon they filled the square about the Federal building, their eyes fastened on the balcony outside the Senate Chambers, where at any moment the new ruler was scheduled to appear to take the oath of office. A hush fell upon the expectant crowd as at last the doors opened and he stepped out. Just one look down over those upturned faces, and George Washington turned as gray as ashes. He closed his eyes and sank into a chair behind him.

"Those people!" he thought. How could he face them, when they expected so much of him and he was sure to fail! But for a man whose duty lay before him there was no turning back. Quickly he pulled himself together, rose to his feet and, placing his hand on the Bible, repeated the words of the vow:

"I do solemnly swear that I will faithfully execute the office of President of the United States, and will to the best of my ability preserve, protect and defend the Constitution of the United States."

His voice had not wavered. In the street below the people cheered: "Long live George Washington, President of the United States!"

VI

WHEN GEORGE WASHINGTON WAS

President

Events that occurred in the World

★★★ Vermont, Tennessee and Kentucky became States.

ALEXANDER HAMILTON was Secretary of the Treasury

JOHN ADAMS was Vice President, and then elected President.

FEDERAL CITY

VIRGINIA

THOMAS JEFFERSON was Secretary of State

DR. EDWARD JENNER Discovered the way to prevent **SMALL POX**

WASHINGTON laid the cornerstone for the new United States capitol

1793

The **COTTON GIN** was invented by **ELI WHITNEY** 1792

ROBERT FULTON Drew this first idea for a Steam Boat and wrote James Watt about an Engine.

The **ROSETTA STONE** key to Egypt's picture writing, was unearthed 1799

EMPEROR CH'IEN LUNG received England's first ambassador to China, and replied to George III

and what other People were doing

when Washington was President

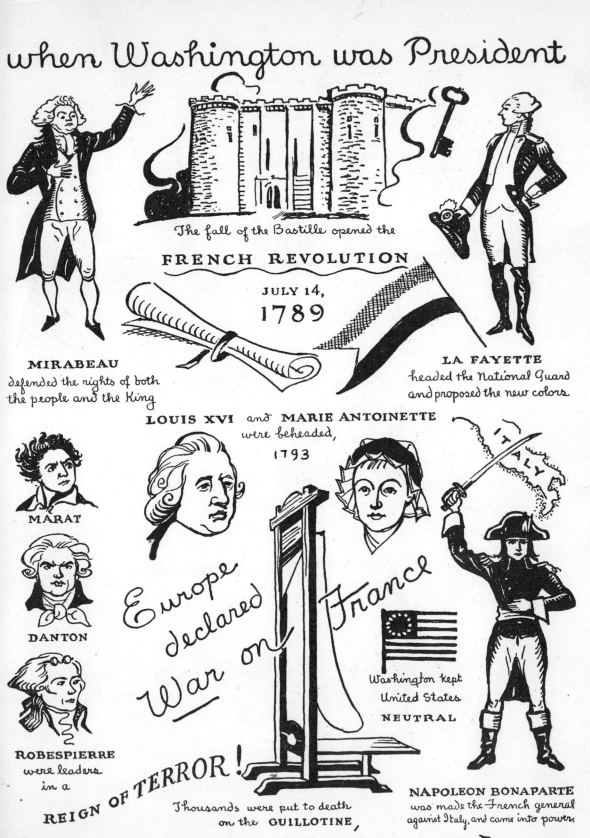

The fall of the Bastille opened the

FRENCH REVOLUTION

JULY 14,
1789

MIRABEAU
defended the rights of both
the people and the King

LA FAYETTE
headed the National Guard
and proposed the new colors

LOUIS XVI and MARIE ANTOINETTE
were beheaded,
1793

MARAT

DANTON

ROBESPIERRE
were leaders
in a

REIGN OF TERROR!

Europe
declared
War on France

Thousands were put to death
on the GUILLOTINE,

Washington kept
United States
NEUTRAL

NAPOLEON BONAPARTE
was made the French general
against Italy, and came into power.

between the Years 1789 and 1799

Versailles

1 The Palace
2 The Avenue leading to Paris
3 The Court where the mob gathered
4 The Church where the Delegates assembled
5 The Hall where the National Assembly met
6 The Tennis Court
7 The Grand Trianon
8 The Petit Trianon
9 Marie Antoinette's play "farm"

VICTORY FOR THE THIRD ESTATE

AY 1, 1789, THE DAY AFTER George Washington was in-
augurated President, was the day that Louis XVI set for
a meeting of the States-General or National Assembly
in France, though it actually convened a few days later.

Summoning of a States-General caused great excitement among the
people, for it called for delegates from the middle class as well as from
the nobility and the clergy—all three classes, or three Estates, as they
were called. Not since 1614 had delegates been summoned from the
bourgeois, or third estate. So it is not surprising that curious crowds
from Paris and all the surrounding towns flocked to Versailles the night
before the great event, to be there on time for the opening ceremonies.

Mirabeau

As soon as the first rays of the sun touched the gold cross on the Church of Our Lady, people in the windows and on the roofs near by could watch the delegates begin to gather, while those on the terraces near the palace saw the royal family as it started for the church to meet them.

High-stepping horses with jewelled harnesses and waving plumes drew the golden coach, sinside of which, against its scarlet cushions, could be seen the King. "Vive le roi! Long live the King!" the people cheered. Another golden chariot followed. The Queen. A dead silence fell; not a voice raised as it moved slowly past.

The Queen was again humiliated as she sat beside the King, facing the delegates. "There is the victim," whispered one man at the sight of her white face. In contrast, the King appeared unmoved. As for the Master of Ceremonies, he was almost bursting with importance as he indicated with his staff just where, according to rank, each nobleman and clergyman should be seated. During that time the third estate were huddled together in a sort of "dog house" or vestibule outside the door. Two hours and a half, it was, before the King could open the meeting.

Even then the meeting could not get down to business, because the King had made no mention in that speech of how the three orders were to vote, whether it was to be as one body or as three. According to the ancient custom, each of the estates had voted separately. But since the nobles and the clergy were sure to vote alike, the third estate said that it would always be two votes against their one, and insisted that the States-General should vote as a whole. Eight weeks went by debating that point. Finally some of the poor parish priests joined with the third estate and together they made the daring announcement that *they* were now the National Assembly. The answer to that was that three days later they found the doors of the meeting hall locked and guarded by the King's soldiers. Where then could they meet? Some one suggested a large hall used for indoor tennis. So there they rushed, lifted their president to the table and surging around him took the famous Oath of the Tennis Court: "Never will we separate," they swore, "until a Constitution for this Kingdom shall be established."

Three days later the three estates were called to a meeting in the original hall. The King appeared. He ordered the three estates to meet separately, and then departed.

"You have heard the King's order," said the Master of Ceremonies. "His Majesty requests that the members of the third estate withdraw."

Then up rose Mirabeau, one of the leaders. Mirabeau, a man with head and hair like a lion, but behind whose shaggy brows there was a brilliant mind. A nobleman born, who had been disinherited, whose life had been a scandal, whose own father had four times thrown him into prison, but who for forty years had written and fought against tyranny. That was the man who now rose and did not fear to defend the rights of the third estate which he represented.

"Go tell your master," he said, "that we are here by the will of the people and shall not leave except at the point of the bayonet."

"They wish to remain?" repeated Louis XVI. "Well, let them."

So the three estates were told to meet and vote together. That victory won, the Assembly then appointed a committee to draw up a constitution. Two weeks later La Fayette proposed a Declaration of Rights as a preamble to the Constitution and also as a guide in drafting it.

"Every man," it read, "is born with certain inalienable rights, freedom of thought, protection of his honor and his life, . . . the pursuit of happiness, resistance to oppression," and so forth.

His draft was patterned after the American Declaration of Independence. Revised, perfected and enlarged upon, it became the since famous French Declaration of the Rights of Man.

La Fayette was full of enthusiasm as to what it would accomplish.

"For the people to love liberty all they need is to know it," he exclaimed. "For them to obtain freedom all they need is to deserve it." How little he dreamed then that this liberty was going to be won by the people, misused by them and so lost again in bloodshed and horror!

July 14th

1789

"TO THE BASTILLE"

EACH DAY SINCE the States-General had assembled, Paris had received news of what was happening at Versailles. Good news and bad news, rumors true and rumors false, followed fast upon each other, each day more and more exciting. Hardly had the good news of the victory of the third estate been received, than the bad news had come that the King had sent for companies of foreign soldiers. They were already marching in Versailles.

"Foreign soldiers! What does that mean?" the people asked.

It meant that the National Assembly was in danger, said the next messenger. Twelve of the leaders were going to be hanged. La Fayette was to be first and then Mirabeau.

What if the King sent those foreign soldiers into Paris? was the

294

next terrifying thought. "What would we do then?" the people cried.

"We'd arm," shouted a young man, one night. Another, wild with excitement, jumped upon a café table. "To arms!" he shouted.

"Aux armes!" shouted the crowd, rushing out to the hot street. As they went surging along, more crowds took up the cry. From every crooked street and corner it was echoed, as the rabble came rushing out, seizing guns, grabbing sticks, stones, whatever they could lay their hands on in their search for weapons.

"To the Bastille!" screamed some one. "The commander of the Bastille has been ordered to turn guns on the city." Up went the cry, "To the Bastille!" "Down with the Bastille!" So to the old fortress they rushed, cut the giant chains that held the drawbridge, swarmed across, overpowered the few guards, murdered the commander, released the prisoners and began to tear down the walls, which they continued until in a few days not one single old gray stone was left upon another.

That was what happened July 14, 1789, in the fight for liberty, and that is how July 14 became the great French national holiday.

That night in Versailles, twelve miles away, Louis XVI was sound asleep, full of food and fresh air from a good day's hunting. The horrified chamberlain woke him up.

"Your Majesty! The Bastille has been taken. The commander murdered! His head! They are carrying it through the streets on a pike!"

"What do you bring me?" said Louis, rubbing his eyes, still half asleep, "the news of a revolt?"

"No, sire, it is a revolution!"

"A revolution?" queried Louis. "What made the people revolt? . . . Could it have been the foreign soldiers . . . ?"

The next day he assured the National Assembly that he had not the slightest intention of sending the foreign soldiers against his own people. Thereupon the Assembly appointed La Fayette to go to Paris and report to the city council what the King had said. In the Hôtel de Ville, the city hall, La Fayette found the council at work designing a new form of government for the city of Paris. That no such outbreak might occur again, they were planning to organize the soldiers into a National Guard to guarantee law and order. "Vive le La Fayette!" they cheered when he delivered the King's message. Then they realized that here was the very man they needed to head the soldiers. So La Fayette remained in Paris as commander of the new National Guard.

"I have now the utmost power my heart could wish," thought La Fayette the following day, as, amid cheering crowds, he escorted the King to the city hall, when Louis XVI came in person to Paris.

The King was cheered by the city council when he told them he approved of the changes they were making, and he was also cheered by the people as he later appeared on the balcony of the Hôtel de Ville.

"Long live the King!" they cried as they saw the fat man standing in the hot sun patient and obliging, with a cockade of red and blue, the city's colors, stuck up in his hat.

Red and blue are the colors of Paris, thought La Fayette, white with golden lilies is the royal flag. Why not have a new symbol now that will combine them both? A tri-colored badge of red, blue and white, representing both the King and the people.

"I bring you here a new cockade," he said as he later presented it to the city council. They approved, and so the red, white and blue cockade was adopted as the national symbol, and red, white and blue became the flag of France.

The whole world heard of the fall of the Bastille. It was most dramatic. It was spectacular and noisy. And it was truly the climax of the rebellion against tyranny, but in itself it accomplished little. Similar uprising among the peasants who attacked and tore down the castles of their lords and masters was also rebellion, but not the real revolution.

The real French revolution took place quietly. Three weeks later in a night meeting of the National Assembly, traditions and evils that had existed for centuries in France were wiped out in a single night. Generously, for the good of the country, the great lords signed away ancient feudal rights and privileges that had come down to them from their grandfathers and great-great-grandfathers since the Middle Ages. Their lands, they said, were no longer to be exempt from taxes, no more feudal dues were to be collected from their tenants. Not even the titles of nobility were any longer to be used. No longer would one man be a marquis and another man a serf. There was to be no more unfair imprisonment. From then on Justice and Equality were to be the rule. Resolution after resolution was proposed and passed and the session closed with a Te Deum in the Palace chapel. No one who was present ever forgot that thrilling meeting. There occurred that night the most complete social revolution, and the greatest, it is said, that had ever taken place in so short a time in the history of the world.

OFF WITH "THE BAKER" TO PARIS

MARIE ANTOINETTE it was, who had insisted that the King
send for the foreign soldiers. Descended from a long line
of absolute monarchs, she believed that rebellious subjects
should be punished like impudent children who defied
their parents. The National Assembly she considered a "pack of idiots
and rascals." As for the rebellious riff-raff that had stormed the Bastille,
they were beneath contempt.

That "riff-raff" of Paris returned her contempt with hate. They
blamed her for all their suffering. Starving mothers standing in long
lines outside the bakery windows blamed her because they could get
no bread. They cursed her when their little ones clutched at their skirts
and cried that they were hungry, or died in their arms. It was no task
for agitators to stir those hungry people into action.

One bleak October morning when the food supply had been held
up for days, word passed among the people that the King and Queen
had given a great banquet the night before for the foreign soldiers.

"Food that belongs to us," cried the women of Paris, and in a
mob thousands set out on foot for Versailles to demand that food.

Marie Antoinette was sitting alone in the garden of the little Trianon, idly watching the yellow leaves drifting along the path, when toward noon a page brought word that a mob of angry women dragging cannon was on its way from Paris. The Queen went back to the palace immediately. Clouds had gathered and it was about to rain by the time the King arrived. He had been hunting and was not at all pleased to have his sport, as he said, "interrupted by events." Besides, what could he do about it? He looked vaguely from one minister to another until it was too late to take any advice. By dusk the hoarse voices of the mob could be heard approaching with the cry of "Bread!"

In no time the court outside was filled with women. Muddy, soaked to the skin, they held their bedraggled skirts over their heads to keep off the rain, though rivulets ran down the lank strands of black hair that hung about their faces. Soon, six of them were inside the palace. Accompanied by the head of the National Assembly, they sloshed up the glistening marble steps in their muddy shoes, to meet the King.

Bread was what they wanted? asked the King. Certainly they should have bread. Yes, and meat too! The six left, surprised and satisfied. But the mob outside were scornful.

"Easy promises; let's see the bread. Let's take the 'Baker' King and his wife to Paris and the food will go along you may be sure!"

The mob milled about the streets or slept where they could that night. If the Queen slept at all she was wakened at dawn by the sound of a shot, followed by the cry "To the Queen's apartments." Then came the sound of running feet, a guard's dying scream: "Save the Queen!" and the wrenching and crashing of wood as doors were battered down. Quickly throwing a shawl about her night robe, Marie Antoinette opened a secret panel, and ran barefooted down the dark, narrow passageway to the King's apartments. There in a few seconds the governess brought the Dauphin and the Princess. La Fayette arrived. Already the mob in the court below were calling for the King. They cheered as Louis XVI did their bidding and stepped out upon the balcony.

"The Queen," they cried, then, "The Queen to the balcony!"

"Madame, it is necessary," said La Fayette. Marie Antoinette was white with rage, but, giving a hand to each of the children, she stepped out and faced the crowd. Muskets were pointed toward her.

"No children," screamed the mob, "the Queen alone." Expecting to be shot, she pushed the children back and stood alone. Touched by her courage, La Fayette stepped quickly forward, bent and kissed her hand, and from below came the surprising cry, "Long live the Queen!"

That afternoon the strange procession started.

"We bring them back, 'The Baker,' the 'Baker's' wife . . . the 'Baker's boy.' Ha," the women laughed and shouted, pointing their dirty fingers at the royal coach. Some of them rode astride the cannon, some swarmed along beside the carts piled high with sacks of flour. Some marched arm in arm with the more ragged of the National Guards, each man with a loaf of bread carried high on the point of his bayonet.

Crowded together in the slowly moving coach rode the royal family. It was dark when they reached the old palace of the Tuileries. Its gloomy corridors were full of echoes. The little Dauphin was tired.

"I don't like this ugly place, Mother," he whimpered.

"Louis XIV, a great King, once lived here," said his mother proudly. "You, my son, must not be more particular than he."

"Make the best of it," yawned his father, lying down.

The National Assembly now also left Versailles and moved to **Paris**.

Nine months later, on July 14, 1790, the city celebrated the first anniversary of their storming of the Bastille. The King then ratified the new Constitution and swore to uphold it. Thus France became a *Constitutional Monarchy*.

AMERICA AND THE KEY TO THE BASTILLE

GEORGE WASHINGTON, President of the United States, held in his hand the great wrought-iron key to the Bastille which he had just received as a present from La Fayette. It had come with a letter from Thomas Paine, who was then in Europe. "When he (General La Fayette) mentioned the present he intended for you," the letter read, "my heart leaped with joy. That the principles of America opened the Bastille is not to be doubted."

Washington's heart, however, had not been especially filled with joy at the sight of the key, for the interests that stirred his heart lay not in France but in America. With his note of thanks he enclosed for La Fayette a pair of silver shoe buckles.

"Not," he said, "for the value of the thing, but because they are the manufacture of this city." Those buckles, showing what was now being manufactured in the United States, seemed more important to its President than an old French key forged in the Middle Ages.

From his first day in office, Washington had applied himself diligently to his new work and centered his whole interest upon it. He felt a grave lack of education for the great task which he had undertaken, but began apparently with the simple determination to act cautiously and rely upon his good common sense to make as few mistakes as possible. At the same time he fully appreciated the abilities of other men, and regardless of personal likes or dislikes, tried to appoint to office in each case the man best suited for the job. These are the appointments he made for his cabinet:

Secretary of War, General Henry Knox

Secretary of State, Thomas Jefferson

Secretary of the Treasury, Alexander Hamilton

There were just those three main departments into which the government was then divided, and the nation itself, according to the first census taken in 1790, numbered only 3,929,000 people.

from a portrait

Alexander Hamilton had risen very fast since that day, seventeen years before, when he had landed in America, a poor unknown orphan from the West Indies. Now, seated at his mahogany desk in his New York law office, in white satin waistcoat and lace ruffles, he tried to forget the days spent in the old island counting-house.

For he was now one of the aristocrats, the father of four young Hamiltons, whose grandfather was Philip Schuyler. Eliza, his wife, idolized her young husband and like all the ladies found his sparkling eyes and gay wit irresistible. His tendency to overwork, however, gave her constant worry, for though he was not very strong, Alexander Hamilton possessed that rare ability to work hard for endless hours at a time and still keep his interest keen, which is three fourths of genius.

As soon as he was appointed treasurer, he set to work on his plans at once. Always completely sure of his own ideas, and positive that those who disagreed with him must be either jealous or stupid, he went ahead without consulting any one.

His first plan was based on his belief in honesty. Aside from being scrupulously honest himself, Alexander Hamilton also knew that honesty paid. Long ago in the counting-house he had learned that those customers who paid their debts were trusted again. So, said he:

"States like individuals who observe their engagements (that is, pay their debts) are respected and trusted, while the reverse is true of those who pursue the opposite conduct." Therefore, first and foremost, and absolutely imperative:

The United States must pay its debts!

The soldiers who had fought, the people who had furnished goods for war, the foreign nations who had loaned money, in short, all to whom the new government was indebted, both at home and abroad, must be paid. He made a report, and had the exact figures to a penny:

$ 11,710,378.62   was the foreign debt.

$ 42,414,085.94   was the home debt.

$ 54,124,464.56   total.

More than fifty-four million dollars! A staggering sum for the little nation to pay.

"It is impossible!" exclaimed some of the people. "The nation will be ruined."

The nation would be ruined in the eyes of the world, if the debts were not paid, said Alexander Hamilton. Then he showed conclusively how it could be managed, and so in spite of objections won his way, and established the United States as an honest and a creditable nation.

State Debts — The Capitol

Then he brought forward his second idea:

The United States must pay the State debts also.

That suggestion caused a terrific storm of protest from those states which had already paid their debts. Why should they now have to help pay the debts of other states?

"If South Carolina and Massachusetts have got themselves involved in debt, that's too bad. They'll just have to get out the best they can," said the delegates of Virginia, and also many others.

That attitude showed plainly that the states were still jealous of one another and unable to get the idea that they were *united*.

Because he was not a native of any state, Alexander Hamilton could take an impartial view and think only of the united nation. At the same time he saw how he could make use of that very jealousy to gain his point. Just at the opportune moment, Thomas Jefferson arrived.

Thomas Jefferson had left France shortly after the royal family had been taken to Paris. He was in Monticello for Christmas, and then after Patsy's wedding to her cousin Thomas Randolph he had set out the first of March for New York to take up his new duties.

On the way he had stopped in Philadelphia to see Benjamin Franklin and give the old gentleman word of his many friends in France. Franklin, then bed-ridden, was distressed over the violence of the revolution but was eager to hear all details, still so fresh and vivid in his visitor's mind. For it was less than a year since Thomas Jefferson had walked among the ruins of the Bastille, three days after it had been torn down, and had rejoiced with La Fayette that the principles of liberty and equality were henceforth to govern in France.

"How can we in America help but rejoice?" asked Thomas Jefferson. "We who were first to establish a government founded on the will of the people?"

With those feelings, he bade farewell to Benjamin Franklin, and left for New York City, where he found to his amazement what he called a "republican court" established. To his dismay, he found the people of the new republic based on the principles of equality aping the pomp and ceremony of a royal court! The President rode out on state occasions to Federal Hall in a magnificent cream-colored coach drawn by six horses. The newspaper, which no longer called itself *The Gazette,* but *The Court Journal,* spoke of the President's wife as "Lady Washington" and actually referred to the President's reception as a "levee," taking the word from those getting-out-of-bed receptions of the French kings. It was astonishing to Thomas Jefferson.

It was not entirely in accord with Washington's ideas, either. A certain amount of form and dignity seemed necessary to Washington, to inspire the common people with respect for the new government, but with undue pomp and ceremony he had no patience. The year before, after Martha had arrived in May, they had held the first presidential reception and to Washington's disgust, when the company was assembled, the doors had been flung open wide by flunkies, and his aide had boomed out like a court chamberlain: "The President of the United States!" Washington had been furious. "You've taken me in once," he stormed afterward, "but you'll never do it again." Accordingly, after that the receptions were more simple, though they were always dignified and formal, too much so to accord with Jefferson's strictly democratic ideas.

One May afternoon shortly after his arrival, Jefferson walked to the President's house on Broadway for an informal reception, and there met the Secretary of the Treasury. It was the first time Thomas Jefferson and Alexander Hamilton had met. They left at the same time, the small, dapper young man, and the tall, loose-jointed older man with the sandy hair and the turned-up nose, walking down the street together. Mr. Hamilton seized the immediate opportunity to speak to Mr. Jefferson of what was uppermost in his mind: the Bill for the Assumption of State Debts. Briefly and to the point he sketched in the situation. There were two questions under consideration at that time. One was, should the nation assume the debts of the states? The other was, where should the permanent capital be located? Among the southern states Virginia, particularly, was opposed to the assumption of state debts. But she was eager also to have the national capital located in her territory. On the other hand, the northern states, who also would be glad to have the capital, threatened to secede if the Assumption Bill was not passed. The union itself was in grave danger, Mr. Hamilton believed, if some satisfactory solution could not be arrived at.

Jefferson preferred to see the states take care of their own debts, but not at the expense of the union. "To see our credit burst and vanish and the states separate to take care every one of itself" was a tragedy which he could not contemplate.

A few days later at a dinner in Jefferson's house, the subject was discussed again, and very shortly thereafter the bargain agreed upon. Jefferson would secure enough southern votes to pass the Assumption Bill. In return, the south would have the nation's permanent capital. For ten years the temporary capital was to be in Philadelphia. After that, Federal City, as it was then called, was to be in some district ten miles square on the Potomac River, to be selected by President Washington, as "most central to all parts of the union."

So Hamilton won, and by that bill won the support of big business men for the new government, and made it stronger and more centralized.

At his success the young man was so elated that he behaved much as if he were the Prime Minister to a king, which truthfully he would have preferred to be. A monarchy like that of England seemed to Alexander Hamilton a form of government superior to a republic.

In 1790 came Alexander Hamilton's third proposition:

The United States must have a National Bank!

That opened a hot argument, as to whether the Constitution gave Congress the power to establish a National Bank, or whether it did not.

Hamilton said it did, and quoted the 8th section of Article 1, since then called the "Elastic Clause," which said that Congress had the power "To make all laws which shall be necessary and proper for carrying into execution the foregoing powers."

Jefferson said Congress had no such power and cited Article 10 of the Amendments which said that "the powers not delegated to the United States by the Constitution, nor prohibited by it to the States, are reserved to the States respectively or to the people."

The arguments between the two men grew very bitter. Washington listened carefully and weighed the arguments, and in the end did not veto the Bank bill.

That victory, which established a National Bank, gave still more power to the government, which Hamilton strenuously favored, and Jefferson opposed. Jefferson feared that Hamilton and the Federalists leaned too much toward monarchy, that their principles put in force would break down the republic, and make lords of the rich men in the country. Hamilton, on the other hand, feared that Jefferson's democratic ideas about the rights of the people would put the government in the hands of an irresponsible mob. Both ideas were right in part. Both were necessary to check each other, for it is that balance between the two extremes, which began at this time, that has made the United States what it is today. The principles of Alexander Hamilton made the nation strong and united. The ideals of Thomas Jefferson made it free and democratic.

Washington was distressed to see this argument over the National Bank and the rights of Congress grow bitter, and feared that it might divide the whole country into two parties.

As he had feared, the people did split into two parties, but it was the French Revolution that caused the real break, not the argument over the National Bank. Most of the people didn't care much whether there was a National Bank or not. Most of them, outside of the cities, had never seen a bank. If they ever had any money, they kept it in a cookie-jar or a sock. As for technical points in the Constitution, they were beyond their comprehension. But troubles of the people in France were something that every one could understand and appreciate.

It was Thomas Paine who again started the excitement, with a pamphlet called *The Rights of Man*. It had been written by him in England, and was an answer to Edmund Burke who had written an essay damning the whole French Revolution.

"Oh! what a revolution!" cried Edmund Burke. "What a revolution! The glory of Europe is extinguished forever!" he wailed, "shuddering with horror" as he contemplated the acts of the "swinish multitude." With pride he referred to the government of England, as an example that France might have done well to copy, and where, he was happy to say, they still looked "with awe to kings, with affection to Parliaments, and with respect to nobility."

Thomas Paine replied:

"When it can be said in any country in the world: My poor are happy; neither ignorance nor distress is to be found among them; my jails are empty of prisoners, my streets of beggars; the aged are not in want, the taxes are not oppressive; when these things can be said, then may that country boast of its constitution and its government."

England had suppressed the pamphlet and declared Paine an outlaw. James Madison secured the first single copy to arrive in America for Thomas Jefferson, who had heard of it and had been eager to read it.

Thomas Jefferson included a short note when he sent it to the printer:

"I am extremely pleased to find it will be reprinted here," he wrote. "I have no doubt our citizens will rally a second time around the standard of *Common Sense*."

And when it was printed, most of the people all over the country did "rally a second time." Their sympathy, like that of Jefferson, was with the people of France who were making a fight for freedom. "Their cause is ours," they said, remembering how short a time it was since they too had been trying to get rid of the tyranny of a king.

That was the feeling of the small tradespeople and the farmers, but not of the bankers and big merchants of New York and Philadelphia, nor of Alexander Hamilton, nor of John Adams.

"Too many Frenchmen, like too many Americans, panting for equality of persons and property," blustered John Adams. He wrote articles, as did also young John Quincy, denouncing Paine, and the French Revolution, and upholding Edmund Burke and the government of England.

Thomas Jefferson had not expected the pamphlet to start such a commotion and was pleasantly surprised to see the people taking such an active interest again in the principles of equality and liberty, upon which the Declaration of Independence had been based.

Thomas Paine had dedicated the pamphlet *The Rights of Man* to George Washington, who had replied courteously but with no great enthusiasm. Theories and principles of equality and liberty didn't seem as important to that practical man as how his country, based on those ideas, was prospering. What was happening in France was of far less interest to him than the factories and workshops of New England, the farms of Pennsylvania, the shipyards of New Hampshire, the fisheries along the coast, the rice and tobacco fields of South Carolina. Whenever he could get away he took long dusty trips in his coach to see for himself just what was the condition of the country, and how the people were prospering under the new form of government.

George Washington's heart and interests lay in the United States.

I N MASSACHUSETTS George Washington had visited a "Cotton Manufactory" which he was glad to see was "carrying on with spirit."

"In this Manufactory," he wrote in his diary, "they have the new Invented Carding and Spinning Machines" and a "number of Looms and the Cotton stuffs w'ch they turn out seem excellent of their kind."

On his trip to the three southernmost states, however, he had very little to say in the diary about Cotton, for in 1791 cotton had not yet become the great crop of the South.

The "new machines" were those invented by three Englishmen, Hargreaves, Arkwright, and Cartwright, about the middle of the century, and by now were beginning to take the place of spinning and weaving by hand. They had so speeded up the manufacture of thread and cloth that the supply of raw cotton lagged far behind.

In 1792, the year after Washington travelled through the South, Eli Whitney was graduated from Yale University and went to teach school in Georgia. He found the cotton planters there discouraged.

"Easy enough to raise and pick the cotton," they told him. "But the trouble comes in tryin' to get out the seeds."

A good Negro, they said, could pick about two hundred pounds of cotton in one day, but then it took another whole day for a man to clean the seeds out of just one of those pounds.

The new teacher from the North was very skillful at rigging up useful gadgets, and set out to see what kind of a machine he could make that would take out the cotton seeds.

So it was that Eli Whitney invented the Cotton Gin, a simple little machine, but one which marked another step forward from the age of handwork and homespun into the coming age of machines and factories.

BEWARE THE TYRANTS!

IN FRANCE the revolution still continued. Even though the nobles had sworn away their unjust privileges for the good of the nation, even though France now had a constitution, and the conservative members of the third estate were satisfied, the revolution still went on. And why? Because of false play by the King, who accepted the Constitution and then plotted with the Queen and the refugee nobles to destroy it and re-establish the old absolute monarchy.

Because, too, of spite and revenge stirred up in the people by violent agitators who twisted the word liberty into strange meanings.

Marat, one of the most violent, issued horrible warnings.

"Beware of the tyrant," he cried. "Our liberty is in danger! The King should be put under lock and key!"

This Marat, a small, dark man with a wild look in his eye, was such a troublemaker that the city council of Paris had ordered his arrest. But though he had to hide underground and live like a rat in the basements and sewers, his voice was heard. He kept on writing his paper *Friend of the People* and warning them to beware.

"We are betrayed," he cried in 1791. "There is a plot on foot to smuggle the King and Queen out of France." That was the truth.

By spring of 1791, thousands of nobles had fled from France. Those over the Rhine in Prussia and Austria were urging the King and Queen to try and make their escape and join them. Louis XVI hesitated, as usual. Marie Antoinette was positive.

"It is the only path open to us, if we are to escape destruction," she declared, sensing that the masses were no longer under control.

Mirabeau, who had defended the rights of the King as well as the people, had died in March. La Fayette, always condemned by the Queen as a friend of the people, was now also condemned by the people as too great a friend of the King, and had lost all power over them.

"We must attempt to escape," the Queen kept urging the King, and finally Louis XVI gave his consent to the dangerous undertaking.

Marie Antoinette then turned for help to a young Swedish noble-man, who loved her. Count Axel Ferson was his name.

By June the count had everything ready. Money, false passports, wigs, costumes for disguise, all had been smuggled into the Tuileries. Around midnight of the twentieth, the royal family stole from the palace, and rode away dressed in their strange costumes. The governess went as a Russian noble lady travelling with her two children, the Queen in a gray dress and violet veil went as the governess and the King in a green coat and round flat hat was the valet.

Companies of soldiers had orders to meet them near the border, and as Axel Ferson bade the travellers farewell he felt satisfied that he had done all that it was possible for him to do. Unfortunately he had done too much. In his eagerness to give his beloved every comfort he had had a new coach built for the occasion, a splendid affair, so big that it held not only eight or ten people, but a cabinet for the silver dishes, a wine cellar and even a small toilet seat! A plain public carriage might have reached the border in safety, but that huge ark, shiny as a

312

pumpkin, drawn by eight horses, excited the curiosity of all who saw it as it went rumbling along in the early morning.

A little past noon, not far from the border, it came to a dusty stop in front of a posting house. Across the road, Drouet, the master of another posting house, looked out as the strange coach drove up to his rival's door, and suddenly saw a fat face appear in its window. Despite the gray wig and the round servant's hat, that fat face looked very familiar. And that long, bent-over, crooked nose! Who but the King himself had a nose like that? To make sure, the man pulled a gold piece out of his pocket. One glance at the King's face engraved on it confirmed his suspicions. The identical face of the man in the coach!

Saddling his horse, Drouet rode at breakneck speed to Varennes, the next village, to give the alarm. By dark, when the royal coach came lumbering up, the men of the village were ready and waiting.

"Halt!" they cried, "and show your passports." Surrounding the coach, they escorted the suspicious passengers to the house of the village mayor. Above his shop in small stuffy rooms smelling of garlic and sausage, the royal family was forced to spend the night. Louis XVI found comfort in a huge chunk of cheese and a bottle of wine. But Marie Antoinette just sat with set lips hour after hour, straining her ears for the sound of the soldiers who did not come.

Shortly after the sun was up, guarded by officers sent from the National Assembly, the King and Queen left on their humiliating journey back to the city. In every village crowds gathered to hiss and hoot, but when finally they rode through the boulevards of Paris, the people stood in silence. Government signs posted in plain sight read:

"Whoever applauds the King shall be flogged; whoever insults him shall be hanged."

"King?" said the fat man in the flat hat wearily, as he looked out at the signs and the people. "There is no longer a king in France."

The white-faced woman in the violet veil also knew that they were doomed, but she held her head high and her spirit remained firm. "We must maintain a proper bearing to the last," said Marie Antoinette.

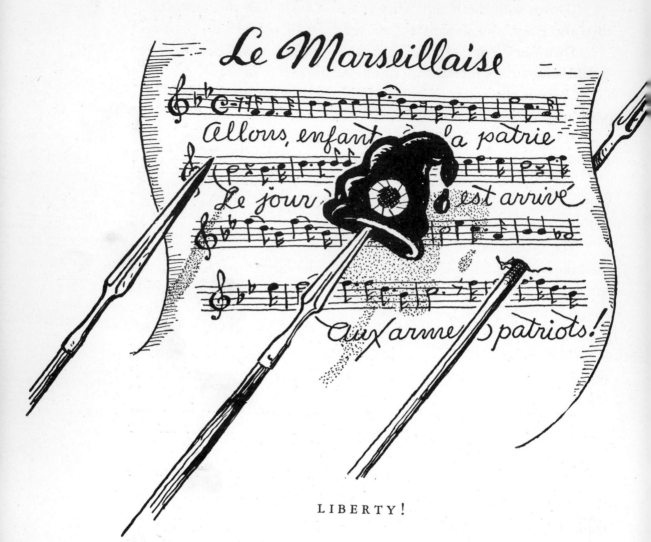

LIBERTY!

"DOWN WITH THE KING!" now became the cry of the radicals, and now for the first time there was talk of doing away with the King and the monarchy and making France a republic. Bright red "liberty" caps were seen on the streets of Paris, caps like those that slaves in ancient Phrygia had been allowed to wear after their masters set them free. Now that old red pointed cap, trimmed with the new red, white and blue cockade, was worn by the revolutionists to show that from now on France would be a land of free men.

314

"Down with the King!" they cried. "Down with the aristocrats!" they also cried, and seized and put hundreds of nobles into prison.

Then came a threat from Prussia and Austria combined, that they would send armies into France to restore the power of the King.

"Beware the tyrants!" cried Marat, ready with his warning. "Beware of your enemies. Attack them before they destroy you!"

"Down with tyranny everywhere!" shouted other leaders, frantic to spread their new-found ideas of liberty to other lands.

The National Assembly also felt that the threat from outside nations was intolerable and forced the King (still the head of the nation) to declare war on Austria.

The Queen, and the royalists, hoping Austria would win, were as well pleased as the revolutionists by that declaration. The Queen, acting quickly, got hold of the secret plans for the French campaign and smuggled them out to the Austrians.

The people became suspicious.

"We are betrayed," the leaders told them. "Behind those windows," they said, pointing to the Tuileries, "they are contriving means of thrusting us back into slavery."

The King, they were told, was not upholding the rights of the people. He had even dismissed some of the members of the National Assembly.

"Traitor!" they cried. "He should be taught a lesson."

One night five thousand workingmen, led by a red-faced brewer, made their way to the palace. Brandishing pikes, swinging their red caps in the air, they strode through the gateway, and, brushing aside the guards, on up to the royal apartment till they stood facing the King.

"There, put that on!" sneered one rough fellow, pushing out his red cap on the end of a pike.

"Drink that to our health!" jeered another, thrusting forward a half empty bottle of wine. Louis XVI put on the cap, drank the wine, and stood taking their jeers for three hours and a half till they finally called it a day, turned on their heels and went lumbering home.

This insult to the King brought Prussia into the war. The Duke of Brunswick, the commander, sent a notice to Paris that if any harm should be done to the King or any one of the royal family he would march into Paris and completely destroy the city!

"Will you people of France let foreign tyrants meddle in your affairs and tell you what to do?" the leaders challenged the people as they plotted another uprising against the King.

Excited, angry people rushed in from all the suburbs. On August 6, six hundred sun-browned men from Marseilles came tramping into Paris to the thrilling rhythm of a new marching song, "The Marseillaise," which was later to become the French national anthem.

With the men of Marseilles in the city, the day to storm the Tuileries, the second uprising plotted against the King, was set for the morning of August 10.

Inside the palace the royal family had known for many anxious days that the attack would come. The night before they had heard the ominous booming of the bell ring out the signal. That morning, beside the National Guard, eight hundred Swiss Guards were stationed in the courtyard ready to defend the King, but up to the last moment, the King couldn't make up his mind whether to defend himself against the mob or let them come. He finally appeared in the balcony.

"You will not fire on your assailants until they have fired on you, I think," he told them uncertainly.

Somewhere lost in the crowd, a shabby young artillery lieutenant by the name of Buonaparte, who still had his way to make, heard the King's remark and sneered at such incompetence. "A few shots and the mob would scatter," he said tersely.

Only a short time after the King went inside the palace, he heard the sound of the mob at the gates. Then came a breathless messenger from the Assembly:

"Sir, your Majesty has no time to lose. The only safe place for you is in the Hall of the National Assembly." So Louis XVI, Marie Antoinette and the royal family, forced to accept protection from the Assembly which they despised, left the palace at once. And never to return.

Meanwhile the Swiss Guards were forgotten. No one remembered to change their orders, so they stood bravely against that mob of thousands and died, almost to a man, defending an empty palace!

Three days later, about sunset, workmen going home in their red caps had the pleasure of seeing their King and Queen driven as prisoners to the Temple, an ancient fortress much like the old Bastille.

That very night the guillotine, a new machine for cutting off people's heads, was moved to the public square, and Marat came up from underground.

On September 2 news came that the Prussians had reached Verdun, the last fort on the way to Paris. Terror struck the city. Tocsins of alarm clanged from the bell towers and a great black flag hung from the city hall bearing the words "Country in Danger."

More troops were ordered to the front at once.

"What!" cried Marat, "send troops to the front and leave an army of aristocrats behind! Three thousand prisoners in this city who may escape, murder our wives and children and bring back the King!"

"We must strike these royalists with terror," cried another leader. "So long as they live we are in danger!"

So a wholesale murder of nobles or aristocrats took place. In four days twelve hundred were hacked to pieces. Those four days Marat's fanatic eyes burned bright and men in red liberty caps jostled each other to get a good view of the bloody heads, now no longer dangerous.

That was the September Massacre.

On September 21, word came that the advance of the Prussians had been stopped. So that danger too was over.

The next day, September 22, 1792, which was later to be spoken of as the first day of the Year 1 of Liberty, the Assembly proclaimed that royalty had been abolished in France and France was a *Republic*.

1 7 9 3

DEATH FOR LOUIS XVI

THE SEPTEMBER MASSACRE was viewed with horror by all conservative French people who were as much opposed to the tyranny of the mob as to the tyranny of the King.

That middle ground was dangerous, however. La Fayette, who had been stationed with the army outside of Paris, had sent letters of protest to the Assembly at the first insults offered the King. So he had been condemned by them as a royalist, and orders issued for his arrest. Escaping over the border, he was then seized as a revolutionist and put into prison by the Austrians at Olmütz.

In his letters to the Assembly, La Fayette had placed the blame for the violent deeds on the Jacobins, the most radical revolutionists.

"The Jacobin Club has caused all these disorders," he wrote.

The Jacobins had grown so powerful that they had overthrown the city council of Paris and set up a new one of their own called the Commune, and were now well on their way toward getting control of the whole National Assembly. Their leader at this time was Danton.

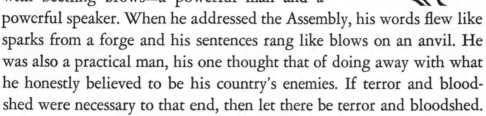

Danton was a lawyer, strong and coarse, with beetling brows—a powerful man and a powerful speaker. When he addressed the Assembly, his words flew like sparks from a forge and his sentences rang like blows on an anvil. He was also a practical man, his one thought that of doing away with what he honestly believed to be his country's enemies. If terror and bloodshed were necessary to that end, then let there be terror and bloodshed.

Opposed to the Jacobins were the Girondists, also a republican club but a very different kind of people. The Girondists were intellectual and romantic, with a beautiful young woman named Madame Roland as one of their leaders. They spent their days discussing how glorious life must have been in the old Roman republic or in ancient Greece, and schemed to establish just such a republic in France, so that they might wear the togas. They loathed the bloodthirsty Marat and abhorred the brutal Jacobins who had allowed the September Massacre.

The fight between the opposing clubs came to white heat over the question of what to do with the King now that he was in prison and no longer head of the nation. The Jacobins said the King should die. The Girondists voted against it. The Jacobins won, and the guillotine got its first royal victim. On January 21, 1793, Louis XVI mounted its steps to his death.

"Gentlemen," he said, "I am innocent of what I am accused. May my blood assure the happiness of the French." His voice was lost in the roll of drums as the knife rose, paused at the top and fell. The King's death plunged France into war with all of the neighboring countries. When the French beheaded their king, all the other kings made it their business to avenge that death, fearing that these revolutionary ideas might spread and their own heads be in danger. Also it appeared to their greedy eyes very much as though France might now be going to pieces, and if that happened they all wanted to be on hand to grab some of her territory.

So Fear and Greed, the two never-failing partners, again brought forth War! In 1793, England, Spain, Holland, Italy, in addition to Austria and Prussia, were at war with the Republic of France.

THE UNITED STATES PROCLAIMED NEUTRAL

GEORGE WASHINGTON began his second term that year of 1793. Sympathy for the French Revolution had then grown very strong in the United States; Liberty poles with red caps on top were to be seen in every small town square. It had also become the fashion to wear the tri-colored cockade and sing the "Marseillaise."

People now formed "republican" clubs, and in their enthusiasm even took to calling each other Citizen and Citizeness, as they had heard that the French were doing, now that their titles of nobility and distinction had been abolished.

On the other hand, the opposition of the Federalists to the revolution had also increased. "It was no more than might have been expected," they said when the news came that those French people whom they spoke of as the "filthy rabble" had beheaded their "noble" King.

320

"But if the King was a traitor he ought to be punished like any other man," said James Madison in his quiet way.

George Washington said nothing. He regretted that the King had been killed, but he was more distressed over the many settlers at home in America who were being killed by the Indians. His problem was how to settle the troubles of America, not of France.

Then came the news of war between France and England, and that divided the American people definitely into two parties: the Federalists who cheered England for trying to stamp out the revolution and its too radical ideas, and the Republican Democrats who wanted to join France in war and help save democracy for the world.

"Their cause is ours," said the Republican Democrats. "We owe them a debt of gratitude. We are in honor bound to fulfill our part of the treaty made with France when she helped us in 1778."

"That treaty no longer holds good," answered the Federalists. "That treaty was made with Louis XVI and not with the government that murdered him." And they went on cheering for England.

People of Philadelphia, while cheering for England, rehung their old portraits of George III, and even sang "God Save the King!" Meanwhile settlers on the frontier were crying: "Join the war with France. Make England give up the western forts."

"Why should England give up these forts," replied those who had been Tories during the revolution, "so long as our property has not been returned to us, according to the treaty of peace?"

And so the heated arguments continued. Young Robert Fulton, the inventor, who was then in Paris, wrote home that it had been much agitated there whether or not the Americans would join the French. But when the French ambassador "Citizen Genet" arrived in America, the feeling for France grew by leaps and bounds.

John Adams said that "ten thousand people in the streets of Philadelphia day after day threatened to drag Washington out of his house and effect a revolution in the government or compel it to declare war in favor of the French Revolution against England."

But though he heard the mob yelling outside, Washington was not frightened, nor was he confused. He looked straight at the one problem before him: what was best for the United States? What was the most sensible way to come to an understanding with England? Arbitration was the sensible answer. Going to war for any reason would be ridiculous and impracticable, and only make matters worse. Common sense said that the United States should remain neutral. Therefore in April Washington issued a neutrality proclamation.

At the same time he also sent an ambassador to England to see what compromise could be made. John Jay, the ambassador, gained promise of the forts, but in return for far too much, the people thought.

The neutrality proclamation had caused enough protest among them, but in 1795 news of the treaty which had been signed with the British brought a perfect storm of abuse down on Washington's head. "He's been made a fool of," the newspapers said. "He doesn't know his business." "Inefficient and treacherous," they called him.

Washington's friends spoke up to defend him, but he himself made no reply. He kept silent as he had done once before at Valley Forge when his enemies reviled him, and again, as it had been then, the storm lashed itself out and subsided.

Once more he had won. But it had been a gruelling battle for the man. He was gray and tired when it was over. When they wanted him to run for a third term, he refused. In his farewell speech he thanked the country for the many honors they had conferred on him, and the opportunity to be of service, and could only say that he had done the best that he could. He also said "the great rule of conduct for us to follow is to steer clear of permanent alliances with any portion of the foreign world" in so far as possible, although "taking care always to keep ourselves . . . on a respectably defensive position, we may safely trust to temporary alliances for extraordinary emergencies." He closed by saying that he was looking forward to the enjoyment, amid his fellow citizens, "of good laws under a free government, the happy reward," he trusted, "of their mutual cares, labors and dangers."

THE REIGN OF TERROR

Enemies of those violent revolutionists the Jacobins had risen on every side at the beheading of the King, inside of France as well as out. None were more infuriated than the Girondists, their opponents in the National Assembly, which had now moved into the Tuileries, and held its meetings in that former home of the kings. All the Girondists, now more shrill in their berating of the Jacobins than ever before, condemned Marat. So Marat, backed by the City Council of Paris, schemed to do away with them by force. The day was set for an insurrection. At the appointed hour Marat scuttled up the crooked steps to the tower of the City Hall and clanged the alarm. As the brassy voice of the bell boomed out an army of soldiers surrounded the Tuileries and terrified the Assembly into arresting the leaders of the Girondists. That was Marat's great day, June 2, 1793. That day the Jacobins gained complete control of the Assembly, with Danton the undisputed leader, and bloodthirsty Marat his right-hand man.

But that attack on the delegates elected by the people was treason to the nation, and only increased the enemies of the Jacobins. In the outlying provinces, and in the cities of Lyons, Bordeaux, Marseilles and Toulon, there were uprisings against the revolution, while on the frontier foreign armies kept advancing.

"Our enemies are everywhere," cried the head of the City Council. "To be safe we must kill all of them! Terrorize them!"

"Terror!" cried Danton. "Let terror be the order of the day."

So the Reign of Terror began.

To speed up the work of terror, the Constitution (the second one, made to fit the republic) was set aside, and in its place a Committee of Safety was established to round up all possible enemies, and a Revolutionary Tribunal to try their cases.

Every day "enemies" were found guilty, the guillotine got its victims, and Marat's feverish eyes burned brighter. But he did not live long to enjoy his triumph. Suffering now from a skin disease caught in the sewers, he had to spend many hours each day in a tub of medicated water. One morning in July, as he sat in his tub, he was stabbed to death in the back by a beautiful girl from Normandy named Charlotte Corday, who had hoped by killing Marat to end the Terror.

But with that death the terror only increased. From then on the iron monster was never idle. It became the center of a bloody carnival featuring Death. Every day men in red caps crowded each other for a good place to see, and the market women brought their knitting and sat in the square, as if it were a gala occasion. Miniature guillotines were worn by the women, and sold as toys for children to play with.

One day late in October, the former Queen of France was trundled in the crude wooden cart over the cobblestone streets from her prison cell to the guillotine. Her hands tied behind her, Marie Antoinette, once the golden-haired little Archduchess of Austria, but now a grave-faced woman of thirty-eight, mounted the steps to her death, her hair turned white but her head held high with courage to the end.

Meanwhile soldiers with guillotines had been sent to the provinces to crush the uprisings there and execute the "enemies" of the nation. But killing one at a time on the guillotine was too slow for the soldiers. Thousands of citizens were lined up and shot by wholesale in the city of Lyons. With that example, rebellion in most of the other cities subsided. Toulon had, however, appealed to England and Spain for help, but, by a clever placing of his cannon, Lieutenant Napoleon Bounaparte subdued that city also.

An enormous number of soldiers had at the same time been rushed to the front. Each young officer knowing that he must win a victory or lose his head, word from those armies was now also encouraging. Danton began to think that Terror had done its work and that the need for terror was over.

But not the Commune. They were still not satisfied. They had abolished the monarchy, now they set about to abolish the Christian religion. They knocked the spires from the churches, destroyed the images of the saints, and in the Cathedral of Notre Dame tore down the cross and set up in its place a model of the "Holy Guillotine," and declared from then on Reason was the god. Even the calendar was abolished. Months were renamed. Years were no longer to be numbered from the Birth of Christ, but from the great day of the September Massacre when "Liberty" was born!

"Enough!" cried Danton. "Enough of terror. Terror has done its work! Let the terror cease!" But too late now for words of moderation.

The Committee of Safety now turned on Danton himself, con-

325

demned him as an enemy of the nation, seized and imprisoned him.

"A year ago I proposed the Revolutionary Tribunal," he mourned just before he was taken to the guillotine. "I ask pardon for it from God and man. I leave everything in terrible confusion; not one of them understands anything of government. Robespierre will follow me."

And so it was. When Danton's head rolled from the guillotine, Robespierre, with his pale greenish skin and eyes like a cat, sneaked warily into the long-coveted place of supreme power. Robespierre now became Prime Minister to the Guillotine, and High Priest of still another new religion, which he himself thought up according to ideas of Rousseau which had been squeezed out of shape in his narrow mind.

"Reason shall not be the god," he said, but Virtue, virtue, of which he considered himself the "Incorruptible" example.

Now it was all the unvirtuous and irreverent who must be put to death. The government must be purged of all its "immoral" enemies.

The Committee of Safety sent spies sneaking about to listen at every keyhole, and round up all citizens who seemed suspicious, and bring them before the Revolutionary Tribunal to be tried. Every day hundreds of people went to the guillotine, who were guilty of nothing except the crime of being alive. But, said Robespierre in his thin cold voice, "There are times in a revolution when to be alive is a crime."

Before long no one was safe who displeased Robespierre, not even members of the Committee.

Finally, the Assembly in terror turned on the leader himself, declared him an outlaw, and when he took refuge in the city hall, seized and dragged the coward to the guillotine, his jaw half shot away. An enormous crowd burst into applause as the knife fell on the worst enemy that France ever had, and the Reign of Terror ended.

Then the third Constitution was drawn up. Hoping to safeguard against any more dictators, the executive power was placed not in the hands of one president but in a body of five men called the *Directory*.

This cartoon ridicules doctors' crude methods,

DOCTOR JENNER AND THE SMALLPOX GERM

WAR AND THE GUILLOTINE destroyed thousands of lives in the eighteenth century, but not so many as were wiped out in those same years by the minute germ of smallpox. Smallpox took the lives of 36,000,000 people it is said, between 1700 and 1799. Seven of Maria Theresa's children died of it. The disease would often wipe out a whole town, so little was known about preventing the spread of epidemics.

Doctor Edward Jenner was a surgeon in a small town in England. For some time he had noticed that dairymaids never caught smallpox. He finally decided that cows must have a mild form of the disease, which the dairymaids caught and which made them immune to the more serious form. People scoffed as people always do.

But Doctor Jenner made vaccine from the cow pus, and in 1796 discovered, by trying it first on his own son, that vaccination was a safeguard against smallpox. He thus defeated an enemy which threatened not one nation but the whole world, and so saved the lives of thousands of people in his own lifetime and millions in the centuries to come.

CATHERINE: THE GRANDMOTHER

CATHERINE OF RUSSIA had been absolutely opposed to the French Revolution, from the beginning to the end.

"I am an aristocrat," she said, "that is my business."

From the beginning Catherine had also predicted much that was going to happen. Before trouble began, she had urged Louis XVI to do something to appease his people or they would rise against him. When the people took the King from Versailles to Paris, she predicted: "They will string him up to a lamppost next." When the era of Liberty was declared she laughed.

"Liberty! They will soon weary of this 'Liberty,' those French, and then they will become as gentle and obedient as lambs. But a clever and courageous leader is needed. Does that man already exist? Will he soon appear?"

Much as Catherine hated the French Revolution, she did not join the war. It was more profitable to her to attend to Poland, to put down any revolution that might be spreading there, and to discourage the new Constitution the Poles were trying to make!

Thaddeus Kosciuszko, Polish nobleman and soldier, who had then returned from America, tried to defend his feeble country, but in 1791, the second division of Poland took place. After leading still another bold uprising in 1794, Kosciuszko, wounded and captured, was taken prisoner to St. Petersburg. The third and final partition of his country had occurred when he was released. He was then offered a sword.

"I have no need of a sword," he said, declining the offer, "I have no longer a country to defend."

In 1794, Catherine of Russia was sixty-five years old, but still, she said, as spry as "a water wag-tail." "Fifty years ago," she wrote a friend in February, "I arrived in Moscow with my mother. I do not believe there are ten people left who remember that day . . . [but I] am as eager as a five-year-old child to play blindman's buff, and my children and grandchildren say that their games are never so merry as when I play them."

The children loved to have the merry old lady show them how she could wiggle her ears, and then she laughed as much as they did.

"I have been able to endure much because I have always laughed whenever I had the occasion," she said.

And Catherine met death as she had life. After a hearty laugh, she was seized with colic and soon gone.

Catherine, the Empress, left Russia at the end of her reign of thirty-six years much as she had found it, still half-civilized, and half asleep, too big a giant to reform.

"To accomplish anything in Russia I'd have to live to be as old as Methusaleh," had been her words.

Catherine II died in the year 1796.

And that was the year that the clever and courageous new leader to whom she had predicted that the French would surrender their liberty stepped forward into the limelight, with his Italian name now spelled in the French manner—not Buonaparte—but Bonaparte without the "u."

NAPOLEON BONAPARTE

NAPOLEON BONAPARTE had been made Brigadier General, in fighting for the Jacobins. But when the Jacobins went out of power, he turned about-face and defended the Directory. What difference to him? All he fought for in either case was the glory of Napoleon Bonaparte.

In the year 1795, France made peace with Holland, Spain, and Prussia. England still remained an enemy, and there were still Austria and the Sardinian army in Italy to conquer. Young Bonaparte then brought forward a new and daring plan for invading Italy.

"Let the lunatic who thought up the plan carry it out," said a skeptical older man. So, taking that advice, the Directory appointed Napoleon Bonaparte commander of the French Army of Italy in 1796.

The time was early spring. The newly appointed general, alone in his room, paced madly back and forth, then stopped, sat down suddenly at his desk, pushed back maps and papers and began to write:

"Sweet incomparable Josephine, what have you done to my heart? In three hours I shall see you; till then, my dear love, a thousand kisses—they burn my blood!" He threw down his pen in disgust. No more idle

330

words. With that intense young man, to think a thing was to do it.

On March 9, 1796, Napoleon married his Josephine. Josephine Beauharnais was a countess of thirty-three, a widow with two children and a great many debts. Napoleon Bonaparte was then twenty-seven years old, and owned nothing but the uniform he wore. "But," said he, "my sword is at my side and with it I shall go far!"

Two days after the marriage he was off for Italy, in despair at parting from his bride, but entranced by his chance of winning glory!

TO ITALY

THREE YEARS the French Army of Italy had been in the foot-hills of the Alps. Napoleon found the men ragged as beggars, underfed, disgruntled, and undisciplined. At their first sight of the young, undersized new general who had come to take command, the toughest among them were ready to mutiny. At the first few sharp commands, however, issued in no uncertain terms, officers and men fell instantly into line and realized that in spite of his size, here was a general of generals. He even seemed to grow taller when he addressed them.

"Soldiers," he cried, and his voice rang like metal. "You are ill fed and almost naked; the government owes you much, it can give you nothing. I will conduct you into the most fertile plains in the world. Rich provinces, great cities will be in your power; there you will find honor, glory, and wealth. Soldiers, are you lacking in courage?"

Lacking in courage? No! They even forgot they were lacking in food and shoes, so fired were they with the glorious prospect.

But between that army of ragged soldiers and the fertile plains and rich cities of Italy rose a tremendous barrier—the Alps. Beyond the Alps also guarding those plains and cities were two armies, the Italian army of Sardinia and the Austrian army. Twice as many soldiers as the French. But neither mountains nor men daunted the young Corsican for a moment. His mind was set. His plans were made. Hannibal and Cæsar had crossed the Alps. Napoleon went around them. Successfully he threaded his army along the narrow strip of land where the Alps come close to the shore of the Mediterranean Sea.

The mountains behind him, Napoleon kept his two enemy armies separated and attacked one of them at a time. His speed was phenomenal, and completely baffled the enemy generals. Inside of two weeks he had the Sardinian army cornered, bluffed and defeated.

"Soldiers," said Napoleon, "in six days you have won six victories and conquered the richest part of the Piedmont. But, soldiers, you have done nothing! You have more battles to fight, more towns to take, more rivers to cross. Is there one among you whose courage fails?"

Courage failing? No! They were filled with courage.

The Austrians must be defeated—and without delay. "I may lose battles, but no one will ever see me lose minutes," boasted Napoleon, and down the River Po he rushed the French troops, chasing the Aus-

332

trians back to the Adda River and over the bridge at Lodi. Austrian cannon fire swept that bridge, but regardless, Bonaparte shouted his order to cross. Seizing the banner he rushed to the head of his faltering troops, who then followed him over, drove back the Austrians and captured their cannon. From the day of that remarkable victory, he was the soldiers' idol. Their "Little Corporal." From then on, wherever he led, they followed and luck was with them.

By the following April, the Austrians had sued for peace and the campaign was over. Napoleon Bonaparte had conquered Italy.

"People of Italy," he then announced to them, "have confidence, your property, your customs, your religion shall be respected."

That said, he overthrew the republic of Venice, robbed and plundered Italy like a thief or a bandit. He forced each captured city to pay enormous sums of money, and shipped the finest of their paintings and sculpture back to Paris. When the enormous wagons rolled through the streets of that city, each bearing its label, Apollo Belvedere, Venus de Medici, the bronze horses of Venice and so forth, enthusiasm, already great over the news of victory, burst all bounds. The people were wild to see the hero himself.

But the "hero" wasn't ready to go to Paris. He spent that summer of 1797 in a magnificent villa near Milan. Joined by Josephine, surrounded by his admiring family, adored by the soldiers, gazed on with wonder by the citizens, Napoleon Bonaparte lived like a king, but took his amazing good fortune as a matter of course.

"What I have done so far is nothing!" he said. "I am but at the beginning of my career."

He behaved, however, as if he were already ruler of France. While arranging the treaty with the Austrians, he regarded or disregarded instructions from the Directory as he saw fit.

"Does any one imagine that I have triumphed in Italy in order to advance the lawyers of the Directory?" he exclaimed. "Let the Directory try to deprive me of my authority and they will see who is the master. What France must have now is a head made illustrious by glory!"

TO EGYPT

NAPOLEON, when he did return to Paris, accepted the cheers of the people with cleverly affected modesty. He knew that still more glory must be his before the time was ripe for him to seize the power or give any sign of his intent to do so. "If I died today," said he, "ten centuries hence my record would not occupy more than half a page in history."

What fame was that? No fame worth having. His glory must be like that of Cæsar or of Alexander the Great. And where had Alexander gone? To Egypt—to the Orient!

"That is the place for me to go," said Napoleon, "to the Orient.

334

This little Europe has not enough to offer me. I shall go to Egypt!"

The idea of Egypt possessed him, and having determined to go, he persuaded the Directory that a campaign into Egypt was the way to defeat England, their one remaining enemy.

"Our government," Napoleon told the Directory, "must destroy the English monarchy or it must expect itself to be destroyed by those active islanders. Let us concentrate our energies on the navy and annihilate England. Let us invade Egypt."

Egypt belonged, of course, to Turkey, not to England. But it lay on England's route to India, and so French control of Egypt would block off that great source of England's wealth and power!

The Directory approved, eager to get this too popular hero out of the country. In May, 1798, Napoleon and his expedition set sail for Egypt. It was a dangerous trip, for the English navy under the young commander Horatio Nelson was guarding the Mediterranean. The French fleet managed to escape detection, however, and the soldiers landed safely in Alexandria.

Leaving the fleet of seventeen ships in Aboukir Bay, one of the mouths of the Nile, the army marched inland along the great river to Cairo. After three weeks on the scorching sands, many of the men dressed in their heavy woolen uniforms dropped dead with the heat. Many went blind in the glare of the sun. But what were heat and sun to Napoleon, when there ahead rose the great sphynx and the pyramids, soon to behold in him another great conqueror?

"Soldiers, from these pyramids, forty centuries look down upon you," cried the man in mad excitement. Spurring his soldiers on, he led them to victory against the native horsemen, and the capture of Cairo, in what has since been called the Battle of the Pyramids.

But disaster followed that victory. One week later the whole French fleet left in Aboukir Bay was attacked and destroyed by the English under Horatio Nelson whose fame was made by the spectacular victory.

That left Napoleon and his army of soldiers stranded in Egypt. The Sultan, greatly encouraged, declared war on France, at which

335

Napoleon set out on a mad march to Syria with the idea of attacking the Turkish fort of Acre near Jerusalem.

"After I have seized Acre, I shall take Constantinople, make an end of Turkey, and found a new and great empire. This will bring me immortal fame," he boasted as they started out. It was a horrible march for the soldiers. Choked by blinding sandstorms, parched for lack of water, taken ill with the plague, five thousand died. Napoleon returned, defeated, having accomplished nothing. Except for Cairo and one other victory, the whole Egyptian campaign was a dismal failure. But he didn't admit it. As soon as he reached Cairo, Napoleon sent out bulletins, announcing a spectacular victory.

Then came news from France that the Directory were in difficulty. Good news for Napoleon, just such news as he had long been waiting for. Fleet or no fleet, he must return at once. Deserting his army, leaving the soldiers to live or die as they could, he set sail one dark night in a small boat headed for France.

The moment he landed he sent on this advance publicity:

"Egypt is wholly ours and safe from invasion. When I heard of your troubles I instantly set out for home. I had to take all risks, for my place was the spot where I could be of most use."

So, having prepared for himself a hero's welcome, he was hailed with delight. "Glory, peace, and happiness follow in his train," were the words with which the Paris newspaper heralded his arrival.

"I have returned at the right moment," he observed to himself. "Now shall the nation have its head made illustrious by glory."

The Directory of five men had made themselves very unpopular. They had been corrupt and inefficient and had completely disgraced themselves and lost the confidence of the people. Napoleon's time had come. He chose his conspirators warily, then by plots, trickery and the use of military force he seized the power. His title was First Consul (one of three) but actually he was Dictator of France.

And true enough, the French people were ready for him.

"The people are so sick and weary of revolutionary horrors," said

336

the Swedish envoy in Paris, "that they believe any change cannot fail to be for the better. Even the royalists are sincerely devoted to Bonaparte, for they think he intends to restore the old order of things. The indifferent cling to him as the one most likely to give France peace. The enlightened republicans, although they tremble for their form of government, prefer to see a single man of talent possess himself of the power than a club of intriguers."

That was November, 1799. The new century was to begin in France with a new ruler, and the letter N on the documents of state.

(Cleopatra)

THE ROSETTA STONE: CLUE TO AN ANCIENT RIDDLE

ONE VERY IMPORTANT DISCOVERY resulted from this expedition into Egypt—how to read the old Egyptian picture-writing. For centuries visitors to Egypt had seen the ancient inscriptions and had known that if they could but understand their meaning the early history of Egypt would be revealed. Up to 1799, no clue had been discovered.

Then, one day, an engineer who was building a fort at the town of Rosetta, near a mouth of the Nile, unearthed an old black stone. On it the same message was written in three different languages—the old picture-writing, another less ancient Egyptian writing, and Greek. By carefully comparing the three, Champillon, a French scholar, was able to decipher the old hieroglyphics and solve the ancient riddle.

CH'IEN LUNG'S REPLY TO GEORGE III

THE YEAR that Louis XVI was beheaded was the fifty-seventh year of Ch'ien Lung's reign in China. His cycle of sixty years was drawing to a close. June found him in his summer palace at Jehol in Mongolia, fifty miles north of the Great Wall among the pines and mountains. There word came to him one day that ambassadors from England had arrived at Canton and desired audience.

"Let them be received as my guests," said he, "and escorted hither to this 'Seat of Grateful Coolness.' "

One hundred men made up the English delegation, which included artists, scientists, musicians and a guard of soldiers. When refreshed from their journey, they were told that on a certain morning at daybreak, the Emperor Ch'ien Lung would receive them. It was customary, the Mandarin reminded them, to kow-tow to the Emperor, that is, to kneel before him and bump the head three times upon the ground.

"When I approach my own King, to whom I owe my deepest loyalty," replied the English ambassador, "I kneel on one knee. I shall be glad to show the same respect to his Imperial Majesty."

"I am satisfied," said Ch'ien Lung. And under the swaying lanterns of the audience tent he received the English guests, and with feasts and gifts and entertainment assured them of their welcome.

338

It was also to his pleasure, he told them, that they remain a week longer to enjoy with him the celebration of his eighty-third birthday. More than delighted by his hospitality, the English ambassadors then took their leave, feeling confident that the requests which they had made would certainly be granted. This, however, is part of Ch'ien Lung's letter of reply addressed to George III:

"You, O King, live in a distant region, far beyond the borders of many oceans, but desiring humbly to share the blessings of our civilization, you have sent an embassy respectfully bearing your letter. . . . Every country under Heaven and Kings of all nations have sent their tribute by land and sea. We possess all things . . . we have no use for your country's products. . . . I have accepted your tribute offerings only because of the devotion which made you send them so far. I have read your letter; it shows respectful humility.

"As to your request to send an ambassador to live at my Heavenly Court, this request cannot possibly be granted . . . there are many other nations in Europe beside your own; if all of them asked to come to our court how could we possibly consent? . . . Your ambassador asks us to allow your ships to trade at other ports beside Canton. There are no interpreters at any other port, so that your barbarian merchants could not carry on their business there. Your request is refused.

"Your ambassador has asked permission to have your religion taught in China. Since the beginning of History wise emperors and sages have given China a religion, which has been followed by millions of my subjects. We need no foreign teaching. The request is most unreasonable.

"I have always shown the greatest kindness to tribute embassies. To you, O King, who live so far away, I have shown greater kindness than to any other nation. But your demands are contrary to the customs of our dynasty and would bring no good result. I have therefore answered them in deail. And it is your duty to understand my feelings and reverently to obey my instructions henceforth and for all time, so that you may enjoy the blessings of peace."

乾隆

339

NEW RULERS FOR A NEW ERA

TRUE TO HIS VOW, when the sixty imperial years were spent, Ch'ien Lung abdicated in favor of his fifteenth son. That son, an unworthy follower of his great ancestors, was no longer interested in upholding either the virtues or the great traditions of China. Before many years of the next century had passed, China, for good or evil, was to be thrown open to Europeans.

Then in 1911, when the United States of America, the youngest nation, but the oldest republic in the world, was one hundred thirty-five years old, the people of that most ancient Empire of China were also to declare their nation a republic.

In 1796, however, the year Ch'ien Lung abdicated, George Washington, first President of the United States, was just completing his second term in office. The next year, John Adams succeeded him as President, and Thomas Jefferson became Vice-President.

There were farewell cheers and tears for Washington as he left the room after the inauguration ceremony. Men crowded around him to

340

shake his hand, women wept, and Washington himself was too moved to speak. John Adams saw clearly, however, that the tired man was greatly relieved to be free of the responsibility of the high office.

"He seemed to enjoy a triumph over me," John Adams wrote to Abigail that night. "Methought I heard him say 'Aye! I am fairly out and you fairly in! See which one of us will be the happiest!'"

John Adams took up his new duties seriously, fully realizing that the science of government was an "art or mystery, very difficult to learn and harder still to practice."

"The great art of lawgiving," he said, "consists in balancing the poor against the rich. But the controversy between the rich and poor, the laborious and the idle, the learned and the ignorant, is as old as creation and as extensive as the globe."

No ruler, he knew, and no nation in the history of the world, had ever more than partially solved the problem, no system of government yet devised had achieved the perfect balance.

George Washington was indeed glad when his service to the government was at last completed. He felt as light-hearted as a boy again when the coach left the outskirts of Philadelphia and the horses' heads were turned toward home. With him were Martha, cosy and cheerful as ever, pretty Nelly, who was then eighteen, and a young Frenchman about her own age, his guest and namesake, George Washington La Fayette. The dog completed the family party. The parrot, to the master's great relief, had been sent by boat with the household furniture. A courier on horseback preceded the carriages, while following came the saddle horses and the baggage wagon piled with trunks, making a small cavalcade. At every town bells rang and cannons boomed, and guards of honor rode out to meet and escort the great man and his party. After leaving Baltimore, Washington looked forward eagerly to the next stop.

It was Federal City. The Capitol, of which he had laid the cornerstone himself in 1793, still had no roof, but was fairly well along, and it seemed possible that the government might indeed be moved there from Philadelphia before Mr. Adams' term was over.

At Georgetown on the Potomac, a company of his home town friends from Alexandria were waiting to accompany their illustrious fellow citizen across the Potomac River into Virginia.

On the evening of March 15, the coach passed through the west postern gate at Mount Vernon, up the long lane, around the serpentine drive, and George Washington was home.

How fresh and sweet the evening air was with the smell of moist earth and the new leaves and first spring blossoms! Washington looked forward to his morning ride out through the fields and woods.

"Grandpa is very well and much pleased with being once more Farmer Washington," wrote Nelly Custis to a friend a few days later.

That summer Nelly's young brother, George Washington Parke Custis, described his grandfather to a visitor who inquired where the general might be found: "If you see an old gentleman," he said, "in plain drab clothes, a broad-brimmed white hat, a hickory switch in his hand, and carrying an umbrella with a long staff which is attached to his saddlebow, that person, sir, is General Washington."

Every morning Washington went for his ride, and every afternoon as regular as the sun, he was back at the house for three o'clock dinner. The afternoons were spent with guests, or writing letters, looking back over his old records and putting his accounts in order. How many changes there had been since he first had come there to live with Lawrence, bringing his new surveying instruments and his copybook. . . . Sally Fairfax! The thought of her wrought the same magic in his heart that it had always done. He sat down one day and wrote her a letter. Sally was living in England. Her husband, his old friend, was dead. George Washington thought of him and of their first surveying trip together—of old Lord Fairfax—of his own brother Lawrence, and of his three young brothers—and his sister Betty—all gone—now—none of his family left. . . .

"I am the last remaining of my father's children," he thought as he stood one day by the Potomac watching a ship that was also being carried along by outgoing tide. "When I shall be called upon to follow them is known only to the Giver of Life. When the summons comes I shall endeavor to obey it with good grace."

The months passed pleasantly by to his birthday, which was his sixty-sixth. With Martha and Nelly and his nephew Lawrence Lewis, he attended his birth-night ball in Alexandria.

On February 22, 1799, George Washington's next birthday, there was a wedding at Mount Vernon, that of Nelly Custis and Lawrence Lewis. In honor of the joyful occasion, and to please Nelly, Washington wore again his Continental uniform. After the wedding, the young couple continued to live on at Mount Vernon. These are silhouettes, which Nelly cut, of the Master of Mount Vernon and his wife on the last Christmas which they all spent together.

Christmas, 1799, George Washington was gone.

Late on a December afternoon, as the sun hung low over his Virginia hills, the great man was borne slowly down the pathway and laid to rest in the quiet tomb beside the river. As the last echo of the guns' farewell salute died into silence, there followed the peaceful words of the Service for the Dead. The wind that stirred the leafless branches of the trees caught those living words and carried them away. None but the little group standing there upon the hillside heard them:

"Lord, thou hast been our refuge from one generation to another. Before the mountains were brought forth, or ever the earth and the world were made, thou art God from everlasting. . . . For a thousand years in thy sight are but as yesterday. . . . The days of our age are three score years and ten, . . . so soon passeth it away and we are gone. . . . So teach us to number our days, that we may apply our hearts unto wisdom. . . . Glory be to the Father . . . as it was in the beginning, is now and ever shall be, world without end. Amen."

The sun dropped behind the hills and the dusk came early, for the year, too, was drawing to a close. Each sunset of that month would cut the daylight shorter and bring the twilight earlier, until day and night were equal and the sun seemed to stand still. After that the days would grow longer.

The snow would melt, the insects awaken, the trees and shrubs burst into leaf and blossom. Though the master was gone, the fields of Mount Vernon would grow green again, to every land the seasons would return in their regular order, and men would sow the grain and reap the harvest as each season came. For that is the law of life.

INDEX

*"The social, friendly honest man, whate'er he be
'Tis he fulfils great Nature's plan, and none but he."*

ROBERT BURNS

Montgolfier (mŏnt-gŏl-fyä'), Etienne and Joseph, inventors of balloon, 255

Morris, Robert, appointed Treasurer, 232

Mozart, composer: with Marie Antoinette, 128; in Italy, 135

Mustapha III, Sultan of Turkey, 140, 144

Napoleon, *see* Bonaparte

Nelson, Horatio, 335

North, Lord: tea tax, 122

Orlov, Alexis: aids Catherine, 100, 145

Orlov, Gregor: helps crown Catherine, 100

Paine, Thomas: with Franklin, 123; writes *Commonsense*, 180; Rights of Man, 309

Peter III, Emperor of Russia: marries Catherine, 37; crowned, 98; murdered, 101

Piranesi (pē rä nä zē), Italian artist, 137

Pitt, William: enters British Parliament, 54; in power, 79; defends colonies, 121, 169; dies, 211; on holding colonies, 241

Pompadour, Mme. de: favorite of Louis XV, 42; plots, 77; dies, 125

Pontiac, Indian chief, 83

Portola, military governor of California, 156

Potemkin, Russian field marshal, 272

Pulaski, Polish patriot, 142

Putnam, Israel, at Bunker Hill, 171

Priestley, Joseph, discovers oxygen, 112

Revere, Paul: engraving by, 163; rides, 166

Reynolds, Sir Joshua, 117, 135

Robespierre (rŏbĕs-pyär'), French Revolutionist: Reign of Terror, 323; beheaded, 326

Rochambeau (rŏ shän'bŏ'), French general, 223

Ross, Betsy, seamstress, 176

Rousseau (rōō-sō'), French philosopher, 263

Salomon, Haym: leaves Poland, 142; helps Robert Morris and the United States, 232

Serra, Junipero, Spanish monk: reaches Mexico, 29; goes to California, 156

Spode, maker of china, 66 (mentioned)

Steuben (shtoi'bĕn), von, Prussian general: in America, 185; Valley Forge, 208

Stuart, Gilbert: leaves Boston, 174; portrait of Washington, 284

Vergennes, French foreign minister, 185, 219, 261

Voltaire, French philosopher: early life, 45; in Switzerland, 102; meets Benj. Franklin, 188; opposes Rousseau, 263

Washington, George, first President of the U. S.: boy, 5; accused of murder, 70; messenger to Fort, 71; married, 89; offers help to Boston, 168; goes to Congress, 169; made Commander, 173; in New York City, 195; crosses Delaware, 197; in Philadelphia, 200; Valley Forge, 206; Benedict Arnold, exposed, 224; Yorktown, 228; refuses absolute power, 229; returns home, 247; trip to Northwest, 280; President of the Constitutional Convention, 282; elected President, 284; his receptions, 305; visits the South, 310; proclaims neutrality, 322; retires, 342; dies, 343

Washington, Lawrence, brother Geo., 7, 342

Washington, Martha, wife of President, 87; in camp, 188; home, 247, 284; presidential receptions, 305; home again, 341

Watt, James, Scotch inventor: boy, 50; invents steam engine, 113

Wedgwood, Josiah, maker of china, 66, 265

West, Benjamin, American painter: boy, 18; in Italy, 136; court painter to George III, 116, 183, 229, 265

INDEX OF PLACES, NATIONS AND EVENTS

*"Knowledge is of two kinds. We know a subject ourselves
or we know where we can find information about it."*

DR. SAMUEL JOHNSON

American Revolution (1775–1783): events leading up to it, 118–123, 162–164; *Rebellion:* Lexington and Concord, 166; Bunker Hill, 170; Washington general, 174; *War for Independence:* battle of Long Island, 195; crossing Delaware, 197; Burgoyne's surrender, 202; Valley Forge, 205; French alliance, 209; Northwest Territory, 212; campaign in the South, 226; Cornwallis surrenders, 228; peace, 237

Australia: discovery, 111; settlement, 241

Aviation: first balloon, 254

Bastille: torn down, 294; key to, 301

Bon Homme Richard, ship, 218

Boston: map, 162; harbor, 16; tea party, 164; massacre, 163

British Empire: American colonies (map); Parliament and the king, 53; map before and after addition of Canada, 82; map of territory in 1763, and 1940, 86; in India, 67, 80, 241; Australia added, 111; Canada settled, 240; loss of American colonies, 241; Australia settled, 241

Bunker Hill, battle of, 170

Calcutta, Black Hole of, 80

Calendar, new and old, Introduction

California: first missions, 156

Canada: settlement, 241

China: map, 62; hongs established, 65; first English ambassadors, 338

Committee of Correspondence, U. S., 167

Committee of Safety, French, 324

347